ALBAN BERG

Alban Berg and his wife, *c.* 1925

ALBAN BERG
The Man and his Music

by

H. F. REDLICH, Ph.D.

LECTURER IN THE HISTORY OF MUSIC
UNIVERSITY OF EDINBURGH

ABELARD-SCHUMAN LIMITED
NEW YORK

PRINTED IN GREAT BRITAIN FOR THE PUBLISHERS
ABELARD-SCHUMAN LIMITED, 404 FOURTH AVENUE, NEW YORK 16, N.Y.
BY THE DITCHLING PRESS, HASSOCKS, SUSSEX

CONTENTS

Preface

PART I
Introduction

PART II
The music of Alban Berg

PART III

PART IV
Appendices

ACKNOWLEDGEMENTS

PUBLISHED
BY ARRANGEMENT WITH
UNIVERSAL EDITION
LONDON AND VIENNA

The music examples mentioned below have been reproduced by courtesy of the following publishers:

Messrs Birnbach, Berlin (from Schoenberg's Opus 7).

Messrs Boosey & Hawkes, London (from Richard Strauss's *Salome* and *Rosenkavalier*).

Messrs Bote & Bock, Berlin (from Mahler's 7th Symphony).

Messrs Hinrichsen Edition Ltd, London (from Richard Strauss's *Tod und Verklärung*).

Messrs Kahnt, Berlin (from Mahler's 6th Symphony).

Messrs Leuckart, Munich (from Richard Strauss's *Heldenleben*).

ILLUSTRATIONS

Ich füh — le luft von an-de-ren pla — ne — ten —

PREFACE

THIS book was written in 1955. It is a transcription and a condensation rather than a literal translation of my somewhat earlier book *Alban Berg—Versuch einer Würdigung*, written in German and published by Universal Edition, Vienna. The later book keeps close to the structural plan of the German publication. Although the analytical sections have been shortened and the number of music examples reduced, it retains all major points of biographical and scholarly interest. In addition it also contains short biographical essays on Georg Büchner and Frank Wedekind, expressly written and inserted for the information of the English reader.

Special thanks are due to all who have made accessible to me Berg's unpublished music, letters, articles, personal documents and photographs and permitted their use or their entire publication in this book. They are: Mrs Helene Berg, Vienna, for *Piano Variations on an Original Theme*, 1908, original photographs of Berg's parents and of himself, letters, documents and comprehensive personal information; Mrs Gertrud Schoenberg, Los Angeles, U.S.A., for Berg's letters to Schoenberg, Schoenberg's article on Berg, 1949, and personal information; Dr Werner Riemerschmid, Vienna, and Mrs Helene Berg for Berg's letters to Webern; Mr Richard S. Hill, Music Division Library of Congress, Washington, D.C., U.S.A., for invaluable help in the selection of Berg's letters to Schoenberg, now deposited in the Library of Congress, and much personal information; Universal Edition, Vienna, and Mrs Helene Berg for permission to study autographs and copies with autograph corrections of Berg's music, articles and lectures, including the unpublished sketches to *Lulu*, Act III, the sketches to the full scores of Lied 4 and 5 of the *Altenberg Lieder* (op. 4), now deposited at the Bodleian Library, Oxford, the autograph of the 'Trio' version of the *Chamber Concerto* (Mvt. 2), the Wozzeck Lecture of 1929 (published here for the first time in an English translation), press-cuttings relating to the first performances of *Wozzeck* and *Lulu*; Mrs Ružena Herlinger, Canada, Mrs Annemarie v. Klenau, Söllhuben-Rosenheim, Bavaria, and Dr A. Kalmus, London, for photographs, letters and documents.

I am also grateful to Dr Egon Wellesz, Oxford, and to Dr Joseph Polnauer, Mr H. E. Apostel, Mr Hanns Jelinek and Mr Oktavian Spitzmüller, all of Vienna, for valuable information.

I feel much indebted to Mr Frank Walker and to Mr John Calder. Both read the book in manuscript and in proof, and suggested numerous improvements in style and presentation. I am equally grateful to Mr Neil Aspinall and to Messrs Clough and Cuming for their unremitting help in the compilation of the Discography.

HANS F. REDLICH
University of Edinburgh
1956   Faculty of Music

PART I: INTRODUCTION

CHAPTER I

The Second Viennese School

IT is the prerogative of the enthusiast to over-simplify historical phenomena. But it is the duty of the conscientious chronicler to describe things as they are, or were, in all their complexity. The triumvirate of the so-called 'Second Viennese School',[1] Arnold Schoenberg, Alban Berg, and Anton Webern, has been so sedulously presented by proselytizing apologists such as René Leibowitz and Joseph Rufer as an artistic unity, with an indivisible community of aims and tendencies, that what are in fact strong contrasts between the musical natures, talents and achievements of these three artists are in danger of being overlooked. The following survey endeavours to supply correctives, necessary for a deeper historical appreciation, especially at those points where the picture drawn by zealous apostles threatens to dissolve in the mists of uncritical admiration.

The creative activity of Schoenberg's school covered a period

[1]In this reckoning, the first Viennese School is considered to have come to an end with the death of Schubert. The 'Second Viennese School' refers here exclusively to Schoenberg, his two disciples and their direct followers. The term has gained currency among continental writers on music, and is not unfitting, in view of the fact that the generation of Viennese musicians preceding Schoenberg, culminating in Brahms, Bruckner, Wolf and Mahler, has continued to exercise influence only through isolated pupils. None of these great composers, flourishing in the Vienna of the late nineteenth century, ever founded a school in the true sense of the word. The younger generation of Schoenberg's followers includes Hanns Eisler, H. E. Apostel, Hans Jelinek, and Joseph Rufer.

13

of fifty years. It began around 1900 with Schoenberg's own earliest songs and chamber music, followed by Berg's first essays in composition. It reached its apogee in the 1920's, when Schoenberg's first compositions in twelve-note technique, Berg's *Lyric Suite* and *Wozzeck*, and Webern's most ambitiously planned work up to that time, the Symphony Op. 21, were written. The glory of that unique creative community and spiritual brotherhood between teacher and disciples was on the wane by 1933. In that year the changed political climate of Germany caused Schoenberg, a baptised Jew, to return to his ancestral faith, and eventually he was driven into exile in America, while his two disciples—not subject to Hitler's discriminatory racial legislation—stayed in Austria but took part in what was called the 'internal emigration' of that time. The earthly bonds linking the members of this triumvirate were cut by the premature death of Berg in 1935 and the tragic end of Webern ten years later. Schoenberg outlived both his followers. His own death on July 14th, 1951, closed an epoch that had begun at the turn of the century, in the shade of the newly-made graves of Brahms and Bruckner.

The common German-Austrian inheritance of all these composers contrasts with the almost irreconcilable diversities of their characters. Schoenberg sprang from the Jewish *petite-bourgeoisie* of Vienna, and was chiefly self-taught. His genius revealed an ambivalent character in the fifty-four years of its creative development. Like C. P. E. Bach at the epochal turning point of 1750, Schoenberg expressed himself, one hundred and fifty years later, with similar originality as ruminating theorist and experimenting composer. He turned periodically from speculative theory to original composition, from performance to the creative re-valuation of the past. His long life divided clearly into two sections, each of two distinct periods, separated by a longer interlude of apparent fallowness (1915-23). The two great style-periods discernible within the first section, the over-ripe romanticism of the gigantic conceptions of 1899-1907, and the aphoristic miniature work of 1908-15, correspond to the two creative periods, after the fallow interlude, dedicated in turn to the consolidation of the twelve-note system (1923-33) and to the late compositions of the years of American exile (1934-51). In this last period dodecaphonic and tonal composition join hands, with his resumption of work on older, uncompleted projects in a final creative effort, deprived of final fulfilment by death. The truly astounding variety of Schoenberg's achievement cannot erase the general impression that only a fraction of his work has so far sunk into the consciousness of his age. The success of Schoenberg, the revolutionizing theorist and teacher, in two continents, is not matched by a similar success of the composer. Only a few works, like *Verklärte Nacht*, the *Gurrelieder*, and the sensational tour de force *Pierrot Lunaire*, have achieved lasting success and repeated performance. Schoenberg's most ambitious conceptions, the oratorio *Die Jakobsleiter*, and the opera *Moses und Aron*, were left unfinished and remain, so far, unpublished. His operas in general are neglected, except for an occasional performance of the monodrama *Erwartung*. In spite of all this, the emanation and 'mystique' of his personality are so great that the first half of the century could fittingly be called 'the Schoenberg epoch'.

To the perturbing, explosive personality of Schoenberg, Anton Webern forms a curious contrast, with his attitude of introspective shyness and the anonymous character of his strangely noiseless creative effort. Webern shares Schoenberg's fate, remaining unrecognized by the multitude, even after death, and with an integral part of his work unknown and inaccessible. A much shorter creative life of approximately thirty-seven years was allotted him, beginning with the surprisingly mature *Passacaglia* Op. 1, of 1908, after which for two decades he was imprisoned in the cul-de-sac of extreme diminution of sound and duration. The miniatures of expression, characteristic of Schoenberg's second period, are subjected in Webern's Opp. 3-17 to a process of dynamic reduction and colouristic note-differentiation in which the original musical impulse seems filtered away almost to physical inaudibility. The integration of this strange sound-world with the twelve-note system, and the development of more generously planned musical organisms (commencing so surprisingly with Op. 21) gave Webern a late phase of development which was shared neither by Berg, in his premature grave, nor by Schoenberg in distant America. The style of fairly late works, such as the *Piano Variations*, Op. 27, has only recently found in René Leibowitz an enthusiastic and competent analyst. The sphinx-like canonic severity and the mysteriously corresponding patterns of sound in the last works remain an enigma to many people, including some of the composer's admirers. In contrast to his mentor, Webern was a distinguished academically-trained musicologist and an experienced professional conductor. But he rarely contributed to musical theory, or indulged in musical polemics. And Webern the editor, arranger, lecturer and writer has been effectively silenced by the continuous *pianissimo* of his creative work.

Berg, dying in 1935 before the completion of his fifty-first year, never witnessed the extreme developments of his teacher or his friend. He was neither a speculative theorist like Schoenberg nor a musical scholar and professional conductor like Webern. As musical journalist with a strong polemic bias, however, and as a musical analyst of philological conscientiousness, he easily surpassed them both. Berg's analyses of Schoenberg's compositions, his articles on the music of his teacher and on his own *Wozzeck*, are among the classics of modern musical literature. He was neither a concert pianist nor a conductor, but as a teacher of composition he raised a new generation of pupils, comparable with those of Schoenberg himself in the 1920's. As a creative artist Berg stands nearer to Schoenberg than to his own contemporary Webern. Most of his work has its roots in late Romanticism and, not unlike his master, Berg attempted in his mature works to reconcile dodecaphonic technique with a feeling for traditional tonality. Like Schoenberg himself, Berg wrote in lyrical, symphonic, concertante and musico-dramatic forms and styles. But where Schoenberg as musical dramatist, after his first attempt *Erwartung*, became entangled in experimental dodecaphony (*Von Heute auf Morgen*) or experimental symbolism (*Die glückliche Hand*), Berg achieved with *Wozzeck* the first great success of an opera, inspired by social consciousness, and conceived in radically modern terms. Berg's early songs, his mature chamber music and late concertante works have all established themselves in the modern concert repertoire. The greater part of his work, like the greater part of Webern's, is not conceived in the twelve-note idiom. On the other hand, the strict logical consistency of the Altenberg-Lieder, Op. 4, and of parts of the String Quartet, Op. 3, and *Wozzeck*, contrasts strikingly with the free tonality of certain contemporary works by Schoenberg and Webern. It seems unprofitable to speculate on the extent to which Berg, had he lived, might have identified himself with Webern's late works or those of Schoenberg's American compositions in which dodecaphony is temporarily abandoned. He had in fact anticipated some elements of both phenomena in his own development, but he never abandoned his psychological roots in the

B 17

revolutionary stratum of the nineteenth century. His position as mediator at this historical turning-point gives Berg and his music special powers of persuasion, which have only become fully evident to a later generation.

CHAPTER II

The Problem of Tonality

ONE of the tasks of this book will be to determine Berg's place in the history of the musical revolution which began with the Viennese Classics. Paradoxically, the feeling for tonality and for the logic of the cadence was seriously weakened for the first time in the works of just those classic composers who are usually considered the high priests of the concept of diatonic tonality. The innovations of Schoenberg and his disciples have their origin, in point of fact, in the late works of Haydn and Mozart.

In 1790, in the Trio of the third movement of his String Quartet in B flat, K. 589, Mozart wrote the following modulatory transition:

Example 1

Bars 1-3 contain a cadence to D flat: V7-VI-II$_5^6$-I. Bar 4 gives the impression of intending to supply the delayed cadence IV-V-I. But what happens? I (D flat) fails to materialize; it is replaced by

*Fictitious resolution

19

the rest bar 5. The music recommences in bar 6 with the $\frac{6}{4}$ of G major, treated at once as the dominant of C major: V-I$\frac{6}{4}$-V. What has happened to the carefully prepared tonic on D flat? It is meant to be only imagined, not heard, and must be supplied mentally during the rest bar 5. The ancillary function of that chord of D flat as supertonic of C and as its SD deputy becomes clear in bar 6, the modulation of which uses the imagined D flat chord as a kind of harmonic swing-door, interpreting it *a posteriori* as the Neapolitan sixth of C major.

Mozart here presents an early example of elliptic modulation and of a selective sequence of harmonic events; both are typical features of the modulatory processes of the 'Second Vienna School' of the early twentieth century.

Mozart calls here (as in many similar cases) for the active participation of the listener's musical imagination, to supply the additional harmonies which implement the modulatory process. Exactly the same participation is called for in the following examples from Berg's *Lyric Suite:*

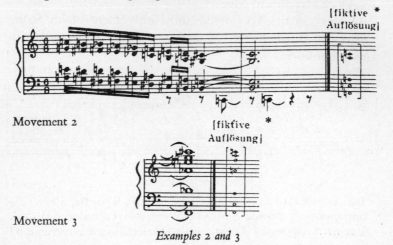

Movement 2

Movement 3

Examples 2 and 3

*Fictitious resolution

In these cases the inner ear supplies the implicit, tacitly accepted, yet never sounded, tonic of F major, which is used as a sort of harmonic converging-point in this particular work.

In the same String Quartet, K. 589, Mozart goes a step further. In the Finale he writes:

Example 4

Here the process of silent implementation in the rest bar 2 is more complicated. Chord '*x*' is the dominant seventh of the tonic B flat. This tonic is suppressed, as the D flat tonic had been in example 1. How can Mozart justify the dissonant false relations in the seemingly incoherent sequence E flat—E natural in bars 1 and 3? Only if the listener can be persuaded to understand the A minor tonic of bar 3 as the ultimate goal of the modulation which had started in bar 1. And this is only possible if the inner ear implements the elliptic modulations by an interpolated Neapolitan cadence in which the tonic of B flat is used as 'Neapolitan Sixth' of the real tonic A minor:

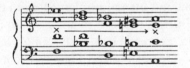

Example 5

The E flat at * and its harmonic basis could also be interpreted as an enharmonic 'swing-door'. In that case E flat becomes D sharp, which in turn becomes the leading note to A minor. The first chord becomes then *a posteriori* an augmented $\frac{5}{6}$ chord on F (the lower Mediant of A minor).

From Mozart's imaginary Neapolitan cadence it is only a step to the subtle technique of deliberate elision used in Wagner's *Parsifal*:

Example 6a

Example 6b   *

Kundry's famous passage 'O ewiger Schlaf' (II/I) can be easily understood as a chain of suppressed Neapolitan *Zwischenkadenzen* (intermittent cadences), conceived in exactly the same way as Mozart's examples of 1790. The difference is only quantitative: Mozart uses harmonic elision once, whereas Wagner uses it a number of times within a few bars. The time given for the inner adjustment and mental implementation (already severely curtailed in *Parsifal*) is reduced to a mere flash in the following examples, from Schoenberg's early song, *Schenk' mir einen gold'nen Kamm*, Op. 2, No. 2. This, too, contains an elliptic cadence which materializes with the aid of a chord of the Neapolitan sixth. Here the first chord becomes *a posteriori* (i.e. in the light of that Neapolitan sixth) the fifth step of a B

*C flat = B

22

minor tonic which is replaced by its own diminished seventh:

Example 7

The revolution begun in Mozart's day reached its culmination in the works of Schoenberg, whose technique of allusive harmony and elliptical modulation became Berg's point of departure.

The Basic Elements of Berg's Music

In the course of nearly forty years Berg's music progressed from the over-ripe Romanticism of 1900 to the etherealized dodecaphony of *Lulu* and the Violin Concerto of 1934/5. Despite all the changes of style which this implies, certain elements of his musical idiom remain constant and immutable. They make it possible to visualize clearly the characteristic silhouette of Berg's musical personality.

These constant elements are:

1 The interval of the fourth, as decisive factor in melodic shapes and chordal structures.

2 The interval of the seventh, as the source of continual implicit tension, in melody and harmony.

3 Schoenberg's principle of perpetual variation.

4 A deliberate neglect of cyclic sonata-form, except in telescopic abbreviation and condensation.

5 A predilection for aphoristic brevity.

6 A deliberate weakening of the tonal effect of cadences, leading up to the phenomenon of the elliptical cadence.

7 A continual endeavour to compensate for the weakened

feeling for tonality, resulting from the above six elements in his music, by establishing associations with historic musical forms and techniques.

8 A partiality for musical anagrams.

9 A partiality for allusive musical quotation.

10 The use of preconceived schemes of tonal organization (serial technique).

The use of the interval of the fourth as constructive element can be studied to advantage in the following three examples, from compositions written at different stages of Berg's career:

Example 8

Example 9

Example 10

24

The fourths, introduced in Example 8 (Piano Sonata, Op. 1) into the sphere of romantic chromaticism, act like acid in a chemical solution. They considerably weaken the cadential potentialities of the triplet melody in the treble. These bars and their continuation at the end of the telescoped recapitulation, despite their episodic character, form a turning point in the processes of harmonic thinking.

The connection between Example 9 (*Lyric Suite*) and the principal motive of Schoenberg's Chamber Symphony, Op. 9, seems self-evident. Berg's version is bolder than Schoenberg's; it traverses a greater octave span, with the help of inverted fourths.

Perhaps the most convincing use of the interval of the fourth is to be found in Marie's Lullaby in *Wozzeck* (Example 10).

These cases of the constructive use of the fourth in the music of Schoenberg and Berg could easily be supplemented by examples from Mahler, Scriabin and other composers of the early twentieth century.[1] The phenomenon as such is, however, not confined to the last fifty years. Schoenberg[2] has repeatedly drawn attention to the fact that the revolutionary use of the fourth really starts in certain experimental works of Beethoven (*Pastoral Symphony*) and Wagner (*Tristan*), where a pre-impressionistic use of the fourth may be found. Another such example is found in the so-called 'Sirens' Chord' in Wagner's *Tannhäuser* Bacchanale (Dresden version of 1845), which could be called the archetype of all later combinations of the interval of the fourth, as discussed in this chapter:

[1]Cf. the chapter 'Quartenakkorde' in Schoenberg's *Harmonielehre*, p. 446 ff. According to this Schoenberg first used chords of the fourth in 1902 in *Pelleas und Melisande*. Cf. also Zofja Lissa, 'Geschichtliche Vorform der Zwölftontechnik', in *Acta Musicologica*, VII/1, 1935; cf. also Mahler's seventh symphony (first movement), with its perpetual use of fourths, especially in chordal combinations.
[2]*Harmonielehre*, pp. 447-49.

Example 11

The interval of the perfect fourth is here still used as a dissonant suspension, deliberately delaying the resolution in a chord of the diminished seventh (*x*). However, in the following examples, taken from Liszt's *Mephisto Waltz* (1863) and from Wagner's *Die Meistersinger*, the chordal qualities of the fourth are for the first time savoured in full:

Example 12

Example 13 a and b

These examples were suggested by the order of the strings on, respectively, the violin and the lute. They also illustrate dramatic situations (the fiddling Mephistopheles, and Beckmesser serenading with the help of his lute). However, in the following

Example 14, taken from a piano quartet by Brahms, the contrapuntal and, as it were, dialectic value of the interval of the fourth is already used in a manner clearly anticipatory of Schoenberg and Berg. In fact, Example 14, with its tendency to avoid the traditional diatonicism of the third, in favour of a modulatory system of fourths, must be regarded as the model for certain processes in Schoenberg's Op. 9 and Berg's Op. 1 and *Lyric Suite*. These bars are taken from the Finale of the Piano Quartet in A major, Op. 26, composed in 1856 and published in 1863:

Example 14*

Serial Technique before Berg and Schoenberg

The fact that Berg adopted Schoenberg's twelve-note technique with alacrity in 1925—after having divined its advent and consequences in some early works—proves that serial technique was part of his musical heritage. For him, it contained no element of surprise, as for so many of his contemporaries. Actually, experiments in something like serial technique date back to Beethoven. In the late String Quartet Op. 132 a four-note motive determines the whole first movement.

*[Sketch]

27

Example 15

The Allegro motive 'x' derives from it, as may be seen in the following sketch of bars 10-15:

Example 16

Schoenberg's principle of allocating parts of a serial motive to different instruments, playing in different octaves, is fore-shadowed in the following bars, taken from the Coda of the first movement:

Example 17

28

The four notes linked by arrows are parts of a row:

Example 18

which, of course, is only a variation of the 'Basic Set' 1 (cf. Example 15) in its fourth permutation. Beethoven's 'rows' are usually short (mostly only four notes). Liszt, however, the great experimenter of the Romantic movement, produced a veritable twelve-note theme in the chief subject of his *Faust* Symphony (1854). Its tendency to arrange its intervals in chordal formation and to avoid note-repetition points towards Schoenberg's later principles of dodecaphony:

Example 19

The 'Faust' theme easily yields the following dodecaphonic 'Basic Set':

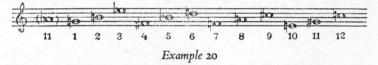

Example 20

It is interesting to note that Liszt invented this serial theme to express Faust's speculative, philosophical disposition. Similarly, Richard Strauss in *Thus spake Zarathustra* (1896) invents an 'impure' twelve-note theme for the section 'Von der Wissenschaft', probably taking his cue from Liszt's work.

Dodecaphonic experiments are also to be found in certain early works of the triumvirate of the 'Second Viennese School'.

An eight-note row forms the basis of Webern's *Passacaglia*, Op. 1 (1908). The Variation theme of Schoenberg's *Serenade* Op. 24 (a work which is strictly dodecaphonic only in parts) shows eleven notes with three note-repetitions. In Berg's early works tendencies towards serial techniques are noticeable— quite apart from the outstanding case of Op. 4, No. 5, which will be dealt with in a later chapter. In the early song *Nacht* (1907) the basic thematic cell contains seven notes:

Example 21

which correspond to their implicit harmonies:

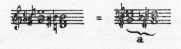

Example 22

These, in turn, represent a sequence of augmented chords in parallel movement at the interval of a whole-tone step.

A six-note series can be recognized in the early String Quartet Op. 3, if one reduces the chief subject of part I and its riposte:

Example 23

30

to its serial foundation:

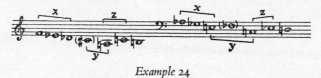

Example 24

This can easily be reduced to a six-note row and its transposition into the lower sixth. The whole-tone step '*x*' determines the whole movement; the interval of the major third at '*y*', and that of the minor third at '*z*', form part of the thematic substance of the piece. They are treated as the constitutional intervals of a series. The Basic Shapes of the dodecaphonic series on which Berg's latest works, *Der Wein* and the Violin Concerto, are based, derive clearly from ancestral archetypes mentioned earlier in this chapter. The fact that they are so firmly rooted in historic phenomena explains their indisputable tonal implications. Thus Berg, for all the apparent novelty of his materials and methods of construction, is seen to be the heir to a venerable music tradition.

PART II: THE MUSIC OF ALBAN BERG

C

CHAPTER III

Early Works

Arnold Schoenberg, whose influence on Berg's musical development was decisive from the year 1905 onwards, was a born lyrical composer. The twenty-three compositions which he completed before his fortieth year include no less than thirteen song-cycles—among them the *Gurrelieder*, which were originally conceived on a small scale as a romantic *Liederspiel* with piano accompaniment, only to develop, during their long gestation period, into a score of truly monstrous dimensions. Schoenberg's peculiar gift for finding the perfect musical equivalent of the most evanescent poetical moods, and his predilection for the song-cycle, were shared by his pupil Webern. Webern, right from the start, inclined towards the aphoristic miniature, and he, too, composed thirteen song-cycles, out of a total of thirty-one opus numbers.

Berg differed from his mentor and his fellow-pupil in that he was never a song-writer by inclination. His period of song-writing is confined to the preparatory years of adolescence (1900-1909). The eighty-two songs and duets he wrote during that time represent an emergency solution of the problems of an apprentice-composer rather than a genuine lyrical outburst. These eighty-two songs (of which fourteen are accessible in print to date) might be called 'veiled operas' with as much justification as the early Piano Sonatas of Brahms had been called 'veiled symphonies' in Schumann's famous article. The parallel with Brahms is confirmed by the course of Berg's subsequent development: the mature Brahms never returned to the piano sonata, and the mature Berg never returned to the *Lied*. The songs written before 1909 attempt to re-organize the relationship between voice and instrument. In Op. 2 (composed in 1909 and, except for the second setting of *Schliesse mir die Augen beide*, the last of Berg's songs with piano accompaniment) the romantic *Lied*, with its symmetrical periodization, becomes finally transformed, in the third Mombert song, into 'dissolved prose'. This song forms a natural link with the Altenberg songs, Op. 4, themselves precursors of *Wozzeck* and employing experimentally serial technique. After the Altenberg songs, written in 1912, Berg only twice returned to lyrical composition. However, neither the second Storm song of 1925 nor the Concert Aria *Der Wein* of 1930 can be discussed in terms of traditional song-composition. Both were preliminary studies in a novel idiom, the forerunners of greater works: the *Lyric Suite* and *Lulu*. Both, moreover, share a rigorous formal discipline. Berg's early song-style reaches its apex in the beautiful lyrical enclaves of Marie's part in *Wozzeck* (*e.g.* the Lullaby, I/3). The preparatory nature of his early songs, as well as their implicit operatic qualities, were recognized and revealed in retrospect, as it were, by Berg himself, when in 1928 he prepared the orchestral version of the *Seven Early Songs*.

Once caught up in the maelstrom of operatic composition, Berg abandoned song-writing altogether. Similarly brief was his excursion into the realm of the musical miniature. Only the four pieces for clarinet and piano, Op. 5, bear witness to the temporary attraction of Schoenberg's experimental piano pieces, Op. 11 and Op. 19, and of Webern's early cyclic compositions.

★　　★　　★

The eighty-two early songs and duets comprise:

(a) The first setting of Storm's *Schliesse mir die Augen beide*, written in 1900, the earliest composition of Berg's that has survived.[1]

(b) Seventy songs and duets composed between 1900 and 1908.

(c) The *Seven Early Songs* of 1905-08, published in 1928, in an edition with piano accompaniment and in an orchestral version.

(d) The four songs, Op. 2, composed in 1909.

Berg's earliest song is deliberately irregular in metre. It skilfully avoids the obviousness of traditional four-bar periodization by means of interstitial joins (*x*) and 5/4 rhythm (Example 25):

Example 25

This first Storm song shows the influence of Schumann; the absence of the chromatic style of Hugo Wolf, fashionable at the time of its composition, is noteworthy.

All but one of the early songs in group (b) have remained unpublished so far.[2] They include a number of settings of poems by Alfred Mombert and Peter Altenberg, to whom Berg was to return in his Opp. 2 and 4. Most of the songs in group (b) were composed before 1905, the year in which Berg became Schoenberg's pupil, but some of them, including *An Leukon*, which has been published, were evidently written in 1908, the year of the piano Variations and the Piano Sonata.

[1] Published together with the second setting in 1930. See p. 130.
[2] A complete list of the titles is given in Appendix 4. Berg's widow is unwilling to publish these songs.

37

The printed title-page of the *Seven Early Songs* bears the date 1907, but this is misleading. The first song to be composed, *Im Zimmer* (words by Johannes Schlaf), dates from 1905, while the remaining six songs were written between the summer of 1906 and the spring of 1908. The choice of poets, from the Romantics Storm and Lenau to the modernists Schlaf, Rilke and Hartleben, reveals the same divided loyalty as group (*b*) had shown. The music shows similar traits. *Im Zimmer* and *Die Nachtigall* still betray the influence of Schumann and Brahms, while *Traumgekrönt* (words by Rilke) is already fashioned as an impeccable sonata-form movement. Its chromaticism, as well as the emotional impetus of *Sommertage*, disclose the extent to which the young Berg abandoned himself to the idiom of early Schoenberg, under the impact of his teacher's overpowering personality. The most progressive song of the whole group is undoubtedly *Nacht*. It opens the whole cycle in the published version of 1928, but was actually the last to be composed (Spring, 1908). It is remarkable for the degree to which Berg had already integrated Debussy's technique of the whole-tone scale with his own post-romantic idiom. All the melodic particles and all the harmonies of this song grow quite naturally out of the subject given out by the singer in bar 1:

Example 26

'*a*' and '*b*' in vertical form become the chords '*x*' and '*y*'. The latter in turn represent a row of augmented triads, in the order of a descending whole-tone scale. They are identical with the chordal crystallization of the chief thematic subject of Liszt's *Faust* Symphony. '*x*' and '*y*', made to oscillate regularly, are

converted into an accompanying figure which clearly fore-
shadows the cadential chords of *Wozzeck*:

Example 27

The structural logic of this song is demonstrated by the fact
that the instrumental phrase:

Example 28

represents nothing but a telescoped diminution of '*a*' plus '*b*'
of Example 26.

The orchestral version of 1928 provides different sonorities
for each song. *Nacht*, *Liebesode* and *Sommertage* are scored for a
large orchestra with double woodwind, four horns and much
percussion, while *Die Nachtigall* is set for divided strings only.
Im Zimmer, on the other hand, dispenses with string tone
throughout, relying exclusively on woodwind, horns, harp and
percussion. Berg's economical use of a rich orchestral palette,
as seen later in *Wozzeck*, is already apparent in the orchestral
version of this early song-cycle. The first performance of the
Seven Early Songs took place in Vienna on November 6, 1928.
Schoenberg attended the first performance in Berlin in the
following spring and sent Berg a congratulatory wire. Berg
replied enthusiastically on May 7, 1929:

'... Your telegram delighted me, as also the mere fact that you
attended the concert. These songs have for me greater value than
they really possess because of their close association with my years

of study with you. And the fact that I succeeded in orchestrating these songs so that they impressed you as sounding well, brings this past still nearer to me. . . .'

The song *An Leukon* (words by Gleim, an eighteenth-century poet) was written in the spring of 1908, together with the last three of the 'Seven Early Songs'. It culminates in the cry 'Flüchtig ist die Zeit'—*Vita fugax*. This re-echoes through several octaves of tempestuous piano accompaniment. The words have an ominous ring, in retrospect. They clearly express an ardent desire for creative fulfilment, welling up from the subconscious in Berg's adolescence, instinctively sensing the brevity of the life-span the Gods were willing to grant him.

* * *

Of the four songs Op. 2, composed early in 1909, only the first (words by Hebbel) belongs to the romantic type of Lied, such as Wolf and Mahler were writing at or just before the turn of the century. In the three following songs (words by the remarkable pre-expressionist poet Alfred Mombert, taken from the volume *Der Glühende*), Berg abandons the tradition of the romantic Lied more decisively than Schoenberg did in his early song-cycles. Mombert's poems are mystical visions in free metre. They renounce the traditional means of rhyme and rhetoric. On the other hand, they contain enclaves of realistic impressions, strung together like photographs on a film-strip. Their brand of pre-surrealistic poetry approximates already to the peculiar type of 'prose-poem' cultivated by Peter Altenberg. Both types of allusive poetry call for a musical complement utterly different from the symmetries of rhyme and stanza in the romantic Lied of the past. Berg's discovery of Mombert and Altenberg, at a time when Schoenberg and Webern were strongly addicted to the German 'Parnassian' Stefan George, shows him instinctively heading for the dramatic psychology of a new type of opera. It has often been remarked that Berg's Op. 2 is a work of crisis and stylistic transition, typographically apparent in the fact that only the first three songs have key signatures, whereas the fourth dispenses with them for the first time. More revealing, however, than these easily recognizable signs of change is the fact that all four songs are derived from a single chord. This is the chord of fourths which concludes the fourth song, but also plays a determining part in the other songs, and notably in the Hebbel song. This common basic harmony for all four songs is a strange phenomenon in a composition of pre-dodecaphonic days. The chord as such attracted Schoenberg so much that he quoted it in his *Harmonielehre* of 1911,[1] without clearly indicating the work from which it was taken. He must have been under the impression that the chord had been used for the first time in Berg's Op. 2. Schoenberg himself used it in his Opp. 11 and 16, composed in 1908-09. Moreover, Leibowitz has discovered that the chord occurs already in Schoenberg's own early song, *Erwartung* (Op. 2, No. 1). The reason why Schoenberg apparently failed to recognize his own harmony of 1900 in Berg's work of 1909 lies perhaps in the fact that the chord is treated in Schoenberg's Op. 2 as '*Alterationsharmonie*' of the chord of the diminished seventh on E flat. This is proved by its immediate diatonic resolution:

Example 29

[1]Cf. p. 469, Example 346.

In Berg's song the same chord, however, is used in complete isolation, bereft of any modulatory logistics. It is the juxtaposition of this chord (*x*) and the following one (*y*) which may have opened Schoenberg's eyes to its future constructional possibilities:

Example 30

It was the constructive element of the fourth, and the integration of altered parallel sevenths into a sequence of chords of the fourth, which paved the way for a new concept of harmony. That Berg himself was aware of these constructive implications can be seen from the identical sequences of harmony for which this chord gives the signal in both No. 4 and No. 2 of Op. 2:[1]

Example 31

[1] The final bars are identical with Schoenberg's quotation, as reproduced in Example 30.

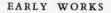

Example 32

The same chord becomes the pivot of modulation in No. 1 (bars 5 and 7), at the words 'sleep' and 'awake'.

Is this chord '*x*' really only a derivative of the chromatic scale, as Schoenberg argued in 1911? A close investigation reveals Example 31 as a sequence of harmonies based on a chain of consecutive fourths. (Cf. the bass '*z*' in Example 31, which is identical with the piling fourths in the introductory bars of Schoenberg's Chamber Symphony, No. 1, Op. 9.) But this sequence is, in turn, only the basis for a chain of chords of the dominant in chromatic alteration:

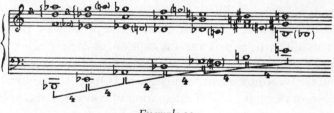

Example 33

By alternative augmentation and diminution of these chords Berg avoids the parallels of the tritone (cf. Example 33 at '*a*') and achieves through a re-arrangement of intervals the parallel fourths of Example 31 (at '*γ*'). There the 'latent' fourths in '*γ*' correspond to the succession of intervals in '*z*'. The harmonic

43

events of these bars are reflected in the vertical, chordal use of the bass 'z'. Berg had thus discovered, at the age of twenty-four, one of the principles of the future twelve-note technique. The chordal sequence of Example 31 is also used as if it were the formula of a preconceived series. This may be observed in No. 2, bars 1-4 (in the piano part), bars 9-10 (in a telescoped version in the vocal part) and bars 15-16 (in extremely condensed form in the piano part). The curious thematic interdependence of voice and instrument, seen in these bars, may owe something to Schoenberg's remarkable song *In diesen Wintertagen*, Op. 14, No. 2, composed in 1907.

In the light of these brave exploits in the 'uncharted sea' of the harmony of the fourth, occasional reminiscences in these songs of Schoenberg's *Gurrelieder* and Wagner's *Tristan* become almost irrelevant.[1]

$$\star \quad \star \quad \star$$

Berg's early instrumental music is conceived in the spirit of Vienna's classical tradition. It derives ultimately from the forms of variation and sonata-form cultivated especially by Brahms. But its ultimate aim is the conception of a new telescoped sonata-form, achieved in the one-movement Piano Sonata Op. 1 and the two-movement String Quartet Op. 3. The ambivalent process of shrinking and condensation of content, noticeable in both works, was in time to prohibit altogether any large-scale

[1]The quasi-orchestral effect of the violent *glissando* for the piano in No. 4 anticipated the numerous *glissandi* in Berg's first orchestral score: the Altenberg songs Op. 4. It also underlines the fact that the composition of songs always retained, for Berg, the character of a solution *pro tempore* only. The later orchestral version of the *Seven Early Songs* of 1928 may in turn have prompted René Leibowitz to provide his orchestral version of Op. 2, known through a gramophone recording. The translation of the music into Berg's orchestral idiom is very skilfully done, except for the *glissando* of No. 4, which unaccountably falls back on Berg's own pianistic emergency solution.

composition on these lines.[1] It was to lead to a condition in which the thematic material tended to pile up vertically instead of unfolding horizontally in time. In the short run that development led to temporary congestion, expressed in the aphoristic miniatures of Op. 5; in the long run it resulted in a style of thematic integration of unparalleled severity, culminating in *Wozzeck* and *Lulu*.

Berg's earliest extant instrumental composition, the Variations for piano on an original theme, had a single public performance in Vienna on November 8, 1908. The work remained in manuscript, and is published for the first time in the appendix to this book. It is rather doubtful whether 1908 (the year in which the Piano Sonata was completed) can be accepted as the year of the actual composition of the Variations. However, it is possible that both works—the Variations as schoolwork in connection with his studies with Schoenberg, the Sonata as free composition in his leisure hours—progressed, as it were, on parallel lines. In a letter written in late July, 1907,[2] Berg refers to his study of counterpoint, mentioning in that connection choral pieces and a fugue with three subjects, adding as a kind of postscript: 'I am working for my own pleasure on a Piano Sonata'.

Berg's Variations are evidently modelled rather on Brahms's Piano Variations Op. 9 and Op. 21, with their emphasis on canonic experiments, than on the more brilliant Handel Variations Op. 24. Berg's theme creates at once a Brahmsian mood, with its ponderous parallel sixths and clogging octave-arpeggios in the left hand. The theme is dualistic, exactly as is the theme of Brahms's Op. 21 and the 'cobbler's patch' of Beet-

---

[1]The instrumental works of Berg's maturity are based on entirely different structural principles.
[2]Cf. W. Reich, *op. cit.* p. 7.

hoven's 'Diabelli' Variations. The sequence of harmony to which the theme's incipit '*a*' is subjected, points back to Beethoven's similar procedure in the case of the 'Diabelli' theme:

Example 34

Example 35*

The twelve variations are full of conventionalities. However, in some of them anticipations of features of Berg's future creative personality are found. The mature composer's delight in contrapuntal complexities is foreshadowed in the skilful handling of two-part and 'infinite' canon in variations 3, 4 and 5. Schumann and Brahms, the former in the concertante episode of Variations 11-12, the latter in the magyar melancholy of variation 7, remain Berg's stylistic models for a great part of the work. However, Variation 12, with its tendency towards irregular metre, its Reger-like harmonies and the startling double intrusion of the whole-tone scale in bar 8 and again eight bars before the end, suddenly reveals a secret link with the progressive song *Nacht*. This passage proves that the latent tension in

*[Sketch]

Berg's music could not long remain suppressed. Its creative release in a work remarkable for originality of method and the individual character of its idiom was close at hand.

★   ★   ★

Berg's Piano Sonata Op. 1 was written in the summer months of 1907 and 1908. It was completed in the latter year on the family estate of 'Berghof' in Carinthia. It was published (together with the songs Op. 2) in 1910[1] and first performed (together with the String Quartet Op. 3) on April 24, 1911, in Vienna, with little apparent success. This Sonata consists of a single movement, in classical first-movement sonata-form, with repeated exposition, expanded development, varied recapitulation and a short coda, growing out of certain residual elements of the exposition. The fact that Berg's Op. 1 is a one-movement work might lead to comparison with Liszt's and Strauss's type of symphonic poem in one movement, or with Schoenberg's early instrumental music, where the traditional four movements of the classical symphony are telescoped into one (*Verklärte Nacht*, String Quartet Op. 7, *Pelleas und Melisande*, Chamber Symphony Op. 9). However, Berg's work was actually planned as a Sonata in three movements, with slow movement and finale to follow the traditional first movement in sonata-form. When Berg complained to Schoenberg that inspiration for these later movements was slow in coming, the latter concluded that Berg had said all there was to say and persuaded him to let the completed first movement stand for the whole sonata. A family-likeness between theme-fragments in its first and thirty-first bars and motives in Schoenberg's Op. 9 has elicited frequent comment. The common thematic link is,

[1]Revised versions of Op. 1 appeared twice during the composer's lifetime, in 1920 and 1927.

47

of course, the interval of the fourth. However, while Schoenberg treats the fourth as thematic raw material, Berg presents already in the very first bars a highly organized combination of motives, the thematic possibilities of which determine the plan of the whole sonata:

Example 36

The peculiar quality of motive 'a' depends only to a lesser degree on its division into two intervals of ascending fourths. Its character is chiefly determined by the interval of the augmented seventh, which becomes the incipit of the second theme of the expository group A:

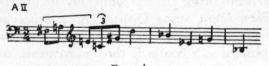

Example 37

The ubiquitous interval of the seventh can be recognized in the *cantabile* group B I (bar 30 ff) as well as in B II (bar 39 ff) and in the concluding group C (bar 50 ff), where it gives the impression of being a deliberate quotation from A I:

Example 38

48

Berg's endeavour to achieve structural integration despite thematic complexity is brilliantly successful. The numerous variants cropping up in the course of the expanded development section can easily be traced back to their origin in the exposition. Sometimes these variants appear as fascinating retrospective self-revelations (and as such they are typical products of Berg's introspective nature[1]). One such case is the transformation of *A* I *a-b* at the beginning of the development section:

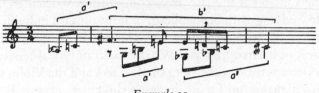

Example 39

Finally, attention should be drawn to Berg's emphatic way of confirming the Sonata's inherent B minor tonality. A tonal cadence occurs already in bars 3-4 and a repeated plagal cadence rounds off the work (bars 176-177) without a trace of tonal ambiguity. Berg's predilection for tonal cadences, even towards the end of compositions with considerably diminished tonal implications, became in time an unmistakable feature of his personal idiom.

★   ★   ★

Berg's first String Quartet Op. 3 was written in the earlier part of 1910. Already on May 30 of that year the first movement was put into rehearsal; by the early summer the whole work was being rehearsed in private. After the solitary performance in April 1911 the Quartet seemed to slip back into

---

[1] Cf. the late disclosure of the full possibilities of the *Seven Early Songs* in the orchestral version of 1928.

oblivion, until in 1920 Webern planned to rehearse and perform it in public. Stimulated by this renewed interest in his early work, Berg decided to revise and publish it, together with the pieces for clarinet and piano,[1] and thus Op. 3 and Op. 5 (together with revised editions of Op. 1 and Op. 2) were issued in the autumn of 1920. The Quartet was again revised in 1924 and this final version was subsequently published by Universal Edition in miniature score.

The Quartet is the last 'free' composition written by Berg while studying with Schoenberg. In it his musical individuality asserts itself with explosive vehemence. It includes all the features of his mature style. What it lacks in lyrical tenderness —so characteristic of the Berg of *Wozzeck* and the Violin Concerto—it makes up for in dramatic directness of appeal. The most unusual feature of this work is the fact that it is written in two movements only. A closer analysis reveals that the relationship of these movements is that of a development section to its exposition. The thematic interdependence of the two movements clearly suggests their stylistic models. They are to be found, outside the world of Schoenberg's one-movement works, Opp. 7 and 9, and Webern's early cyclical 'Five Movements' for string quartet, in Mahler's later symphonies, which made a deep and lasting impression on Berg in his years of early manhood. Mahler's Fifth Symphony (in five movements) begins with two movements (a Funeral March followed by a tempestuous Allegro) based on the same thematic material and complementary to each other. Similarly, Mahler's Eighth Symphony consists of only two movements, whose thematic and spiritual interrelationship becomes clear in the following juxtaposition of the fiery 'Accende lumen' motive of Part I and its

---

[1] Letter to Webern of April 14, 1920. In a previous letter, on March 16, 1920, Berg had confessed to an inexplicable partiality for the Quartet.

mystical transformation into the symbol in sound of the Mount of Anchorites of Part II:

Example 40

If the basic structure of Berg's Quartet owes something to these thematically interdependent works of Mahler, the thematic material itself, and its motivic proliferations, seem equally indebted to certain processes in works by Strauss and Schoenberg. This becomes particularly evident if the main subject of Berg's first movement is confronted with its ancestors: Schoenberg's own Quartet Op. 7, and Strauss's *Death and Transfiguration*:

Example 41

Similarly, a blood-relationship is apparent between the chief subject of Berg's second movement and certain historic thematic types in works by Wagner, Strauss and Schoenberg. *A a*, in Example 41, is clearly apparent behind *B a* in Example 42 below. Motive *b* spawns new elements and begets a motive *c*, which functions as an appendix-like growth *A c* in Example 41:

Example 42

Apart from these models, certain characteristics of Schoenberg's second String Quartet, Op. 10, may have affected the work of his disciple. However, Schoenberg's emphasis on tonality in that work (F sharp minor in the first movement, D minor in the second, E flat minor in the third and a return to F sharp minor in the coda of the fourth movement) is contradicted by the younger composer's equally emphatic insistence on tonal ambiguity. Although Berg's Quartet seems rooted in the polarized conflict between the tonal centres of F and D, their natural affinities are neglected or deliberately ignored. Although, for instance, the coda of Berg's first movement (after bar 160)

develops in the direction of a clear F major, with all its dominant implications (bars 165-168), the movement ends with an
unresolved dissonance:

Example 43

To be sure, this harmonic ellipsis clearly arouses the desire and
expectation of an F major resolution. The denial of this resolution is one of Berg's most typical stylistic features.[1] It was later
to play an integral part in the deliberate tonal ambiguity of
sectional closes in the *Lyric Suite*, *Wozzeck* and *Lulu*. The most
startling application of this new device occurs in the last bar of
the first movement of this Quartet. The bar contains the basic
chord of D minor, a Neapolitan sixth, and an octave-leap into,
as it were, indeterminate pitch on the last semiquaver. The collapse of the tonal structure of the music on this last note anticipates the effects of sheer noise of modern 'bruitisme'. This last
bar has its place among the critical turning-points in the musical
development of this century:

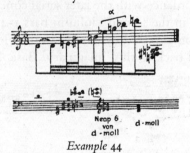

Example 44

[1] It became later one of the most hackneyed effects in modern **harmony,** and plays
a considerable role in modern jazz music.

Berg's bold experiment may have been suggested by certain contemporary works by Webern, in which similar elliptic final cadences occur. Webern's Opp. 3 and 5, both composed in 1909, about a year before Berg's Quartet, provide examples. Schoenberg quoted in his *Harmonielehre*[1] bar 5 of the first movement of Webern's Op. 5. This quotation contains *inter alia* a chord which had been played already in the previous bar as a pizzicato conclusion of a certain phrase. Played 'arco' on its repetition, it can be understood as a synchronized sound of blurred root triads of A flat and B flat. The blurring is created by the deliberately 'missed' octaves of their tonics:

Example 45

Another phenomenon important for Berg's future development remains to be discussed—the anticipatory occurrence of serial technique in this early Quartet. It becomes evident when the chief subject of the first movement (cf. Example 41[1]) is analysed in accordance with the later serial concepts. This main subject appears in the second violin in bars 1-4 and continues, in a transposition a sixth downwards, in the viola (bars 5-9). It could be traced back to this 'imaginary' Basic Shape:

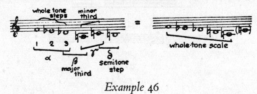

Example 46

[1]p. 468 ff.

The most important feature is the whole-tone character of 'α', which is kept intact through all thematic transformations. On the basis of Example 46 it is possible to understand melodic ideas such as those in the first movement, bar 7, 1st violin, or the second movement, bar 25, as serial derivatives from this source.

*   *   *

The four pieces for clarinet and piano were written in the summer of 1913. They were first performed on October 17, 1919, at one of the concerts of Schoenberg's 'Society for Private Performances' in Vienna, and published in the following year. They were the first of a group of works which Berg dedicated to Schoenberg after he had ceased to be his pupil. These repeated dedications are expressive of Berg's strong personal attachment to his friend and mentor, but they also hint at the continued active interest taken by Schoenberg in the development of his former pupil. Each one of the compositions dedicated to Schoenberg marks the beginning of a new creative period for Berg.[1] The pieces for clarinet are deliberately modelled on the musical miniatures produced by Schoenberg and Webern in 1908 and 1912 as a kind of implied protest against the mammoth-scores of the new century's first decade. It seems worth while recording that this reaction began to manifest itself exactly at the time when Mahler, Scriabin and Schoenberg himself completed their outsize 'symphonies of the thousand'. The work of Schoenberg and Webern on a miniature scale was, of course, no isolated musical phenomenon. Contemporary works of an aphoristic nature, such as Busoni's

[1] Other works dedicated to Schoenberg were the *Three Orchestral Pieces*, Op. 6, the Chamber Concerto and *Lulu*.

Elegies for piano and his Piano Sonatinas of 1910/12, Bartok's
Bagatelles Op. 6 and easy Piano Pieces of 1908 (one of which is
quoted in Schoenberg's *Harmonielehre*) show a similar outlook.
However, more interesting than the parallels between the
Vienna school and other progressive European composers are
the intrinsic differences which exist in the work of the Vienna
school itself, between the musical miniatures of Schoenberg and
Webern and those of Berg. They become especially noticeable
if one confronts one of Berg's clarinet pieces with its obvious
stylistic model. Comparison of the second piece with Schoenberg's piano piece, Op. 19, No. 2, reveals that whereas the latter
relies entirely on the motoric motive of the continuously repeated third, the 'espressivo' motive of bars 2-3 being treated as
a passing phase without thematic consequence, in Berg's piece
a thematic conflict ensues already in bar 2, through the combination of the reiterated piano chords and the melody in the
clarinet. That conflict leads ultimately to an alteration in pitch
of the 'constant' third D-F sharp, which at the end of bar 5 has
become D flat—F natural. The *status quo* is only restored
through the tail-end of the phrase of the clarinet, bar 7. But
that phrase is set against the now diminished 'constant' third on
the piano which, according to the composer's expression marks,
must be clearly audible so as to underline the condition of permanent conflict of harmony. In Schoenberg's piece the 'constant' third really *is* constant, from the first to the last bar.

Like the middle numbers of the Altenberg songs of 1912, the
clarinet pieces impress the student of today, in retrospect, as
pointers towards the future style of *Wozzeck*. The 'Invention
on a six-note chord' (*Wozzeck*, III/4), with its ghostly harmonic
pedal, expressive of the enveloping mists of the pond scene,
seems foreshadowed in the rigid immutability of the chromatic
suspension chord on the basis of C (Op. 5, No. 4, bar 17 ff),

whose resolution merges with the unreal whisper of a weird effect of harmonics on the piano. The syncopated rhythm

of this fourth clarinet piece recalls the rhythm of the first movement of Mahler's Ninth Symphony, but it also points forward to the sinister rhythmic symbols in *Wozzeck*, *Lulu* and the Chamber Concerto. The overpowering explosion at the end of this piece is comparable with the *glissando* in the third Mombert song (Op. 2, No. 4) and the percussive *crescendo* after Marie's death (*Wozzeck* III/2). The ghostly effect of upper partials produced on the piano may have been suggested by the aeolian harp effect in Schoenberg's Piano Piece, Op. 11, No. 1. However, while that effect remains an episodic impressionistic gesture in Schoenberg's piece, in Berg's composition it clearly expresses with dramatic finality an ultimate catastrophe. The miniatures of Berg's Op. 5 clearly reveal the latent musical dramatist, waiting impatiently in the wings for the decisive cue.

Something might be said, in addition, about the part played by mere note-repetition in these pieces. This can be observed especially in the clarinet part, where the main motives congeal, as it were, out of a welter of trills, 'flutter-tonguing' effects, tremolandi and irregular note-repetitions. Although Berg is anxious to avoid the structural devices of sonata-form, and especially recapitulation, yet even these musical miniatures reveal to the analyst the bony structure of the archetypal sonata pattern. No. 4 represents a telescoped sonata-movement with elliptic reprise and dramatic coda. The content of this final piece goes far beyond the static impressionism of Schoenberg's and Webern's contemporary compositions. It heralds, in fact, future stresses and tensions which will manifest themelves fully in a new musical drama.

* * *

Berg's first opera was preceded by two previous works employing the orchestra: the Altenberg songs, Op. 4, and the *Three Orchestral Pieces*, Op. 6. Two problems of paramount importance for the future composer of *Wozzeck* were the establishment of an orchestra, capable at once of miniaturistic differentiation and of sound-climaxes of shattering intensity, and the establishment of a new relationship between the singing voice and its instrumental accompaniment. Both problems are posed and solved with remarkable originality in Berg's Op. 4.

When he started work on the Altenberg songs in 1912 Berg could benefit by the revolutionary experiments in orchestral sonorities and vocal expression already undertaken by Schoenberg and Webern. The latter's surprisingly mature *Passacaglia* for orchestra, Op. 1 (1908) already made use of the rudiments of a new serial technique; his *Six Pieces for Orchestra*, Op. 6 (1910), followed by the *Five Pieces for Orchestra*, Op. 10 (1913), reduced the musical picture to a pointillistic flash-light snapshot. In Webern's Op. 10, No. 1, sonority, structure, thematic evolution and all the paraphernalia of traditional symphonic rhetoric have been filtered away, leaving a residue of barely twelve bars. At the same time Berg was subjected to the full impact of Schoenberg's *Five Orchestral Pieces*, Op. 16, and the two early operas *Erwartung* and *Die glückliche Hand* (composed roughly between 1909 and 1913). It is in Schoenberg's Op. 16 that the struggle for a new conception of orchestral sonorities becomes manifest. It is here that the antithesis between an enormous orchestra and its application to the exclusive expression of minute and evanescent sound effects creates the basis of a new style. There is, undeniably, a paradoxical discrepancy between the assembling of a huge orchestra and its employment in pieces of aphoristic brevity. Schoenberg's increasing desire to find exact musical equivalents for the most involved psychological experiences led to the discovery of new devices such as the 'flutter-tonguing' effect on the trombones in Op. 16, No. 5, the unique vocal style of *Erwartung* and the introduction of 'Sprechstimme' into the chorus-parts of *Die glückliche Hand*. It led also, in *Erwartung*, to the use of a deliberately asymmetrical music as accompaniment to a psycho-analytical text, devoid of rhyme and rhythmic scansion. The sum total of Schoenberg's achievements in this direction constitutes Berg's point of departure in his approach to the problem 'Singer versus orchestra'. With the unerring instinct of genius he chose for his own experiments the one medium neglected at that time by both Schoenberg and Webern: the song with orchestral accompaniment. The choice was almost inevitable after the quasi-orchestral ebullience of the last Mombert song. There Berg had already taken steps leading away from traditional post-Romantic lyricism. And after the free rhythms of Mombert's asymmetrical prose, it seemed a perfectly logical further step for Berg to discover Peter Altenberg,[1] the eccentric Viennese poet and 'Socrates of the Coffeehouse', who befriended his fiancée Helene Nahowski, and delighted in inventing slightly scandalous texts to picture postcards, in an embarrassing mixture of obscenity and tenderness.

Opus 4 was composed in 1912, the first work of Berg's creative freedom, after the termination of his studies with Schoenberg. But there is good reason to believe that Schoenberg was repeatedly consulted about this work while it was

---

[1] His real name was Richard Engländer. His book *Neues Altes*, of 1911, includes pieces dedicated to Helene Nahowski. Altenberg died in Vienna, half-forgotten, in 1919. Berg valued his books highly, and put them on a separate shelf of his library, next to Strindberg's.

still in the preparatory stage. After its completion in the autumn of 1912 Schoenberg accepted it for inclusion in the programme of an orchestral concert under his direction, given on March 31, 1913, in the Grosse Musikvereinssaal, Vienna. Besides Schoenberg's Chamber Symphony, Op. 9, Webern's orchestral pieces Op. 6 and Berg's Altenberg songs, the programme was to have included also songs by Mahler and Zemlinsky with orchestral accompaniment. But owing to a carefully-planned riot by one section of the audience the concert had to be abandoned during the performance of Berg's songs, which seem to have been drowned in the ensuing general uproar. A free fight between members of opposing musical factions led to a somewhat anticlimactic epilogue in the police court. The disaster of that first performance sealed the fate of Berg's Op. 4. It remained unperformed, unpublished,[1] and almost totally forgotten.[2] Finally, in 1953, Jascha Horenstein resurrected the score for a BBC broadcast programme and after that the cycle was at last published, in piano arrangement.

The conceptual basis of these songs is the contradictory conflict between the vocal part, often reduced to a mere whisper, and an outsize orchestra, excelling in different colouristic combinations and groupings. The orchestra consists of: three flutes, three oboes, three clarinets, bass clarinet, three bassoons, three trumpets, four horns, four trombones, bass tuba, glockenspiel,

[1]Except for the fifth song *Hier ist Friede*. This was published as an appendix to a periodical *Menschen* (Dresden, 1921). It was recently reprinted to illustrate an article on Op. 4 by René Leibowitz (*Musical Quarterly*, 1948).

[2]A first orchestral draft of the fourth and fifth songs found its way to Lincoln College, Oxford, and is now deposited on permanent loan at the Bodleian Library. The story of that autograph has been told by Egon Wellesz in his article: 'An Alban Berg manuscript at Oxford' (*Tempo*, 1946, No. 5). It is possible that sheet 14 of this autograph includes a short vocal phrase (from the second song, bar 5) in Schoenberg's hand. If this could be clearly identified as Schoenberg's hand it would provide definite proof of his active interest and even collaboration in Berg's work, long after the latter had ceased to be his pupil.

xylophone, cymbals, gong, tympani, drums, celesta, harp, piano and strings. However, this tremendous array of players is hardly ever used in a symphonic 'tutti'. Instead, the composer makes every effort to reduce the sonority of each instrument. He uses cunning devices for cushioning the sound impact by frequent *glissandi*, trills, flutter-tonguing, harmonics and mutes, even for instruments of a vigorous nature such as trombones and tympani. Berg's new devices aim to express the faintest stirrings of the soul in tonal symbols of wraith-like evanescence. Characteristic examples are:

The 'mute' *glissando* of harmonics on the violin's E string, whose graphic symbol almost looks like a wind-swept leaf:

Example 47

the weird device of bowing at the string-holes on the 'bridge' (No. 1, bar 38) is nearly eclipsed by the fantastic tympani *glissando* in the final bars of the last song. These devices find their vocal implementation in the unique gradations of tone, in which the very act of singing pierces finally the hard crust of painful silence:

Example 48

Berg's explanatory footnotes to this quotation should be added:
  x Note sung with lightly closed lips (*ppp*).
  xx Note sung with half-open mouth (*pp*).
Both footnotes are bracketed with the remark: 'To start and finish with a mere breath'. The behaviour of the first audience

successfully prevented this hesitant world of sound from materializing at all.

The first song, from which Example 48 above is taken, is also remarkable for its iridescent orchestral prelude. This is based on a self-repetitive series of five notes, and its sonorous mosaic of dovetailing motive-particles results in an almost oriental tissue of sound, reminiscent of the Javan Gamelan orchestras. The purple colours of this first song give way to a chamber music style of elliptic abbreviations in the second. The eleven bars of this song revolve round the descending fourths of bar 2, a motive later to be exploited in *Wozzeck* and *Lulu*. Voice and violoncello end the song in strict canon at the octave, a curious anticipation of future serial severity. The third song starts and ends with a veritable twelve-note chord. It contains, like all the pivotal harmonies of Op. 4, the interval of the tritone at the brackets.

Example 49

During bars 1-7 this static chord is 'spotlighted' by different and rapidly changing combinations of instruments, with an effect like a musical impression of an unruffled but iridescent pond. The same effect is found in Schoenberg's Op. 16, No. 3. It is repeated in Berg's fourth song, in which certain basic features of serial technique appear. The chief melody, as presented in bars 19-21, determines also the two static chords (bars 8 and 22) which are subjected to similar changed 'spotlighting'. This can be studied by comparing the melody itself with its resultant harmony and the two static chords:

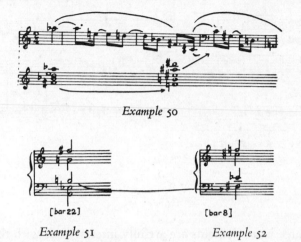

Example 50

[bar 22]   [bar 8]

Example 51   *Example 52*

The last and longest song, No. 5, is an amazing anticipation of future musical developments. It is a Passacaglia, based on a five-note motive in the bass. But it is also a piece of strict dodeca-phonic music, composed long before the official establishment of twelve-note technique. The use of archaic forms like the Passacaglia precedes their re-introduction in Schoenberg's *Pierrot Lunaire* by a few months. The impeccable twelve-note row, however, which enters in the woodwind at bar 5, ante-dates Schoenberg's first serial compositions by more than ten years. The song is strictly organized by the three thematic ele-ments, entering in close succession before cue 2:

(*a*)   the five-note Passacaglia bass (*c*).
(*b*)   the twelve-note row in the treble (*R*).
(*c*)   a theme of ascending fourths, evidently developed from the motive of No. 3 (*c* 1).

63

Key : R = 12 note series
C = Passacaglia theme
C1 = Continuation of C
b = Countersubject of C

Example 53

The three basic elements are artfully intertwined, with the element (*b*) meandering through the whole fabric of the song almost like a Chaconne theme, more and more out-distancing the Passacaglia bass (*a*). The emphasis on rigid adherence to preconceived principles of form, the firm reliance on strict contrapuntal devices and the fact that these devices are employed in the service of a subtle and fleeting emotional experience of wistful longing, link this song with the world of *Wozzeck* and even with the systematic dodecaphony of *Der Wein* and *Lulu*. *Hier ist Friede* remains Berg's most important technical achievement before *Wozzeck*.

★　★　★

Berg's second work for orchestra before *Wozzeck*, the *Three Orchestral Pieces*, Op. 6, probably owes its peculiar form to the tendency of Schoenberg and Webern, before 1914, to replace the traditional cyclic symphonic forms by short self-contained movements with a certain programmatic bias. The sub-headings of Berg's Op. 6—Prelude, Round, March—are similar to those in Schoenberg's Op. 16 and Webern's Op. 10.[1] A further sign of the impact of Schoenberg's *Five Orchestral Pieces* can be found in Berg's adoption of the new structural guides 'H' and 'N' ('Hauptstimme' and 'Nebenstimme'), first employed in Schoenberg's Op. 16, No. 5. In addition, the considerable numerical increase in Berg's orchestra, even beyond that used in the Altenberg songs, may have been prompted by the imposing sonorities of Schoenberg's Op. 16. However, despite these affinities, Berg's Op. 6 is farther removed than any other work of his from Schoenberg's orbit. It represents, rather, his creative approach to Mahler's conception of the symphony. The influence of Mahler, as man and artist, now competes with that of Schoenberg in a protracted struggle for Berg's allegiance. This struggle led to a crisis in 1913, when Berg discarded a planned symphony, saving only a fragment which was later incorporated in the last orchestral interlude of *Wozzeck* ('Invention on a key'). This fragment, with its decidedly Mahlerian flavour, bears witness to the impression made on Berg by the slow movements of the last symphonies of the older composer. The discarded symphony, however, was inspired by Balzac's mystical novel *Seraphita*, which, at the very same time, Schoenberg himself planned to utilize for an opera libretto. Webern told Berg that Schoenberg was planning an operatic trilogy based on Balzac's novel. In his reply, on July 29, 1912, Berg mentions his own projected work:

'. . . Just fancy: this winter I intended to compose a big symphonic movement and I had planned to let it end with a boy's voice

[1] The original sub-headings were eliminated in the published scores of both works. For details consult the German edition of this book.

singing (from the gallery) words from "Seraphita"! Of course it remained a mere project—as so often happens in my case . . .'

The idea of ending a symphony with a vocal solo derives, of course, from Mahler. Berg's dream of a programmatically-based Mahlerian symphony never materialized because he found the solution of his problems in his own new conception of opera. After *Wozzeck* he could not return to the symphony. His later instrumental works are either *concertante* music (Chamber Concerto, Violin Concerto) or lyrico-dramatic (*Lyric Suite*, *Der Wein*). None of them is really symphonic in character. This is regrettable, because Berg could easily have become heir to Mahler's symphonic tradition—a tradition which now lives on only in scattered movements by Zemlinsky and Karl Horwitz, and, in recent time, in the remarkable symphonies of Egon Wellesz.[1] No work written during the first half of this century reveals a deeper affinity with Mahler than Berg's Op. 6.[2]

The psychological roots of the *Three Orchestral Pieces* can be traced back to a personal crisis in Berg's life, during which his relations even with his beloved teacher Schoenberg became strained. A letter dated June 14, 1913, written shortly after he had visited Schoenberg in Berlin, reflects the mental conflict and distress brought about by stern discussions with his mentor and heralds a future creative experience of heart-searching intensity:

'. . . You will surely understand that, together with the loveliest memories of unspoiled enjoyment, there also intrudes the memory

[1] Wellesz, born in Vienna in 1885 and an early pupil of Schoenberg's, like Berg himself, only began to write symphonies at the age of sixty. His five symphonies, composed in England between 1945 and 1956, are the only convincing attempt so far to continue the symphonic tradition of Bruckner and Mahler in the second half of the century.

[2] In marked contrast to Schoenberg and Webern, whose music is surprisingly free from Mahler's influence. An exception is Webern's *Marcia funebre*, Op. 6 (1910). Cf. T. W. Adorno (W. Reich, op. cit., p. 46).

of the last afternoon, with its depressing home-truths. However, I have to thank you for your reproof, as much as for everything else I have received from you, convinced as I am that it was all said for my own good. . . . I don't need to tell you that the deep pain it has caused me is proof of that fact that I have heeded your reproof. . . . I hope to show you by deeds what I am unable to express in words. As soon as I am in the country I will begin the Suite. Perhaps one day I shall be able to compose something serene. . . .'

A year later, by the middle of 1914, the plan for a 'Suite' had resulted in the first draft of the *Three Orchestral Pieces*. Berg intended to dedicate them to Schoenberg on the occasion of the latter's fortieth birthday (Sept. 13, 1914), but on July 18 expressed anxiety, in a letter to Webern, about his ability to complete the score in time. The tension of the 'last afternoon' in Berlin is recalled still, in this as in other letters of the period. Berg suffered greatly from lack of news from Schoenberg. Writing to him on July 20 he referred to this 'prolonged silence' as part of the great punishment he had endured then for two months. In that letter he expressed concern about the fate of the 'orchestral pieces', adding with moving sincerity:

'. . . To be sure, I have to ask myself, again and again, if what I express in them, and what compels me to brood over certain bars for days on end, is any better than my last compositions. . . .'

Berg retired to Trahütten, his parents-in-law's country estate in Styria, but the outbreak of war interrupted work on the full score. On September 8, 1914, he wrote to Schoenberg:

'. . . I am sending you by the same post a registered parcel: the orchestral pieces, dedicated to you on the occasion of your birthday. . . . For years it has been my secret but persistent wish to dedicate something to you. The works composed under your supervision, the Sonata, songs and Quartet,[1] do not count for that purpose, having been received directly from you. My hopes of writing something more independent and yet as good as these first compositions (something I could confidently dedicate to you without incurring your displeasure) have been repeatedly disappointed. Your kind suggestion of last spring (during the journey from Amsterdam to Berlin) gave me the courage to attempt a composition which I could dedicate to you without blushing. I cannot tell today if I have succeeded or if the attempt has failed. Should the latter be the case, then, in your fatherly benevolence, you will have to accept the good intention in place of the deed itself. I really have tried to give of my best and to follow your advice. In this endeavour the unforgettable experience of the Amsterdam rehearsals[2] and the close study of your orchestral pieces was an enormous help and has intensified my self-criticism more and more. *This* is why I have not been able to complete the second of the three pieces, "Reigen", in time, and why I have had to leave it until later, when I shall probably succeed in altering what is wrong in it, about which I am not yet certain. Another reason is that the unavoidable commotion of the last weeks caused slower progress with my work than I had hoped for before the outbreak of war. Please do not take amiss my boldness in dedicating to you something incomplete. I hope to finish the missing second piece soon (it is a piece of dance-character, about 100 bars long, i.e. longer than the Prelude, shorter than the March) and to add the score to the two pieces I am sending you now. . . . I am still working at the piano arrangement of the Chamber Symphony.[3] For this reason I am remaining here for a time and I believe I can curb my impatience and restlessness in connection with the war better here than in Vienna. The urge "to be in it", the feeling of helplessness at being unable to serve my country, prevented any concentration on work there. . . .'

Reigen was not completed until the summer of 1915 and the

---

[1]Opp. 1, 2 and 3.
[2]For the first performance of Schoenberg's *Five Orchestral Pieces*, Op. 16, late in 1912.
[3]This arrangement is lost.

fair copy was sent to Schoenberg in early August of that year.[1] Interest in Op. 6 was only shown after the publication of the vocal score of *Wozzeck* (1922-23). Berg's autograph score was then published in facsimile by Universal Edition, in 1923. The first two pieces were performed in Berlin on June 5, 1923, under Webern. The complete work was first performed in 1930 at Oldenburg, under Johannes Schüler. Berg revised the score for Schüler, and for Scherchen,[2] who performed the whole work at Winterthur in the following year.

★   ★   ★

An unmistakable family likeness exists between the motives and thematic processes of Berg's Op. 6 and those of some of Mahler's symphonies. The models for the second and third pieces are to be found in Mahler's symphonic march-movements and his rustic 'Ländler'-like Waltz-Scherzos. Berg's movements are very much shorter, of course, and it must be added that he presents them as self-contained entities and not, as Mahler invariably did, as sub-sections of one great symphonic concept.[3] But the relationship between Berg's Op. 6 and Mahler's musical world goes deeper than this. It becomes manifest in Berg's re-employment of Mahler's hammer in the third piece, the fatalistic tonal symbol for the hammer-blows of fate, which fell the hero of the sixth symphony in its tragic finale. Preoccupation with sonorities and rhythmic devices typical of Mahler led to the anticipation of the 'Leitrhythmus' used in

---

[1] Letters to Webern of July 13 and August 5, 1915.

[2] This revised version was published in 1954 (Universal Edition, Vienna). It reveals some changes in expression marks and certain improvements in the difficult part for the first trombone. The substance of the music is unchanged.

[3] In 1929 Berg ruled that separate performances of these pieces were permissible. But the fact that the last bars of No. 1 anticipate bars 3-6 of No. 2, and the fact that No. 3 is evidently planned as a kind of development section to No. 1, seems to contradict the idea that the pieces are easily separable.

Wozzeck, Lulu and the Chamber Concerto, as may be seen in the following juxtaposition of passages from the two composers. Mahler's rhythm of death from the first movement of the Ninth Symphony, bar 1, corresponds to Berg's 'Hauptrhythmus' in the Prelude of Op. 6:

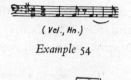

(*Vcl., Hn.)*

Example 54

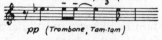

pp (*Trombone, Tam-tam*)

Example 55

Again, Mahler's thrice-repeated fate motive in his sixth symphony (corresponding with the three hammer-blows of the finale), with its tonal inexorability and the lugubrious thud of its drum-taps, anticipates Berg's 'catastrophic rhythm' at the very climax of his third piece:

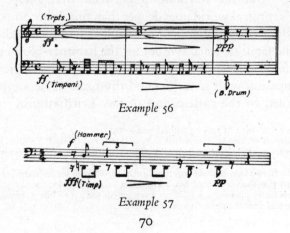

Example 56

Example 57

70

The uncanny 'bruitisme' of the exclusively percussive beginning and end of the 'Prelude' foreshadow the experiments of
'La musique concrete' and the percussive extravaganzas of
Milhaud and Varese, as much as they point back to Mahler's
enclaves of organized noise in the march-sections of the first
movement of his third symphony.

The role played by Mahler's music as model can also be seen
in certain melodic progressions of Op. 6. The lyrical contrasting
subject of the first piece (bars 15-20) seems indebted to lyrical
passages of the first movements of Mahler's sixth and ninth
symphonies. And the following bar from Berg's *Reigen*, which
anticipates the Ländler music of *Wozzeck* (11/4), was clearly
suggested by the scherzo-grotesqueries of Mahler's seventh
symphony (Example 59):

Example 58

Example 59

On the other hand, Op. 6 also contains many felicitous touches
of indisputable originality. These include the six-note chord
of fourths in No. 1 (bar 9), which constitutes a link with No. 2
(cf. No. 1, bar 43). The introduction to the *Reigen* is based
exclusively on two tonal root-harmonies (F minor, D major):

Example 60

the harmonic impurities of which recall similar processes of harmonic-blurring in the Altenberg songs. The structure of Nos. 1 and 2 is based on the principle of perpetual variation. Their architectonic contours are therefore simple, especially in comparison with the ambitiously-planned March. The latter consists of Introduction, Exposition, Recapitulation and Coda, and can compare even in dimensions with a symphony movement by Mahler. The key to the understanding of the involved harmonies of No. 3 is to be found in its very last bar, based on the bare tritone: E natural—B flat. The tritone can be understood as the sum total of three whole-tone steps. It stands for the principle of the whole-tone scale, which is combined with the chromatic scale at the psychological climax of the 'March' (Coda, bar 149 ff). The use of the chromatic scale here anticipates Berg's future serial technique, which seems to be somehow in the air, especially in the octave transpositions and the resulting interval-camouflage of chromatic semitonal steps at bar 149 ff:

Example 61

The little fanfare at the end of No. 2, based on a progression of mediants, plays an integral part in No. 3. The same little motive had occurred at the word 'schöner' in the second Altenberg song (bar 5). It prepares for the harmonic climate of *Wozzeck*, where in turn it will re-appear in the visionary second scene of the first act. Similarly, the murder scene of *Wozzeck* seems to

72

be foreshadowed in the chromatic dissolution of No. 3, bar 161 ff. The link between Berg's Op. 6 and his opera becomes manifest even to the casual observer in the case of the trombone motive of No. 3 (bar 80 ff), which re-appears, slightly varied rhythmically, in *Wozzeck* (I/2, bar 275 ff), where it accompanies *Wozzeck's* sinister words: 'Something wanders with us deep down there. . . .'

CHAPTER IV

'Wozzeck'

The Opera of Protest and Compassion

IN a hitherto unpublished essay on Berg,[1] Schoenberg wrote:

'I was greatly surprised when this soft-hearted, timid young man had the courage to engage in a venture which seemed to invite misfortune: to set "Wozzeck", a drama of such extraordinary tragic power that it seemed forbidding to music. And, further-more, it contained scenes of every-day life at variance with the concept of opera, which still depended on stylized costumes and conventionalized characters . . .'

Schoenberg's insight thus recognized the feature by which *Wozzeck* may be distinguished from its forerunners and models —Wagnerian music-drama and contemporary operas such as Debussy's *Pelléas*, Strauss's *Salome* and *Elektra*, Schoenberg's own *Erwartung* and *Die glückliche Hand*, and Franz Schreker's early opera *Der ferne Klang*. What was new in Berg's opera was determined by his choice of subject. A superficial survey of operas roughly contemporary with *Wozzeck* might easily per-suade one to attach too much importance to one feature they have in common: the librettos of Debussy's opera and the two

---

[1] See Appendix 1, where the essay is printed throughout in Schoenberg's own peculiar variety of English. The passage here quoted has been slightly revised.

works by Strauss named above are based, like that of *Wozzeck*, on existing stage plays. This phenomenon, remarkable in itself, was the result of a general tendency of the time to avoid the symmetrical periods of Viennese classical music, to turn away from the use of regularly corresponding phrases (largely determined by the fact that the old libretto was usually in rhymed verse) towards a free, asymmetrical, musical 'prose' style. The composer of the new century preferred the realistic dialogue of straight plays to the metrical versification of the older libretto. It is surely more than coincidence that Maeterlinck's *Pelléas*, Wilde's *Salome* and Hofmannsthal's *Elektra* had all enjoyed successful runs on the stage before practically renouncing their purely literary existence in symbiosis with music of overpowering vitality. At first glance it might seem reasonable enough to link Berg's *Wozzeck* with these works, although Büchner's fragment—left unfinished at the time of the poet's death in 1837 and published posthumously as late as 1879—can hardly be classified as a contemporary play. The principal difference between *Wozzeck* and these plays lies in its subject matter. Büchner's fragment presents a social problem in dramatic form, whereas the plays of Maeterlinck, Wilde and Hofmannsthal, despite their prose dialogue and realistic tendencies, are still not far removed, in essentials, from the sphere of romantic music-drama.

Debussy's *Pelléas*, although deliberately conceived as 'Anti-Tristan' and differing from Wagner's opera also in its much lower emotional temperature, yet presents another variation of the tragic triangle Tristan-Isolde-Mark. The emotional agent of *Pelléas* is identical with that of *Tristan* and draws the characters as inevitably to their 'Liebestod'. Salome's obscene 'love-death', too, and Elektra's sterile hysteria, result from the same primordial force of frustrated eroticism. Despite certain realistic scenes, like that of Golaud dragging Mélisande by her hair, or Elektra digging up the hatchet, the action of these operas takes place in an atmosphere of legendary remoteness. Although based on modern plays in prose, with none of the traditional operatic choruses, ensembles, arias and duets, they still derive from Wagner's romantic mystery-play of redemption.

Even the immediate forerunners of *Wozzeck*—Schoenberg's *Erwartung* (1909) and *Die glückliche Hand* (1913), and Schreker's *Der ferne Klang* (completed in 1909; first performed in 1912)— differ considerably from it, although they certainly powerfully influenced Berg.[1] The primitive conflict of the sexes lies behind both early operas of Schoenberg, which can still be assessed as emanations of the Tristan legend. Schreker's opera comes much nearer to a truly realistic conception of music-drama. *Der ferne Klang* is based on a libretto, written by the composer himself, of which the contemporary plot and characters anticipate the *Zeitoper* of the 1920's. The story of the modern composer, Fritz, who, chasing a phantom sound, abandons his sweetheart and drives her to prostitution, only to re-encounter the dishonoured girl at the very moment of his despair in his creative faculties, represents an early attempt to depict social environment as the determinant of personal tragedy.[2] Schreker's Fritz and Gretel are seen from the viewpoint of the 'Milieu' theory of the 1890's. Unfortunately, Gretel's emotional debauch usurps too much of the limelight, and Schreker, in his naïvely realistic libretto, fails to achieve a well-balanced presentation of the social implications of his subject. An artist of more profound

[1] Berg's preface to *Wozzeck* points out the determining influence of Schoenberg's 'Sprechstimme' technique, especially as used in *Die glückliche Hand*. The importance of *Erwartung* in this connection will become manifest in the course of this book. Schreker's influence was probably wholly subconscious.

[2] Some of Janacek's operas also call for mention here. *Jenufa* was begun as far back as 1896. Janacek is reported to have recognized *Wozzeck* as the expression of a kindred spirit when he attended the first performances of the opera in Prague in 1926.

feeling and a musician endowed with the gift of structural integration was needed for the creation of a new archetypal species of opera: the opera of social protest and compassion. Only in the spiritual and creative symbiosis of Büchner and Berg could this new kind of opera come into being.

*   *   *

It is clear from Schoenberg's essay on Berg, already quoted, that he thought the stark realism and unrelieved gloom of Büchner's play made it unsuitable for musical treatment, at any rate on anything approaching traditional operatic lines. Karl Rankl reports, even, that Schoenberg at first disapproved of Berg's choice of subject, declaring that the concern of music should be angels, rather than batmen.[1] However, what seemed superficially a commonplace crime-report ('Soldier murders girl in jealous fit') became the basis of a social drama of remarkable penetration. According to more recent research, Büchner seems to have planned, as culmination of his play, a final scene in which Wozzeck was to have addressed a criminal court, and in which the accused was to have become the accuser, delivering a shattering sentence of death on the court of law and on the State itself. If Büchner's fragment (used by Berg in the textually unreliable version published by Emil Franzos in 1879) had represented nothing more than the dramatization of a police report, then Schoenberg's initial scepticism would have been justified. But *Wozzeck* is much more: it is the gospel of a convinced revolutionary and socialist, who succeeds in presenting his murderer as the hapless victim of a system of political tyranny.

[1] Cf. *The Score*, May 1952.

Georg Büchner was born on October 17, 1813, at Goddelau, near Darmstadt (Hesse), the son of a doctor. He belongs, with Richard Wagner, to the generation destined to prepare and to unleash the 'liberal revolution' of 1848 in Germany and Austria. A precocious child, a brilliant scholar, a scientist of distinction, a philosopher of great promise, he became involved in political strife with the authorities of Hesse while studying at Giessen University. Büchner's youth coincided with a period of unrelieved reactionary oppression in Central Europe, increasingly hostile to the liberal movements among students and university teachers. Büchner eventually went to near-by Strasbourg, where he completed his studies with a brilliant paper, 'Sur le système nerveaux du barbeau'. This essay was accepted as a thesis by Zürich University, where in due course Büchner received the degree of Doctor of Philosophy. In October 1835 he arrived at Zürich and was appointed Lecturer in Anatomy. The political persecution to which he and some of his friends were subjected in Hesse, the frustration of exile in Alsace and Switzerland, continuous over-work during his student-days, and the stress and strain of his creative activities undermined his delicate health. He became ill early in 1836 and died in his twenty-fourth year, on February 19, 1837. A political pamphlet, 'Der Hessische Landbote', which circulated clandestinely in 1834-35, stamped Büchner as a forerunner of Marx and Bakunin. The play, *Danton's Death*, characteristically inspired by a great revolutionary subject, was published in 1835 and hailed by Carl Gutzkow as a work of genius. Two more plays, the comedy *Leonce and Lena* and the fragmentary *Woyzeck* (this was the original and correct spelling), were discovered after his death among his papers. Büchner's poetical works, letters and pamphlets, continued to exercise a profound influence on his generation—an influence easily traceable in the dramatic works of Gutzkow, his discoverer, as in those of Friedrich Hebbel (1813-1863), his later admirer. It was left to Emil Franzos,[1] editor of the first collected edition of Büchner's works, to decipher the almost illegible manuscript of *Wozzeck* and to publish this great dramatic prelude to the revolution of 1848-49 for the benefit of a later generation, in 1879.

Wozzeck is the tragedy of the enslaved victims of Metternich's *'Vormärz'*, the dreary epoch that went before the March revolution of 1848. The 'Holy Alliance' during this epoch deprived the generation of Schubert and Grillparzer of freedom of thought and political independence, and thus forced them to withdraw from unpleasant reality into literary clubs and romantic make-believe. Wozzeck is the spokesman of the 'tiers état', which, in belated succession to the storming of the Bastille in 1789, was at length in 1848 to succeed in abolishing at any rate the worst features of that feudal tyranny. In Büchner's drama the sufferings of the humble and the almost dumb find painful articulation in elliptic, ejaculatory sentences and fragmentary exclamations: 'Folk like us are always unfortunate . . . in this world and in any other world.' 'If we should arise to heaven we'd be employed there in helping to make the thunder . . .' 'All our days are spent in endless toiling . . . sweating even in sleep . . . poor, wretched folk.' The importance given in Berg's opera to these sudden, lightning-like illuminations of the darkness in Wozzeck's mind shows the measure of the influence exercised by Büchner's social and political ideas of 1836 on the young Austrian composer of 1914, whose subsequent war-time experiences must have made him particularly sensitive to the ordeals

[1] Franzos was born on October 25, 1848, at Czarkow, in Galicia, a part of Poland which then formed part of the Habsburg Empire. He was a Polish Jew, and wrote novels concerned with Polish or Ruthenian Jews living precariously on the fringes of Germany and Austria-Hungary. He died in Berlin on January 31, 1904.

of Wozzeck at the hands of his ruthless superiors.[1] The tragedy of the poor Prussian infantryman of Polish extraction, harassed to death in the stuffy atmosphere of a Prussian garrison-town, held special significance for the young Berg, called up for the Austro-Hungarian army, which consisted in good measure of enslaved soldiers of Wozzeck's Slavonic type. 'The Bohemian-German Job of the Fourth Estate', as Arnold Zweig called him,[2] became in the end the symbol of the Austrian Slav, gagged and silenced, in an army led by German-speaking officers.

Büchner's fragment was probably written between the Spring of 1836 and October of the same year. To set it to music be-tween 1914 and 1921 was an act of supreme artistic awareness and political conscientiousness. Berg chose to treat this subject at the fateful moment when, to use again the terms of Schoen-berg, the batman changed into the avenging angel of enslaved humanity.

* * *

The revolutionary novelty of the subject of Berg's opera is matched by the entirely new relationship between words and music which he established in it. We must now try to discover the principles that guided the composer in setting to music a drama that even Schoenberg at first believed unfit for such treatment.

The first stage was the construction of the libretto by con-densing and unifying Büchner's loose sequence of short scenes. These were transformed into a closely knit, coherent structure in three acts, each of five scenes. The table of concordances

---

[1] Cf. Kurt Blaukopf, 'Autobiographische Elemente in Alban Berg's "Wozzeck" ', (Österreichische Musikzeitschrift, May 1954).
[2] In his Complete Edition of Büchner's works, Munich, 1923.

between play and libretto (printed overleaf) shows how this was done. Berg set to music fifteen out of a total of twenty-seven preserved scenes of the fragmentary drama. He admitted later that he had used for his opera only the older and unreliable edition published by Franzos, which included only twenty-three scenes. Among those missing was the very effective one, 'The idiot, the child, Wozzeck' (No. 23 in Zweig's complete edition of 1923). On the other hand, Scene 19 ('Junk-shop: the Jew and Wozzeck') *had* been included in Franzos's edition, but was eliminated by Berg; he is reported to have regretted this in later years. More than once Berg telescoped several scenes of the play for reasons of dramatic economy and concentration. Büchner's scenes 10, 16 and 17 were fused together to form Act 2, Scene 5, of Berg's libretto; Büchner's scene 18 and part of scene 20 became Act 3, Scene 1; another part of scene 20 and scene 26 became Act 3, Scene 5, of the libretto. Similarly, the number of characters was reduced. The figure of Margaret (Act 3, Scene 3) stands for Büchner's Käthe as well as for the innkeeper's wife. In Act 3, Scene 4, the Captain and the Doctor have also absorbed the parts of Büchner's 'First and Second Citizens'. In Act 2, Scene 4, Andres takes over the words of the 'other young men' and those of the un-named 'soldier'.

Table of Concordances

between

BÜCHNER'S PLAY	and	BERG'S LIBRETTO
(Zweig's edition)		
1 A room (Captain, Wozzeck)		I/1
2 Countryside		
(Wozzeck, Andres)		I/2

3	The town (Marie, Wozzeck)	I/3
4	The Doctor's study	I/4
5	Open square (People, Wozzeck, Marie)	—
6	Inside a booth (Crier, Marie)	—
7	A street (Marie, Drum-Major)	I/5
8	The Doctor's operating theatre (Doctor, Wozzeck, students)	—
9	A small room (Marie, child)	II/1
10	A tavern (Wozzeck, Drum-Major)	—(but cf. Büchner's No. 17 and Berg's II/5)
11	Street (Captain, Doctor, Wozzeck)	II/2
12	Marie's room (Wozzeck, Marie)	II/3
13	Guardroom (Wozzeck, Andres)	—
14	Country inn (Dance, wandering artisans)	II/4
15	Open country	—
16	Barracks (Andres, Wozzeck)	II/5 } combined with elements of Büchner's Nos. 10, 16, 17.
17	Inner yard in the barracks (Drum-Major, Wozzeck)	II/5 }
18	Marie's room (Bible-reading scene)	III/1
19	Junk shop (The Jew, Wozzeck)	—
20	Street (Grandmother's story)	—(But cf. III/1 and III/5)

Berg added many stage-directions. On the other hand he expunged, or considerably softened, many coarse expressions in the original text. If he had set *Wozzeck* in later years he might have been less puritanical, since he did not hesitate to set to music lines of a much more *risqué* character in *Lulu*. Here and there the composer improved Büchner's text, as in the fourth scene of the first act, where his replacement of 'Wozzeck, let me feel your pulse' by 'Wozzeck, show me your tongue' leads to a 'curtain' of grotesque, daemonic effectiveness. The addition of the out-of-tune upright piano, on which a fast polka is played, to the lurid tavern-scene (Act 3, Scene 3) is another happy innovation.

In *Wozzeck* Berg employed a style of singing and of declamation totally different from the traditional styles of German opera, although foreshadowed in certain passages of the operas of Strauss and Schoenberg. Berg expounded his views on this subject in his lecture on *Wozzeck* of 1929[1]:

> With regard to the treatment of the singing voice in this opera, it has often been observed that it is not exactly a Bel Canto opera. However, there is no real reason why much of what is conceived in terms of *cantabile* singing should not be mastered with the aid of the art of 'beautiful singing'. I have not even forgone the possibilities of ornamental singing. There are, to be sure, almost no recitatives in my opera. But I believe I have liberally compensated for this omission with the so-called 'rhythmic declamation' introduced by Schoenberg nearly twenty years ago in the declamatory choruses of 'Die glückliche Hand' and in the 'melodramas' of his 'Pierrot', which I was the first and for a long time the only person to use on a large scale in opera. The application of this technique to opera has shown that this kind of melodramatic treatment of the voice (while fully utilizing all its purely musical possibilities, which in recitative are abandoned), this kind of melodically, rhythmically and dynamically controlled speech, represents not only one of the best means of conveying the sense of the words (which must at times be the task of language, even in opera), but that by it opera has been enriched by a valuable new musical resource (ranging from the whispered word off-pitch to the 'bel parlare' of its widely ranging 'speech' melodies), at once a welcome complement and an attractive contrast to the fully sung word.
>
> The other result of my present investigations is the way in which I dealt with the necessity of introducing passages in the style of popular song, and thus of establishing in my opera a relationship between art-music and popular-music—something that is a mere matter of course in tonal music. It was not easy to make these different planes clear within this so-called atonal harmonic system. I believe I succeeded by giving to everything that, musically, fell within the popular sphere, an easily perceptible primitive character, practicable even within the atonal harmonic system. The means available for this are: a preference for symmetrically shaped periods; the use of harmonies in thirds and,

---

[1] For a first full publication, Cf. Appendix 3, page 261ff.

especially, in fourths; melodies based largely on the whole-tone-scale and the perfect fourth, in contrast to the diminished and augmented intervals used in the atonal music of the 'Vienna School'. So-called 'Polytonality' is also another such means of creating harmonically primitive music.

Avoiding both Bel Canto and dramatic recitative, in order to explore and exploit the possibilities of the realistic expression of his text, Berg employs in turn different techniques of musical declamation. They range from emotional 'Sprechgesang' in the manner of Wagner (Wozzeck's expressive main motive: 'Wir arme Leut' ')

Wir ar - me Leut'

Example 62

and the style of popular song (the songs of Marie and Andres), to the 'normal speaking intonation' of words spoken to synchronized music (Act 1, Scene 3, dialogue between Marie and Margaret), this last being identical with the 'mélodrame' of classical opera (e.g. Beethoven's *Fidelio*, Act 2, No. 12).

Midway between these two extremes of vocal expression are the transitional types of 'Sprechstimme' and 'rhythmic declamation', used in Schoenberg's Opp. 18 and 21 and expressly mentioned in Berg's lecture. In the preface to the vocal score of *Wozzeck* Berg reprints parts of Schoenberg's explanatory note to his *Pierrot Lunaire*. He also refers to a similar commentary provided in the full-score of *Die glückliche Hand*. It is interesting to note that Berg abstains from any reference to the earlier 'mélodrame' in the *Gurrelieder* ('Des Sommerwindes wilde Jagd'), although this piece is surely the earliest example of Schoenberg's brand of 'speaking voice'; it may well have been put on paper as early as 1901. The subtle differences between

85

the 'mélodrame' in the *Gurrelieder* and the 'Sprechstimme' in
Die glückliche Hand and *Pierrot Lunaire* are revealed in a letter of
Schoenberg's published in Berg's guide to the *Gurrelieder*. The
problem of actual pitch and of clear differentiation of intervals
is evidently a more serious one in the two later works. The
contrast becomes graphically evident in the transition from the
'white notation' of the *Gurrelieder* 'mélodrame' (♪) to the
'black notation' of Opp. 18 and 21 (♪). The latter method of
strict indication of pitch and interval was adopted by Berg in
many parts of *Wozzeck* (ɪ/2, ɪɪ/3-4, ɪɪɪ/ɪ and ɪɪɪ/4). However,
subtle gradations can be found even within the narrow limits
of 'rhythmic declamation'. Whereas Wozzeck's spoken phrase

Du, der Platz ist ver-flucht!

Example 63

represents only an ordinary speaking 'mélodrame' with extra
emotional emphasis, Marie's reading from the Bible

und knie-te hin zu ih-ren Füs-sen

Example 64

re-approaches again the plane of *cantabile* singing. (Observe in
the foregoing examples Berg's endeavour to distinguish graphically between the two vocal techniques.)

The extreme contrast to Example 63 is represented by the
popular 'Lied' style of *Wozzeck*, especially apparent in the
songs of Marie and Andres. In the 'Quasi Trio' section of the
Military March (Act ɪ, Scene 3), Marie hums in the manner of
a folksong in symmetrical eight-bar periods. The result is a
melody that might have been invented by the Mahler of the

'Wunderhorn' songs. This passage seems indeed to have been consciously associated by Berg with Mahler's *Revelge*, from the 'Wunderhorn' songs:

Example 65

In his treatment of the voice parts Berg undoubtedly paid special attention to the question of 'Intonation'.[1] This becomes particularly noticeable in the rare *cantabile* sections. In striving for truly realistic expression and in his dislike of the clear contours of the traditional Bel Canto vocal line, Berg deliberately blurs the outline of his melodies in folk-style by the intrusion of the atmospheric orchestral background-music:

Example 66

The 'atonal' deviation in Andres's song (it is hummed, rather than sung) at '*x*' is as legitimate an artistic device for the creation

---

[1] The use of intervals based on the inflections of the voice in ordinary idiomatic speech, as, for example, by Janacek in his Czech operas.

87

of a realistic sound-atmosphere as are the 'tonally' corresponding echoes at '*a*'. The latter incorporate the involuntary deviation from pitch, customary in unaccompanied singing. This
calculated impurity of pitch saves these popular melodies from
obviousness and all vestiges of sentimentality. Even more convincing is the shaping of the folk-song for chorus 'Ein Jäger
aus der Pfalz' (Act 2, Scene 4). Here the naïve diatonicism of
the tune is countered by the erroneous A flat in the refrain
'Halli, Hallo' and by the burden-like choral parts, clogging and
hampering the nimbly ascending scale-passage in C major:

Example 67

It should not be overlooked, however, that certain extrava-
gances of Berg's vocal style, such as the grotesque squeak of the
apoplectic Captain:

Example 68

have their roots in certain border-line cases of dramatic expression in Wagner and Strauss, approaching near to the realistic
shout. Wagner, in his autobiography, describes Wilhelmine
Schröder-Devrient's transference of the 'cris du fureur' of the
French revolutionary opera to Beethoven's *Fidelio*, Act 2:

Töt' erst sein Weib! —

Example 69

The realistic interpretation of this passage in *Fidelio* probably paved the way for things like these bars from *Parsifal* and *Salome:*

Und   lach te . .

Example 70

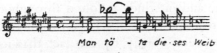

Man tö - ta die · ses Weib

Example 71

which in turn may have influenced certain vocal climaxes in Berg's opera.

★   ★   ★

Wozzeck is scored for an outstandingly large orchestra, offering marked possibilities of differentiation of tone-colour:

4 FLUTES	4 HORNS	TYMPANI
4 OBOES	4 TRUMPETS	CYMBALS, BASS DRUM,
4 CLARINETS	4 TROMBONES	BROOM, SIDE DRUMS,
BASS CLARINET	CONTRABASS TUBA	2 TAMTAMS, TRIANGLE,
3 BASSOONS		XYLOPHONE, CELESTA,
DOUBLE BASSOON		HARP, STRINGS.

A cursory glance at the massive array of wood-wind and brass might suggest a work rather in line with the mammoth scores of Richard Strauss and early Schoenberg. However, that impression would not outlast the very first page of the first scene of the opera, where Wozzeck, shaving the Captain, is accompanied by a mere 'obbligato' of five solo woodwind instruments, harp, muted strings and an occasional touch of percussion. The whole first scene, the structure of which closely corresponds with that of the old harpsichord suite (comprising Praeludium, Pavane, Cadenza, Gigue, Gavotte and Double), is played throughout to the above accompaniment of chamber-music-like dimensions. The first orchestral tutti, of only 9 bars, occurs in the following orchestral Interlude. This relationship between scene and interlude is found throughout the whole score. The orchestral style of *Wozzeck* differs from that of Wagner and Strauss chiefly by the fact that its 'fortissimo' effects are almost exclusively confined to the interludes between the scenes, while the scenes themselves are accompanied by smaller, selected groups of instruments. Berg thus reflects the change of style in writing for the orchestra which took place with Schoenberg's and Schreker's *Kammer-Sinfonien* of 1906-08, Mahler's last vocal compositions and Strauss's *Ariadne* (1912). The solution of the orchestral problems of *Wozzeck* was finally determined by the nature of the libretto, which compelled the composer to provide no less than fourteen orchestral interludes, the basic function of which was to ensure the musical cohesion of the acts as wholes, in spite of the numerous changes of scene. Berg discussed this problem in his lecture on *Wozzeck*:

A further compelling necessity for musical variety arose with the comparatively large number of orchestral interludes, resulting from the fact that each act demanded three changes of scene. To have written here symphonic transitions or intermezzi throughout (such as I was to observe later in another contemporary opera with many changes of scene[1]) would have been at variance with my own conception of musical drama. So I was compelled to aim at contrast and variety by making these interludes partly transitional bridge-passages, and partly giving them the forms of coda to the preceding scene, or prelude to the following scene, or even both at once.

Generally speaking, these orchestral interludes are related to the scenes they connect in a way that recalls the relationship between the development section of a movement of a symphony and its exposition and recapitulation. This organic quality in the *Wozzeck* interludes distinguishes them, much to their advantage, from the orchestral interludes, say, in Debussy's *Pelléas*, which often tend to smother the delicate, athematical lyricism of the preceding scene with their heavy climaxes of, as it were, extraneous orchestral sonorities.

Berg's art of orchestral differentiation is seen at its subtlest in Scenes 3 and 4 of Act 2. Here the orchestral *tutti* is split up into three self-contained and independently organized groups of instruments:

(a) A chamber orchestra of fifteen instruments (deliberately modelled on Schoenberg's Chamber Symphony No. 1, Op. 9) consisting of:
Flute (Piccolo), Oboe, Cor Anglais, Clarinet in E flat, Clarinet in A, Bass Clarinet, Bassoon, Double Bassoon, two Horns and five solo strings;

(b) A band of players in the village inn, on the stage, consisting of:
'Fiddles' (i.e. violins with 'scordatura', tuned a tone

[1] Probably Debussy's *Pelléas et Mélisande* is meant.

higher than normally, like the solo violin in the
Scherzo of Mahler's Fourth Symphony), Clarinet in
C, Accordion, Guitars and Bombardon in F;

(c)   A residuary orchestral 'tutti'.

In the third scene the spoken dialogue between Marie and
Wozzeck is accompanied by group (a); group (c), however,
comes into action as soon as the figure of the Drum Major
begins to dominate their exchanges, and brings in all the
motives associated with that character (Rondo theme, Trio of
the Military March of Act 1, Scene 2). This results in a very
original relationship between *concertino* and *tutti*. In the fourth
scene group (a) is replaced by group (b) which—like the three
ballroom orchestras in Mozart's *Don Giovanni*—enters with a
cadential figure (in Berg's opera on the Bombardon). There is
even a thematic allusion to Mozart at bar 439:

Example 72

For a long time group (b) dominates the scene, with its music
based on Waltz and *Ländler* rhythms, while group (c) is confined to occasional interjections. This relationship between an
orchestra on the stage and the orchestra in the pit recalls that in
Der Rosenkavalier, Act 3 (the waltz in E, cue 101). The music

of Berg's stage-orchestra is, perhaps deliberately, reminiscent of this *Rosenkavalier* waltz, and of the *Ländler-Waltz* from Weber's *Der Freischütz*, Act 1.

Very different is the role allotted to the orchestra in Act 3 of *Wozzeck*. This is organized as a sequence of 'Inventions', beginning with a Fugue on a six-note theme:

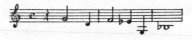

Example 73

accompanying Marie's reading from the Bible. Here the orchestra is again transformed into an ensemble of soloists. In sharp contrast is the treatment of the orchestral interlude ('Invention on one note') following the second scene of this act, which culminates in the famous thirteen bars on the note B (i.e., the persistent pedal point of the preceding murder-scene) ending with a tremendous '*fff*', after the 'fatal rhythm' (the structural backbone of the following scene) has been given out by the bass drum in isolated savagery:

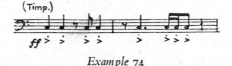

Example 74

Example 74 is the basis of the brutal 'Quick Polka' strummed out on the out-of-tune upright piano at the beginning of the third scene. Here the instrumental accompaniment is again of a dualistic nature. The piano vamps accompaniments to the ballad-like song of Margaret, the barmaid, while the *tutti* orchestra contributes the sinister stammer accompanying Wozzeck's distracted exclamations.

93

In the final interlude ('Invention on a key'), linking the fourth and fifth scenes of this act, the full power of the orchestra comes at last into play, epitomizing the dramatic content of the whole work in the manner of a symphonic epilogue. This is the longest piece of sustained orchestral music in the opera. Its roots go back to a discarded symphonic project of 1912, as already mentioned, and the almost anachronistic recurrence here to the opulent manner of Mahler or early Schoenberg throws the subtleties of the chamber-music-like texture of the *Wozzeck* score in general into bold relief.

Another passage of Berg's lecture of 1929 discusses the problem of musical form presented by *Wozzeck*:

> When I decided to compose a full-length opera I was confronted with a new problem, at least in the harmonic sphere. How could I hope to achieve, without the well-tried resources of tonality and its possibilities of formal organization, the same compelling musical unity? Unity, not only in the short scenes, but in the formal design of whole acts, and, indeed, in the general structure of the entire opera?

The solution of this problem is to be found in the unique formal organization of *Wozzeck*, which has elicited so many commentaries, ever since its publication. In the three main sections of the work, each of five scenes, Berg himself recognized *a posteriori* 'the good old ternary form *A-B-A*'. The following table of corresponding relationships between stage-scenes and musical forms, originally drafted by the composer, is familiar to every student of the opera. It emphasizes remarkably the ternary structure of the work.

'WOZZECK'

Formal Organization of WOZZECK

SCENE	MUSIC

Act 1

Exposition: Wozzeck in relation to his environment.

Scene 1: Wozzeck and the Captain.
Scene 2: Wozzeck and Andres.
Scene 3: Marie and Wozzeck.

Scene 4: Wozzeck and the Doctor.

Scene 5: Marie and the Drum Major.

Musical form: 5 character pieces.

Scene 1: Suite (in 11 sections).
Scene 2: Rhapsody on 3 chords.
Scene 3: Military March—Lullaby—Scena.
Scene 4: Passacaglia (Theme and 21 variations).
Scene 5: Andante affettuoso (quasi Rondo).

Act 2

Dramatic development: Wozzeck becomes more and more convinced of Marie's unfaithfulness.

Scene 1: Marie and the child; Wozzeck (Wozzeck's first suspicions)
Scene 2: Captain, Doctor, Wozzeck (Wozzeck derided)
Scene 3: Marie and Wozzeck (Wozzeck accuses Marie of being unfaithful to him)
Scene 4: Garden of a country inn (Marie dances with the Drum Major)
Scene 5: Guardroom in the barracks (Soldiers, Andres. The Drum Major manhandles Wozzeck)

Musical form: Symphony in 5 movements.

Scene 1: Sonata movement.

Scene 2: Invention and Fugue.

Scene 3: Largo for chamber orchestra.

Scene 4: Scherzo with 3 Trios and recapitulation (2 orchestras).

Scene 5: Introduction and Rondo marziale.

Act 3

Catastrophe and epilogue: Wozzeck murders Marie and atones by suicide.

Scene 1: Marie and the child (her remorse).
Scene 2: Marie and Wozzeck at the pond. (Marie's death)
Scene 3: Tavern. Wozzeck seeks forgetfulness in drink.
Scene 4: Wozzeck's death in the pond.

Orchestral interlude (Epilogue)
Scene 5: Children playing, among them Marie's child.

Musical form: 6 Inventions.

Scene 1: Invention on a theme.

Scene 2: Invention on one note.

Scene 3: Invention on a rhythm.

Scene 4: Invention on a chord of six notes.
Invention on a key (D minor)
Scene 5: Invention on a continuous quaver-movement.

95

Some commentators have hailed the use in opera of the older musical forms (Suite, Passacaglia, Fugue, Rondo, etc.) as a revolutionary innovation. Berg himself disposed of that idea, in an article published in 1928.[1] Actually, the use of the forms of 'absolute music' in opera was much less of a novelty than he and his first critics, thirty years ago, imagined. However, the structural organization of *Wozzeck* is by no means fully illustrated by the above tables. Although Berg discarded the possibilities of formal organization through tonality, he continued to use *Leitmotive*, in Wagner's manner. He also used scales (including the diatonic scale) and serial rows at certain pivotal points of the drama. An assessment of the musical structure of *Wozzeck* must distinguish three basic techniques:

(1) The use of diatonic and non-diatonic scales and serial rows as unifying elements;

(2) The use of characteristic motives (*Leitmotive*), establishing close affinities between character, situation, action and music;

(3) The use of the forms of absolute music.

But does the emphasis on formal organization in *Wozzeck* really represent something new in opera? Surely not. All three basic techniques have been used in opera again and again, from Monteverdi and Gluck to Méhul, Weber and Wagner. *Leitmotive* play an integral part already in Monteverdi's *Favola d'Orfeo* (1607) as in Méhul's *Ariodant* (1799) and Weber's *Freischütz* (1821). The forms of absolute music are likewise no strangers to opera.[2]

When Berg conceived the five scenes of his second act as the movements of a symphony he only turned a fundamental, if

---

[1] 'Das Opernproblem' (*Neue Musikzeitung*, Stuttgart, *Jahrgang* 49, No. 9, 1928).
[2] Cf. the fugues in Wagner's *Meistersinger* (Act 2) and in Verdi's *Falstaff*, the canon in Beethoven's *Fidelio*, the chorale prelude in Mozart's *Magic Flute*.

hypothetical, claim of Wagner at last into artistic reality. In his essay 'Über die Anwendung der Musik auf das Drama' ('On the application of music to the drama'), of 1879, Wagner had traced the conception of his new *Musikdrama* back to the Viennese classical symphony: 'Nevertheless, the new form of dramatic music must have the unity of a symphony-movement, to become a musical work of art. This unity is given by a tissue of basic motives permeating the whole composition. These motives act upon one another, linking up, separating, complementing, like motives in a symphony-movement.'

Berg's *Wozzeck* is neither atonal nor dodecaphonic. Both terms are misleading and inappropriate, although their use could be justified by certain features of the score. The opera is described by Berg himself as 'a work in atonal style', yet it is not strictly atonal in the sense, say, of Schoenberg's *Erwartung*: for there are many passages of tonally organized music in which definite keys are employed.

Traditional major and minor scales are frequently used to express certain moods. For instance: Marie's hummed folk-tune 'Soldaten sind schöne Burschen' (I/2, cf. p. 87, Example 65) in A flat; the frequently misinterpreted chord of C major accompanying Wozzeck's 'Da ist wieder Geld, Marie, die Löhnung . . .' (II/1);[1] or the section in F minor (III/1, Var. 5, 2 bars before cue 35) when Marie tells the fairy-tale about the lonely child.

The final cadential chords of the opera, to which Berg attributes integral importance, also derive from traditional harmony. These chords, which recur at the end of each act, and function there 'like a tonic', are formed, according to the com-

---

[1] A hand-written interpolation in the typescript of Berg's lecture of 1929 refers to this passage: 'How could the detached objectivity (*Sachlichkeit*) of money be better expressed?'

poser himself, of the same notes. Yet they appear each time in different form. Closer investigation shows that their origin may be traced to a certain serial scale-organization. The sequence of chords at the ends of Acts 1 and 3 can be presented in the following reduced form:

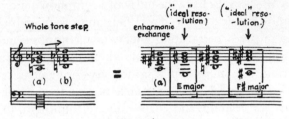

Example 75

Both chords, (*a*) and (*b*), oscillate above the faburden-fifths (*c*), i.e. they are rooted in diatonic harmony. Separately assessed, both (*a*) and (*b*) are chords of the seventh, capable of tonic resolution into E major or F sharp major. To these obvious relationships of (*a*) and (*b*) to diatonic harmony should be added the melodic movements, from C flat to D flat, and from A to B natural, in the highest and lowest parts. These melodic movements are steps of whole tones. This means that the chord sequence (*a*)-(*b*) is related to the whole-tone scale (melodically) as well as to the diatonic scale (as far as modulation and the possibilities of enharmonic change are concerned).

If the variant of the sequence (*a*)-(*b*) in Act 3, bar 390, at the entry of the faburden fifths (*c*), is presented as a cadential formula:

Example 76

98

and is then strung out serially, in the sense of later dodecaphonic practice, the result is the 'Grundgestalt' (Basic Shape) of a G major scale with interstitial whole-tone steps:

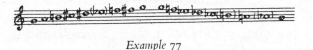

Example 77

Its inversion presents a perfect whole-tone sequence. Kinship exists, undoubtedly, between the chord sequence (*a*)-(*b*) and the chordal pendulum of the introduction to the song *Nacht* (*Seven Early Songs*, 1907):

Example 78

That kinship is seen in the variable sequence of chords of the ninth, as well as in their immutable hard core: the inner sequence of two whole-tone steps:

Example 79

This relationship between *Wozzeck* and the harmonic process of the early song proves anew the organic character of Berg's whole creative development. Those sections of *Wozzeck* based on scale-like serial formations of atonal character are further removed from the logistics of the diatonic scale. They disclose (like the fifth of the Altenberg Lieder, Op. 4) a surprisingly close approximation to the processes of twelve-note music, which was still *in statu pupillari* at the time when *Wozzeck* was completed. This is seen most forcibly in the Passacaglia subject

(I/4), called 'Chaconne' by Berg himself, the basis of the twenty-one variations which express, as the composer says, 'the Doctor's *idée fixe* with purely musical means'. The theme itself is dodecaphonic (as Berg himself discovered later), as is the passacaglia-subject of the fifth Altenberg song, Op. 4, which might have been a preliminary study for it. This passacaglia-theme is first presented on the clarinet as an 'expressionless' symbol:

Example 80

In Variations 6 and 7 this subject is not treated in the traditional manner of the passacaglia. It is not used as a thematic ground-bass, but appears as a vertical chord-condensation. This is a typical process of Dodecaphony, which admits the possibility of transposition of every member of the Basic Shape into different octaves. Significantly enough, a condensation of this twelve-note series (cf. Example 80) accompanies (at the very end of Variation 6) Wozzeck's words 'Wenn was is und doch nicht is. . . .' ('Ah, when it's there, and is not there. . . .') boldly anticipating Variation 7. The vertical presentation of the series telescopes the intervals into simultaneously-sounding harmonies, thus:

Example 81

Variation 7 repeats the process and completes it by including the retrograde version of the series. In Variation 7 the series is subjected to a selective process based on the principles of permutation, which anticipates the serial technique of *Lulu*. The selective sequence of notes may be presented in tabulated form, thus:

$$(a) \quad 2 \ 4 \ 6 \ 8 \qquad 12 \ 8 \ 6 \ 4$$
$$(b) \quad 1 \ 3 \ 5 \ 7 \qquad 11 \ 7 \ 5 \ 3$$

The omitted notes '*a*' and '*f*' (9 and 10 of the series) are presented by the stationary faburden-fifths (*c*).

The passage here analysed contains the principles of Schoenberg's later twelve-note technique in a nutshell—proof at once of the historical inevitability of the development of this technique at this time, and of the creative independence of Berg's exploring mind.

Polytonality also has a part to play among the expressive devices of the opera. Berg effectively blurs the contours of harmony by simultaneously sounding two chords of the seventh, which in turn are related to one another as tonic and dominant. This overclouding of the harmony takes place at Marie's words 'Du siehst so verstört' ('You look so distraught'), which re-echo Wozzeck's visionary imaginings (I/3). Violins, *col legno*, play the following passage, based on a chord of A flat minor, given out by the trombones:

Examples 82 and 83

101

The note sequences (*a*) and (*b*) can be presented in vertical chord formation, thus (cf. No. 83). Their simultaneous sounding, intensified by the alien 'A flat' (a link with the chord of the trombones), results in a nine-note chord:

Example 84

Although *Wozzeck* dispenses with tonality for long stretches, its music remains strictly organized down to its last details, largely owing to the judicious employment of serial techniques.

Referring to the bare fifths in the orchestra which accompany Marie's 'absent-mindedness' (first occurring in Act 1, cue 415):

Example 85

Berg, in his lecture of 1929, said: 'These fifths are closely associated with the figure of Marie . . . their harmonic immobility expresses, as it were, her aimless waiting, which is only terminated with her death. This passage is used several times, almost in the manner of a *Leitmotiv*.' Actually Berg's use of such motives of dramatic characterization is strikingly akin to Wagner's use of *Leitmotive*. The web of motives is much denser in *Wozzeck* than in Strauss's *Salome* and *Elektra*, both based on a comparatively small group of characteristic themes, and compared with other contemporary operas of looser texture Berg's work represents, in this respect, almost a return to Wagnerian orthodoxy. Among the numerous motives of *Wozzeck* may be singled out the group of 'motives of fear' associated with Wozzeck himself, the hunted and miserable victim of his social inferiority. These motives recur also in the music associated with Marie and her child. They express the permanent psychological oppression exerted on them by Wozzeck, even in his absence. Their common structural link is the whole-tone scale:

Example 86

and its inversion:

Example 87

From Marie's threatening gesture 'Go to sleep, boy' (II/1, cue 30) the motive of 'the child's fear' is developed:

Example 88

Example 89

This is condensed into a hasty sequence of which the across-the-bar rhythm and tendency to descend by whole-tone steps suggest a feeling of breathlessness:

Example 90

The same motive returns in slow, dragging tempo when Wozzeck suddenly appears and surprises Marie putting on the compromising ear-rings. The breathless fear of Example 90 has now become the tragedy of the everyday treadmill of the poor, expressed in the sinister lethargy of the canon on muted trombones:

Example 91

In this canon there occurs again the sequence of descending whole-tone steps:

Example 92

A new variant of this motive is heard in Act 2, Scene 2, when Wozzeck is pulled up by the doctor with the words: 'Why hurry so fast and pass us by?' At this point the muted trombones express compellingly the tragic discrepancy between Wozzeck's inner heaviness and his apparent haste:

Example 93

Bereft of its heavy harmonies, Example 93 becomes at bar 313 the third subject of the 'Invention and Fugue on three subjects', in the trio between the Captain, the Doctor and Wozzeck, the climax of which comes with Wozzeck's cry of despair (based on the familiar whole-tone steps):

Dann wüss te man woran man ist!

Example 94

The role of the descending whole-tone scale in the musical characterization of Wozzeck is played by the interval of the fourth in the 'popular' parts of the score. All motives in 'popular' style can be traced back to the basic cell of an ascending fourth:

Das ist die schö·ne Jä ge rei

Example 95

This motive develops in the second stanza of Andres's song into:

Example 96

where the particle 'x' can be recognized as the basic motive of Marie's lullaby:

Mö·del, was fangst du jetzt an?___

Example 97

In the final orchestral interlude in D minor ('Invention on a key') particle 'x' represents once more the central core of the musical idea:

Example 98

Berg was anxious to explain the use of the older musical forms in his opera. In his lecture he said:

> My aim was musical variety and the avoidance of Wagner's method of 'through-composing' every single one of these many scenes. Therefore I had to give to every scene a different structural basis. On the other hand, the dramatic unity of these scenes demanded a similar unity in the music. This could best be achieved by the employment of closed musical forms.

Berg goes on to emphasize that the choice of these forms was determined by the character of each scene and that he employed not only archaic forms, such as Passacaglia and Fugue, but new designs, such as the 'Inventions' based on one note, one rhythm, or one chord. The use of Passacaglia and Fugue, for musico-dramatic purposes, deserves closer scrutiny. There is nothing casual about the choice of these forms for use in *Wozzeck*.

Berg based his deliberations on Hugo Riemann's etymologically dubious but interesting association of the term 'Folia' (ostinato) with the Berliozian term 'idée fixe'. In the passacaglia theme (I/4, Cf. Example 80,) the doctor's mania, as well as Wozzeck's maniacal philosophizings, find their appropriate musical equivalent. The obstinate repetition of one single musical idea under changing melodic and harmonic progressions is

surely the only possible way of representing in notes the omni-
presence of the 'idée fixe'. Büchner's characters all have their
dominating 'fixed idea' (Wozzeck's visions, the Doctor's theory
of nutrition, the 'moral' philosophy of the Captain, Marie's
unbridled sensuality). They almost inevitably suggest the use
of musical ostinato forms.[1]

In this context Schoenberg's use of the passacaglia for 'Nacht'
in his *Pierrot Lunaire* (Part II, No. 8) should not be overlooked.
Berg freely admitted the influence of *Pierrot* on the music of
Wozzeck.[2] This influence becomes evident if Berg's passacaglia
theme (Example 80) is compared with Schoenberg's
theme, the latter being the final result of an initial canonic
stretto of its first link '*a*':

Example 99

However, whereas Schoenberg's *Pierrot* passacaglia, rooted in
the four-note motive:

Example 100

remains a musical miniature of only twenty-six bars, Berg's
Wozzeck passacaglia with its twenty-one variations, based on

---

[1] Manfred Gurlitt's opera *Wozzeck*, composed shortly after Berg's own, also makes
systematic use of ostinato and passacaglia.

[2] In a letter to Webern of August 19, 1918, first published by Willi Reich in 1953.

a veritable twelve-note series, is an impressive structure, in which Schoenberg's own methods of composition of the 1920's are clearly anticipated. It is likely that Webern's passacaglia, Op. 1 (1908), also contributed something to Berg's work. Its eight-note theme contains intervals with striking possibilities of subsequent vertical, chordal treatment. In the final variation of Berg's passacaglia (Variation 21, vocal score, two bars before cue 640) the full melodic series (Example 80) is presented in full twelve-note harmony also—a solution probably suggested by Webern's example.

The use of fugal technique for purposes of dramatic characterization is seen in the 'Invention and Fugue on three subjects' (Act 2, Scene 2). The 'Invention', accompanying the dialogue between the Doctor (B) and the Captain (A), (Act 2, bar 172), presents its two subjects in the manner of a two-part Invention by Bach, with all the implications of double counterpoint:

Example 101

From bar 286 onwards the music becomes strictly fugal, with subjects A and B presented in a double exposition and subject C (Example 93) entering at bar 313, to Wozzeck's sombre threat: 'But why do you ask that question, good doctor? . . .' From her onwards A and B are kept to the level of countersubjects to C, until bar 345, when the tortured Wozzeck rushes away. With the doctor's baffled remark: 'How he runs off, and his shadow runs behind . . .' is heard a ghostly reminiscence of the 'idée fixe', the passacaglia theme, from the scene between Wozzeck and the doctor in the previous act.

Berg first decided to set Büchner's play to music in May 1914.[1] However, work on the *Three Orchestral Pieces*, Op. 6, occupied him until the end of that year. Meanwhile the first World War had broken out, and in August 1915 Berg was called up for the army. By the summer of 1917 he had completed the draft of the libretto and had started on the music. He began with the Invention and Fugue (Act 2, Scene 2), but by August 1918 only two scenes had been set to music. The greater part of the opera was written between the autumn of 1918 and the autumn of 1920, a period of perpetual political crisis in Austria, resulting in much economic hardship, especially for the intellectual stratum of society. Financial embarrassment and the mounting problems of a hand-to-mouth existence compelled Berg to look for a job, and for a time he planned to become general editor of the musical periodical *Der Anbruch*; nothing came of this, in the end. By April 1921 the orchestration of *Wozzeck* was complete, after about eight months' work. In the winter of 1922-23 Berg invited subscriptions towards the publication of the vocal score of his opera and, with the financial support of Mahler's widow, *Wozzeck* was first published in this way in 1923. In the following year it was acquired by Universal Edition, Vienna. Following the advice of Hermann Scherchen, Berg chose three extracts from his score for separate performance and these 'Fragments of *Wozzeck*'[2] were first heard, under Scherchen, at Frankfurt in June 1924, with Beatrice Sutter-Kottlar singing the part of Marie. This

[1] According to a letter from Berg to Webern of August 19, 1918.
[2] They comprise: (1) the orchestral interlude between scenes 2 and 3 of Act 1, with the third scene, including Marie's Lullaby up to Wozzeck's entry; (2) Scene 1 of Act 3, with Marie's reading from the Bible; and (3), from Scenes 2, 4 and 5 of Act 3, a condensation of the two scenes at the pond, the last orchestral interlude and the final scene of the opera.

first performance of any of the music of *Wozzeck* met with remarkable success and the opera was soon accepted for production at the Berlin State Opera. The first stage performance followed after a prolonged interval, during which frantic rehearsals were accompanied by the dissonant noises of polemical pro's and con's in the German press. The *première* on December 14, 1925, in the presence of the composer, was preceded by 137 rehearsals and ended in a complete triumph for Erich Kleiber, the courageous conductor, who had risked his position in championing the cause of this controversial work. Berg was also lucky in his principal singers, Leo Schützendorf and Marie Johannsson. Despite a slanderous press campaign against composer and opera, *Wozzeck* succeeded brilliantly. It totally eclipsed Gurlitt's opera on the same subject, and was twice revived in Berlin under Kleiber, in 1927 and 1928. Meanwhile it had been performed with great success outside the German cultural orbit—in Leningrad and Prague, among other places. It was heard in New York in 1931 and in London, in a concert performance, in 1934. All told, there were 166 performances up to the end of 1936, and the opera was translated into English, French, Russian and Czech. In 1934 the Library of Congress purchased the autograph score from the composer. A production at Oldenburg in 1929 had initiated a new series of spectacularly successful performances in Germany, which stopped abruptly when Hitler came to power on January 30, 1933. After the downfall of Nazism the ban on *Wozzeck* was gradually lifted. It is a remarkable fact that despite heavy protests from Hitler's government the opera had been performed for the first time in Rome in 1942, under Tullio Serafin, at the height of the 'total war'. Since the war, notable performances have been given at Naples, Berne, New York, Buenos Aires, Hamburg, Kiel and many other places in Western Germany. It was given at the Salzburg Festival of 1951, and at Covent Garden in January 1952, the first stage performance in London, under its first conductor, Erich Kleiber. Recently, complete recordings for the gramophone have further increased the wide appreciation and mounting popularity of this great opera.

CHAPTER V

Development of Serial Technique

1. THE CHAMBER CONCERTO

IN the Chamber Concerto, Berg's personal idiom asserts itself vigorously, with all the idiosyncratic features of his mature musical style. Elements of that style which had appeared in *Wozzeck* now become permanent, foremost among them a predilection for strict canon and an ever increasing emphasis on serial technique. To these should be added an extraordinary inclination for allusive quotations and musical anagrams, most forcibly expressed in the motto theme of the Concerto, which makes play with the full names of Schoenberg, Webern and Berg, in so far as they are expressible in musical equivalents:

Example 102

112

Such links between the letters of names and their corresponding tonal symbols had played their part in Flemish polyphony, in Bach's *Musical Offering* and *Art of Fugue*, in Schumann's *Carnival* and *Abegg Variations*, and in some of Brahms' chamber works.[1] The revival of this practice by Berg in his mature compositions, coupled with his mania for allusive quotations from works of other composers, has parallels in modern literature.[2] Berg's use of these devices had its roots in the depth of his subconscious. He evidently tried to establish, with the help of allusions and quotations, a spiritual link with the past, mitigating the sense of isolation from which he increasingly suffered. There was inherent in him a spiritual escapism which at times craved for suspension of the present and for the magic reversal of time. Berg's deep-seated fear of the evanescence of life found a kind of safety-valve in the return of the end of a musical structure to its very source by, as it were, musical black magic, by the use of mirror-reflection, inversion and retrograde motion.

These devices play an integral part in all Berg's works from now on. How seriously Berg took these repeated excursions into the musical equivalent of a topsy-turvy, Lewis-Carroll world is seen from the mystical mood which precedes each one of them. The twelve mysterious chimes of low C sharp, given out by the piano and the double bassoon, which ring in the hour of musical ghosts in the middle movement of the Chamber Concerto (bars 358-363), find their later parallel in *Lulu*, Act II, bar 687 ff, where Lulu's motive of descending fourths, coupled with an improvisational turn of the piano, announces the beginning of the musical reversal which accompanies the filmstrip of her trial and release. Similar retrogressive movements take

[1] The 'F-A-E' Sonata of 1853/54, the String Quartet in A minor, using the same tonal symbols, and the second String Sextet, Op. 36, with its 'Agathe' symbol.
[2] Ezra Pound's *Cantos* and T. S. Eliot's poems, with their copious and polyglot quotations from and allusion to other literary works in poetry and prose.

place in the Scherzo of the *Lyric Suite* (bar 93 ff.) and in *Der Wein* (middle section, bars 141-172).

Another important feature is the use of 'constructive rhythm' (Berg's own term), as first introduced in *Wozzeck*, Act III. It appears, with its graphic symbol 'RH' ('Hauptrhythmus'), in the Rondo Finale of the Chamber Concerto. In *Lulu* it was afterwards to play an integral part (as 'Monoritmica').[1]

The *concertante* element in the Concerto had been foreshadowed in many episodes of *Wozzeck*. The use of a single instrument in this way, and of different combinations of instruments in 'concertino' style, represents the very antithesis of traditional symphonic processes, and helps Berg finally to abandon the outsize orchestras and complicated sonorities of his Opp. 4 and 6. The *concertante* element also allows a certain latitude in expansion, without necessarily involving a dense symphonic texture, and by this Berg's mature instrumental music differs from the symphonic miniature style of Schoenberg and Webern. The character of the Chamber Concerto certainly derives partly from the conception of the chamber orchestra manifested in Schoenberg's Op. 9. But *Wozzeck* had already revealed new possibilities, new devices and sound combinations. Henceforth the *concertante* element determines the nature of Berg's instrumental works,[2] and keeps them clear of the danger-zone of symphonic autobiography where Mahler and Zemlinsky ventured.

The Chamber Concerto is the first of Berg's compositions in which serial technique, albeit of a pre-dodecaphonic type, is

[1] A similar phenomenon in the Finale of Schoenberg's Quintet for wind instruments, Op. 26, composed at the same time, was mentioned by Felix Greissle in *Anbruch*, February 1925. Berg expressly refers to these parallel findings in his 'Open Letter'.

[2] The *Lyric Suite* is in *concertante* style, in so far as it eschews sonata forms and patterns; *Der Wein* is a concert aria; the Violin Concerto, in spite of its tone-poetical leanings, pays tribute to the *concertante* principle in its polyphonic cadenza.

systematically used.[1] Twelve-note technique was to be first used in the second Storm song, in late summer 1925, very shortly after the completion of the Concerto.

Like the clarinet pieces Op. 5 and the orchestral pieces Op. 6, the Chamber Concerto bears a dedication to Schoenberg. Berg planned to present his mentor with the full score on his fiftieth birthday (September 13, 1924), but, as in the case of his Op. 6, he was unable to keep to his timetable. The work, begun in the summer of 1923, was completed in short score on February 9, 1925 (Berg's own fortieth birthday) and in full score on July 23 of the same year. The manifold psychological complications which bedevilled Berg's attempts at new creative work after the completion of *Wozzeck* are vividly reflected in his letters to Schoenberg and Webern. The plan of the Chamber Concerto is discussed for the first time in detail in a letter to Schoenberg, dated from Trahütten, July 12, 1923:

> . . . I have now been here more than a week, well again, and at long last again at work, which however does not flow easily. After all, I've composed almost nothing in the past twenty months;[2] now it seems as if something will come of it. Out of many plans . . . the following has crystallized: a Concerto for Piano and Violin, with accompaniment of ten wind instruments (woodwind and brass)[3]. . . . The old idea of a Piano Concerto (incidentally suggested by yourself), and then the idea of a Double, Triple, and even Quadruple Concerto (forgive my incurable elephantiasis!) has kept me in thrall. When the idea of using wind instruments occurred to me, I tried to accommodate the idea of the Piano Concerto to it by combining the two. However, as you know, that didn't work. Finally I hit on the solution mentioned at the beginning of this letter, to which I hope to adhere, and which at once banishes all the seemingly unsoluble problems

[1] Apart from the exceptional cases of the fifth Altenberg song and the Passacaglia in *Wozzeck*.
[2] i.e. since the completion of the full score of *Wozzeck*.
[3] They became thirteen in the completed score.

115

of an accompanying chamber orchestra. These problems are: (1) What is the relationship of the piano in the chamber orchestra to the *concertante* piano? (2) What is the relationship of the *concertante* violin to the solo strings (first and second violin) of the chamber orchestra? (3) How can the harmonium be used as an instrument of the orchestra in this special case—and can it be used *at all*? I admit that these problems can be solved. However, as you so convincingly said to me: Why choose *beforehand* a difficult combination of instruments? In the combination I have now arrived at, with ten wind instruments, apart from the fact that I'm much attracted by it, such difficulties are, as it were, blotted out. And if work progresses only slowly just now (I've only got about fifty bars on paper, and I am planning to write a big symphonic movement in three sections, extending to perhaps five hundred bars) that is not the result of the combination of instruments, but—as I've told you—of my heavy hand. . . .

Six days later Berg revealed to Webern the structure of the whole Chamber Concerto:

. . . I am also at work, industriously, but struggling with difficulties: a Concerto for Piano and Violin, with accompaniment of ten wind instruments: a big symphonic movement in three parts, Scherzo variations, Adagio and an opening sonata movement...' [1]

By September 1 only the first movement was completed. In a letter to Webern of that date Berg commented ruefully on his slow progress and added:

The second movement is an Adagio. The third, a combination of the two preceding ones, a sonata movement. . . . But when shall I get that far? . . . If only it were July 1 today, instead of September 1. . . .

After that, composition came to a complete standstill and was only resumed on August 11, 1924. The work was completed, as we have seen, on July 23, 1925. Full score and piano reduction

[1]It was eventually turned into a rondo.

were published in facsimile in the year of their completion. Berg also published an analysis of the Concerto in the form of an open letter addressed to Schoenberg, dated February 9, 1925.[1] The Chamber Concerto was first performed on March 20, 1927, in Berlin, under Hermann Scherchen. The published score included special full closes for the first two movements, making possible their separate performance. In February 1935 Berg (whose predilection for making arrangements of his own works became more pronounced as the years went by) completed a version of the slow middle movement as a Trio for violin, clarinet and piano. It was performed in Vienna shortly after his death.[2]

Berg's 'Open Letter to Arnold Schoenberg' includes a detailed analysis of the structure of the Chamber Concerto, illustrated by a Tabular Synopsis in graphic form (reproduced on pp. 124-125). Both the chart and the textual commentary emphasize the ternary principle which forms the basis of the whole composition. The number '3' is something of a common denominator in all the structural features of the work. The Motto Theme (Example 102) unites the names of Schoenberg, Webern and Berg. There are three movements, and the instruments divide easily into three categories: keyboard, strings and wind. The movements:

I. Thema scherzoso con variazioni (piano and wind instruments)
II. Adagio (violin and wind instruments)
III. Rondo ritmico con Introduzione (piano, violin and wind instruments),

---

[1]Published in *Pult und Taktstock* (Vienna), in 1925. Reprinted by Reich, op. cit. p. 86 ff.
[2]It was published in 1955 by Universal Edition. The Trio version includes a cut of seventeen bars (bars 435-452). The bulk of the wind-parts has been deftly cued into the piano-part.

are tripartite entities in themselves. The third movement is one huge recapitulation of the first two movements, the whole forming an organic unit of three interrelated sections. The tripartite basis can also be traced in the thirty bars of the thematic exposition of I, the ternary form of II and its retrograde mirror-reflection, and, finally, in the three basic rhythms of III.[1]

Berg himself acknowledged the relationship between his Chamber Concerto and Schoenberg's Chamber Symphony, Op. 9, stressing the fact that both works were scored for the same number (fifteen) of players. A close scrutiny of the Chamber Concerto, however, reveals the novelty and originality of its orchestral design and reduces the parallel with Schoenberg to the wind section only. Schoenberg's orchestrally subdivided strings are replaced by the two soloists: violin and piano. The wind section moreover is supplemented by trumpet and trombone. Schoenberg's orchestra is, by and large, a pocket edition of the late romantic orchestra, reduced in numbers but not in basic types, and turned into a medium for refined polyphony, not unlike the orchestra in Wagner's *Siegfried Idyll*. Berg's orchestra, however, is a complete wind band, to which two solo stringed instruments are juxtaposed. The *concertante*, yet intimate, character of Berg's composition contrasts fundamentally with the *tutti* character of Schoenberg's Op. 9, which is still conceived in the tradition of the post-Wagnerian era.[2]

In his 'Open Letter' Berg observed that the tripartite principle even determined the harmony of the concerto. He dis-

---

[1] They may have been influenced by similar features in Schoenberg's *Serenade* Op. 24 (1924), but not by the wind quintet Op. 26, which was *unknown* to Berg when he composed his Chamber Concerto.

[2] Berg adopted, however, certain features of Schoenberg's notation, such as the untransposed writing for transposing wind instruments and the distinction of 'Haupt-und Nebenstimme' (main and ancillary theme) by use of the symbols 'H' and 'N'.

tinguished tonal, atonal and, in certain section, harmony 'subject to the laws of twelve-note technique'. This is the very first time Schoenberg's new method of composition is mentioned by Berg who, in the same document, frequently refers to his master's Opp. 24 and 26 and their revolutionizing style.[1]

Berg is, however, very reticent about the serial aspect of the work, beyond an initial remark drawing attention to the role played by the three names of the Motto theme and those of their letters for which equivalents in musical terminology exist. The thematic subjects built from these letter-associations are not yet dodecaphonic, to be sure, but they are certainly related to the type of future 'Basic Sets'. Their serial character can be studied if they are written out in the manner of a dodecaphonic graph:

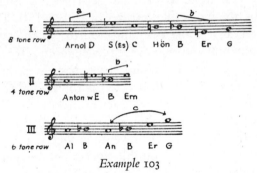

Example 103

The three Christian names (and their corresponding thematic subjects) begin with 'A' (Arnold, Anton, Alban), by which a kind of tonal centre is established. The three themes have certain harmonic potentialities in common, as may be seen from bar 3 of the 'Motto theme'. The chord on the sixth beat has three notes common to all three thematic subjects:

[1]Together with the piano works Opp. 23 and 25, they represent Schoenberg's earliest avowed dodecaphonic compositions.

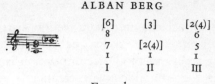

	[6]	[3]	[2(4)]
	8		6
	7	[2(4)]	5
	I	I	I
	I	II	III

Example 104

Apart from this, I and III have the first and the two last notes in common, and I, II and III the last or the last-but-one note in common. Finally, all the notes of II (Webern) and III (Berg) are contained in I (Schoenberg). On the basis of these facts an imaginary 'Basic Shape' of eight notes could be distilled in the sense of strict serial technique. The intimate bonds of friendship linking the three leading composers of the 'Second Viennese School' are hereby subtly and secretly expressed.

The harmonic trend in the Chamber Concerto is chiefly determined by the intervallic features of I, II and III. The determining intervals are the ascending fourth (*a*), the augmented fourth (tritone) (*b*) and the seventh (cf. Example 103).

We have had opportunities in earlier chapters of this book to observe the integral role allotted to the fourth and the seventh in Berg's music. These intervals act as dissolving elements of tonality, which rests normally on structures of thirds. Nevertheless, it is the fourth and the seventh in their harmonic implications which become responsible for certain tonal enclaves in the work, referred to in Berg's analysis. They occur frequently in elliptic cadences, as if aiming at an imaginary tonic, and as if intent to establish a kind of aural 'Archimedes's point' in a confusion of conflicting tonalities. Such episodes show how Berg's most exploratory music is deeply rooted in Viennese classic traditions. Here is the sequence of fourths which occurs as a regular interstitial cadence in the Chamber Concerto:

Example 105

This combination of vertical and horizontal sequences of fourths is not only to be found in Schoenberg's Chamber Symphony, Op. 9, whose main subject (horn, bars 5-7) is closely related to the bass of Example 105. It can be identified in a literal anticipation in the Finale of Brahms' fourth symphony. There it is used as cadential enclave between two variational sub-sections of the Passacaglia, whose bass theme represents, as it were, a Basic Shape of strictly serial character:

Example 106

The bass-line of Example 106 can be understood as a sequence of ascending fourths, if the intervals are transposed into higher octaves. In both examples the chromatic bias of the top part, combined with the chain of ascending fourths in the bass, results in parallel sevenths in the middle parts, here indicated by arrows.

Characteristic of Berg's later music is the demoniacal sultriness of these parallel sevenths at the beginning of the Adagio of the Concerto, which distinctly foreshadow the harmonic aura of *Lulu*:

Example 107

Movement I—*Tema scherzoso con variazioni*—consists of a tripartite theme, thirty bars long (more a thematic group in the sense of Bruckner's and Mahler's symphonies, than a theme in the strictly classical sense of the word) and five variations. In his 'Open Letter' Berg emphasizes the Scherzo character of the six sub-divisions of this movement. He all but fails to draw attention to the *concertante* character of large parts of it. In particular, Variation I represents, by and large, a *concertante* interpretation of the thematic exposition, given out *con bravura* by the piano.

The 'Tema' itself, played by the entire wind band, consists again of three sections in different tempi:

(1) Leicht bewegt   (Tempo I)
(2) Schwungvoll   (Tempo II)
(3) Meno allegro   (Tempo III).

The derivation of (1) from the tripartite Basic Shape I-II-III (cf.

Example 103) clearly reveals the prominent part played by serial technique in this, strictly speaking, pre-dodecaphonic work. Here are the first bars of the thematic outline of (I) (Tempo I), of which bars 1-4 can also be understood as a twelve-note theme based on the Basic Shape of the naturally dodecaphonic chromatic scale[1]:

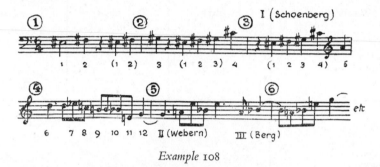

Example 108

Variation 2 brings the melodic outline (but not the actual notes) of the 'Tema' in inversion. Its character differs noticeably from the pianistic solo of Variation 1. It is a slow Waltz, in which piano and wind instruments are combined for the first time. Variation 3 and 4 use the 'melodic' notes of the theme in inversion and in the retrograde motion of the inversion. Variation 4 represents the development section and the main axis of the whole movement. It bristles with canonic imitation, like the preceding variation, and yet manages to remain diaphanous. How ingeniously the cancrizans motion of the thematic inversion is made to grow out of the very tail-end of Variation 3, can be seen in the graph on pages 124 and 125.

---

[1]Cf. R. Leibowitz: 'Introduction . . .' (cf. Bibl.). Leibowitz's numerical organization has been utilized for Example 108.

	Theme	Var. 1	Var. ll
I Tema con Variazioni	in its basic shape (Exposition)	(1st recapitulation)	in retrograde motion (Develop-
	Number of bars: 30	30	60

		Tripartite				
II Adagio	Al		B		A2 (Inversion of Al)	
	bars: 30	12	36	12	30	

	Introduction	Exposition
III (= I + II) Rondo ritmico con Introduzione	(Cadenza for violin and piano)	
		(da
	bars· 54	96
		repeat:

This tabulated survey is taken from Alban Berg's analysis of the Chamber Concerto, contained in an 'Open Letter' to Arnold Schoenberg, and published for the first time in the music periodical

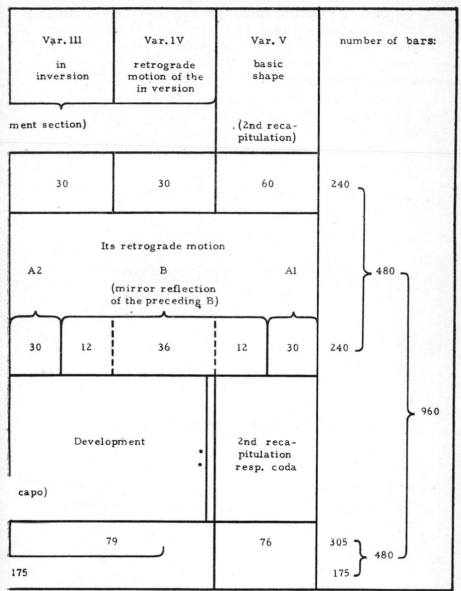

Var. III	Var. IV	Var. V	number of bars:
in inversion	retrograde motion of the inversion	basic shape	
ment section)		.(2nd recapitulation)	
30	30	60	240

Its retrograde motion

A2   B   A1

(mirror reflection of the preceding B)

30	12	36	12	30	240

480

960

Development	2nd recapitulation resp. coda
capo)	
79	76	305
175		175

480

PULT UND TAKTSTOCK, Universal Edition, Vienna, 1925. An English translation has been prepared by the author of this volume.

Variation 5 goes back to the thematic exposition, in the manner of a sonata recapitulation. The treatment of the theme itself evolves a technique of detaching thematic splinters and sub-dividing such motives into 'peak-notes' and 'ancillary notes'—a process of thematic atom-splitting developed to a high degree of virtuosity in *Lulu* and the Violin Concerto.

The thematic subject of Movement II—Adagio—is given out by the solo violin. It is sixteen bars long and shows pre-dodeca-phonic features similar to those in the 'Tema con variazioni':

Example 109

The above example follows the analysis of Leibowitz,[1] who points out a deviation from strict dodecaphony at NB. From this subject a twelve-note series can be deduced *a posteriori*:

Example 110

which is nothing else than a thematically pre-organized series of the dodecaphonic Basic Shape derived from the chromatic scale:

[1]Cf. Op. cit. p. 78 ff.

126

Example 111

This second movement forms a telling contrast to the first. It is an extended Cantabile-Adagio lasting fifteen minutes, from which the piano is rigidly excluded (except for the twelve mysterious chimes at bars 358-63), just as the violin had been excluded from the first movement. It is full of magical sonorities, with distant echoes from *Tristan* and *Pelléas*. The sweltering vagueness of its cadential sequences of chords of the ninth already anticipates the erotic morbidity of *Lulu* (cf. Example 107). The treatment of the solo violin contributes markedly to the opalescent coloration of the movement, the player being asked to use a *glissando* intonation, as if deliberately to blur his own melodic contours. Berg even attempts to fix in notation the *Zwischentöne*, between the intervals of the tempered scale, akin to Haba's quarter tones. These he indicates by the sign 'z':

Example 112

It is in this second movement that Berg's 'constructive rhythm' (indicated by the sign 'R.H.') is introduced for the first time (cf. p. 68 of the full score):

Example 113

127

It grows out of an accompanying figure in the brass:

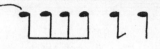

and breaks out dramatically in the cancrizans part of the movement with the formula:

As already mentioned, the twelve mysterious chimes in the piano lead to the fascinating reversal of the whole exposition of the Adagio.

Berg himself characterized Movement III—*Rondo ritmico con Introduzione*—as a combination of Movements I and II (Cf. pp. 124-125). He distinguished three important types of thematic treatment:

(1) A free juxtaposition of sub-divisions of these movements which correspond thematically to one another;

(2) The juxtaposition of single phrases in literal quotation almost in the manner of a duet;

(3) The linking together of whole sections of Movements I and II.

The special character of this movement is to be found in its emphasis on rhythm and in its reliance on the three rhythmic Basic Shapes. It also differs markedly from the two earlier movements in its varied metre. Its thematic material is as dependent on that of the preceding movements as the music of *Götterdämmerung* is dependent on the themes of the preceding parts of the *Ring*. Although Berg calls the movement a 'Rondo', the rondo-character is not determined by a recurring theme, but by the recurring utilization of the 'constructive

Alban Berg and Anton Webern

rhythm', in support of themes of differing character.[1] The movement could with equal justification be classified as a Sonata movement, preceded by a long introduction in the manner of the Cadenza. In this Cadenza, which anticipates certain stylistic features of the much later Violin Concerto and its polyphonic Cadenza, the *concertanti* violin and piano are brought together for the first time—an effect deliberately saved up for this late stage of the work. The 'Rondo' itself is built up as an ensemble of the wind band in combination with the two soloists. It is full of felicitous touches in its diaphanous texture and novel *concertante* style.

The Chamber Concerto characteristically ends on a chord of the tritone:

Example 114

The chord is presented in expanding sonorities by use of the piano pedals and a fleeting *pizzicato* arpeggio on the solo violin:

Example 115

This bar, with its wistful romantic undertones, is like a premonition of the last bar of the Violin Concerto. The very last chord (bars 780/85, cf. Example 114) contains the tritone, which is implicit in all three Basic Shapes of the Chamber Concerto, as well as the pivotal '*A*' with which all three Basic Shapes begin. The chord itself in its dreamy vagueness seems to long for a resolution in the haven of an imaginary C major tonic.

---

[1]This technique had its origin in Schoenberg's *Serenade*, Op. 24.

The feeling of suspense created by the denial of this resolution is one of the unmistakable characteristics of Berg's personal idiom—an idiom convincingly employed in every bar of this Chamber Concerto.

2. 'SCHLIESSE MIR DIE AUGEN BEIDE'

Two Songs; 1900 and 1925

The two settings of Theodor Storm's poem 'Schliesse mir die Augen beide' were published as a musical supplement to an article by Willi Reich, in Die Musik for February, 1930. Reich's article, mainly biographical in content, referred only briefly to the songs, but in this first publication they were prefaced by a commentary by Berg himself;

> The twenty-five years of Universal Edition's existence have coincided with music's enormous development from tonal composition to the 'method of composing with twelve notes related only with one another', and from the C major triad to the so-called 'Mother-chord' (the twelve-note chord, containing also all twelve intervals, discovered by F. H. Klein). It is the imperishable achievement of Emil Hertzka, the publisher, to have followed that development from its very beginnings. To him the two songs printed overleaf, settings of the same poem by Theodor Storm, are dedicated. They are intended to exemplify that musical transformation and are here published for the first time. One of them was composed at the beginning, the other at the end of the first quarter of the century (1900-1925).
>
> ALBAN BERG

Some confusion has been caused by the fact that the dates of composition of both songs are given wrongly in Reich's book of 1937. Berg refers to his contribution to the silver jubilee of Universal Edition in a letter to Webern, dated October 12, 1925, and written at Trahütten:

I, too, sent a (love) song, the words of which have no connection whatsoever with the jubilee, or rather, I sent *two* songs, on the same poem, a very old song, and a brand-new one. The latter I composed up here—my first attempt at strict twelve-note composition. However, in that art I am unfortunately not as far advanced as you.

The second setting was thus written shortly before Berg started to compose the *Lyric Suite*, which the song anticipates thematically. The *Lyric Suite* was completed in the summer of 1926. The relationship between the second Storm song, in which an entirely new mode of musical expression was first explored, and the *Lyric Suite* resembles that between Wagner's two Wesendonk songs *Im Treibhaus* and *Träume*, of 1857, and the score of *Tristan* completed in 1859.

The stylistic antithesis of the two songs demonstrates convincingly the fundamental dialectic tension inherent in Berg's musical idiom, which ranges from the late romanticism of Schumann and Wagner to the constructivism of Schoenberg's twelve-note system. Both songs are interesting for what they foreshadow. The first successfully blurs the outline of Schumann's lyrical four-bar periods by extended 5/4 bars, and so anticipates the rhythmic flexibility found in Berg's first opus numbers of 1908. The relationship between the second song and the *Lyric Suite* is of fundamental importance for the understanding of Berg's mature style. The song, the composer's first attempt to employ the twelve-note system, as the letter quoted above establishes, is based on the same Basic Set as the *Lyric Suite*.

Here is the Basic Set common to both works, in its Basic Shape[1]:

Example 116

Its intervallic analogies, as well as its harmonic implications, become evident in the notation suggested by Hanns Jelinek:[2]

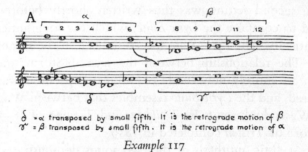

Example 117

If the Basic Set, in its Basic Shape *A*, is consistently unfolded in one direction, it stands revealed (as Berg pointed out in his analysis of the *Lyric Suite*) as Klein's 'twelve-note row, containing all twelve intervals':

Example 118

---

[1]Schoenberg's own English terms are 'Basic Set' (*Grund-Reihe*) and 'Basic Shape' (*Grundgestalt*). The less preferable term 'series' is occasionally used in this book in deference to Berg's own terminology.

[2]Cf. H. Jelinek, *Anleitung zur Zwölftonkomposition*, Vienna, 1952, p. 14 ff.

Klein had discussed this discovery of his in the preface to his Variations, Op. 14, published in 1924.

Basic Shape *A* represents the dodecaphonic base for the first bars of the vocal part of the song and for bars 2-4 of the first movement of the *Lyric Suite*:

Example 119

This juxtaposition of the initial bars of both compositions makes apparent their melodic and atmospheric kinship. Obviously both are based on the same thematic organism, subjected only to certain changes of phrasing and rhythmic scansion. It is highly interesting to observe the different processes of composition, by which widely divergent results are obtained. The vocal part of the song consists of several permutations of the intervals of Basic Shape *A*:

133

Example 120

Of the five sections into which the whole song may be divided, the first and fifth sections are identical, while the second, third and fourth form the links of a chain of variations. These five permutations of the intervals of *A* involve no transposition, nor do they show any deviation from the basic order of the twelve notes within the Basic Set. The song thus shows a comparatively primitive application of twelve-note technique. The *Lyric Suite*, on the other hand, as early as bars 7-8 of the first movement, by anticipatory use of the last four notes of the set and by free transpositions into other octaves, achieves an impressive variant of *A* :

Example 121

Similarly a variant of *A* may be traced in the piano part, bars 9-11, the second half of which (*x*) is constructed in the sense of Example 117;

Example 122

Thereby it anticipates the 'Mother-chord' of the last bar, which may be presented in a horizontal chain of intervals:

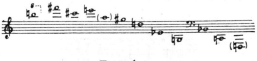

Example 123

While the song in its last bar brings the intervals of the basic set to rest in the 'Mother-chord', the first movement of the *Lyric Suite* develops out of the disorder of intervals in its first bar, the notes of which, strung out horizontally, present the complete chromatic scale, and from this in the second and following bars, grows the Basic Set in its thematic shape:

Example 124

The function of the first bar of the *Lyric Suite*, to serve as source for the dodecaphonic development of the rest of the movement, becomes evident here, as does the startling finality of the 'Mother-chord' in the last bar of the song, in which the last note added, the low F, establishes, as it were, a tonal relationship with the note F with which the vocal part of the song began. This subtly-suggested, immanent 'F' tonality in the second Storm song may be considered to bear a ghostly relationship to the C major tonality of the first song, whose subdominant F is already decidedly touched-on on the fourth beat of the first bar. And on the fourth and fifth beats of that bar the vocal part of this earlier song gives out the motive:

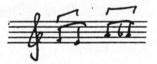

which consists of integral elements of *A*.

The ingenious canonic dove-tailing of the Basic Set between vocal part and piano part in the second song, bars 4-10, and the elliptical series (commencing with the fourth note) in the piano part, bars 8-9, may also be mentioned. Finally, the fact should not be overlooked that even quasi-impressionistic harmonies such as:

136

in the second song, bar 11, represent strictly functional chord clusters, derived from the Basic Shape *A*, or from certain sections of it.

Berg's masterly employment, at his first attempt, of a technique of composition then still in its infancy is convincingly seen in the second song. The inner relationship of the two songs, of 1900 and 1925, symbolizes the gradual integration of late Romantic methods of composition with a style of musical expression based on entirely novel principles.

3. THE LYRIC SUITE

The *Lyric Suite* for string quartet was composed in 1925-26, almost immediately after the completion of the Chamber Concerto. The stages of its genesis are vividly reflected in a spate of letters to Webern between September 18, 1925 (the approximate date of the first sketch), and October 8, 1926, when Berg wrote: 'My Quartet is finished; now I'm getting on with the fair copy, to which the last polish will be applied and all traces of the workshop eliminated'. But that post-creative process dragged on into the later autumn. The same letter mentions casually: 'I was very ill and am evidently far from recovered, which is very embarrassing at the present moment'. Actually, the composition of this profoundly inspired work took place during a period of grave physical suffering, culminating in attacks of asthma, which laid the composer low for several weeks.

The *Lyric Suite* is dedicated to Alexander v. Zemlinsky, whose *Lyric Symphony* had influenced the choice of title and the formal organization of Berg's work. The successful first performance, by the Kolisch Quartet, took place on January 8, 1927, in Vienna. When the same players performed the work at the Baden-Baden Festival on July 16, 1927, it had to be repeated. Several prominent quartet teams incorporated the *Lyric Suite* in their repertory and assured its spectacular success everywhere. The miniature score issued by Universal Edition in 1927 was followed in 1928 by an arrangement of the three middle movements for string orchestra, which Berg had undertaken at his publisher's request. This arrangement was first performed under Jascha Horenstein on January 31, 1929, in Berlin. It became a favourite in Erich Kleiber's programmes in the U.S.A. from 1930 on.

The return to lyricism in the Suite is perhaps best understood as a reaction following the tremendous cerebral effort entailed in the creation of *Wozzeck* and the Chamber Concerto. It is a typical Bergian paradox that this temporary return to the lyrical haunts of his adolescence should also be the point of departure for new adventures, in dodecaphonic fields. The second Storm song, which preceded the first draft of the *Lyric Suite* by only a few weeks, is the first composition of Berg using twelve-note technique, and the *Lyric Suite* itself adopts it, not exclusively, but quite determinedly. The very title indicates the a-symphonic character of this work. Earlier analysts have stressed its lyrico-dramatic mood and even called it a 'veiled opera'. Such a view finds corroboration in the sub-titles of the

138

six movements of the Suite, which evidently outline a psychological experience of great intensity:

I. ALLEGRO GIOVIALE
II. ANDANTE AMOROSO
III. ALLEGRO MISTERIOSO
TRIO ESTATICO
IV. ADAGIO APPASSIONATO
V. PRESTO DELIRANDO
TENEBROSO
VI. LARGO DESOLATO.

The fact that Berg deliberately avoided sonata-form and its implications of corresponding tonalities,[1] and gave his work more than four movements, should not blind us to its classic-romantic derivation. The number of movements can find justification in Mahler's symphonies and Beethoven's late string quartets. Both these types of cyclic composition tend to spread out fan-wise, in order to reflect a psychological, largely autobiographical experience in a multitude of phases, in up to seven movements. The parallel between Berg's *Lyric Suite* and Beethoven's late quartets is surely more than fortuitous. A predilection for serial technique, for fugal processes and contrapuntal rondo-patterns, is common to both composers. Even such a peculiarly Bergian phenomenon as his tripartite Scherzo-Trio type (on which Movements II, III and V of the Suite are based) is anticipated in Beethoven's Opp. 130 and 132 (second and fourth movements of both quartets). Even Berg's penchant for cancrizans motion (cf. Movement III, bar 93 ff.) can be detected in Beethoven's Op. 132. Similarly his mania for self-quotation is foreshadowed in Beethoven's Opp. 130, 131, 132 and 133, which are all based on a common four-note series. Finally, the

[1]Herein undoubtedly prompted by the dodecaphonic bias of the whole work.

semi-operatic passages of the *Lyric Suite* can claim a parallel in the Recitativo-episode of Beethoven's Op. 132 (Introduction to the Finale), and in the similar bridge passage, the 'schwer gefasste Entschluss', of Op. 135. No less numerous are the parallels between the *Lyric Suite* and typical features of Mahler's last symphonies. The emphatic 'Largo' character of Berg's music, its deliberate slowing down and the utter despair of its last movement, fading out in the melancholy whisper of a quaver-motion on the viola, recall Mahler's *Lied von der Erde* in general and its heart-searing 'Farewell' section in particular. Berg's middle movements, based on violent antithesis of mood and character, may have taken their cue from the ambivalent and demoniac Scherzo type evolved in Mahler's last three symphonies. However, the Mahlerian affinities of the work are rooted deeper, in the artistic subconscious. Mahler's *Lied von der Erde* and Berg's *Lyric Suite* share a deception inherent in their title-pages. Mahler's 'Lied' is as little a classical symphony (as its sub-title expressly claims) as the *Lyric Suite* is a 'Suite' in the pre-classical sense of the term. Both works camouflage their lyrical or dramatic nature by a titular claim to a formal pattern, in open conflict with their actual musical content. Mahler's 'Lied' is emphatically *not* 'a symphony for Tenor and Alto voices and orchestra', simply because such a formal hybrid does not exist and because the work does not show a single biological feature of the accepted symphony-type. It is rather a cycle of orchestrally accompanied songs, the action of which takes place between its sub-sections, exactly as in Schubert's song-cycles. Likewise, Berg's *Lyric Suite* is emphatically *not* a Suite in the older sense, but a cycle of instrumental movements, the tone-poetical content of which is conveyed in quotations, thematic allusions and programmatic hints.

Berg's six movements correspond in many ways to the six

movements of Mahler's *Lied von der Erde*. The three Scherzos of the *Lyric Suite* (Movements II, III, V) correspond to the three gay middle sections of the 'Lied', just as the two slow movements (IV and VI) correspond closely to the structural position and general mood of Mahler's *Solitary in Autumn* and *Farewell*. That *Das Lied von der Erde* is the real archetype of Berg's *Lyric Suite* can also be deduced indirectly from the fact of its close and freely admitted association with Zemlinsky's *Lyric Symphony*, Op. 18. The latter work, composed in 1923 and published in 1926, shows a family-likeness to Mahler's 'Lied' (first performed in 1911) which is anything but casual.

The *Lyric Symphony* is based on a cycle of oriental poems which are sung alternately by male and female singers to a richly coloured orchestral accompaniment—exactly like Mahler's 'Lied'. Zemlinsky's beautiful but neglected work exudes the same mood of wistful farewell, the same melancholia and nostalgia for escape from the world, the same self-tormenting longing for death and annihilation. The fourth movement[1] of Zemlinsky's symphony is especially remarkable as a synthesis of Wagner's ecstatic *Tristan* style and the strange oriental tranquillities of Mahler's 'Farewell' section. The two quotations which occur in Berg's Movement IV (bars 32/33 and 46/50) refer to the third section of Zemlinsky's symphony. They were evidently modelled on the following phrase, sung there by the baritone:

Example 125

[1]Zemlinsky's work only differs from those of Mahler and Berg in that he bridges his sub-sections with orchestral interludes which give the whole the deceptive aspect of a single movement.

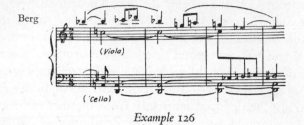

Example 126

Rabindranath Tagore's poem, the refrain of which is twice quoted in Berg's *Lyric Suite*, exhales a Tristanesque nostalgia for love-fulfilment and death. It attempts to express the unattainable goal of love's deepest desire and the incompatibility of love's fondest dreams with the hard reality of Wagner's 'öder Tag'. Zemlinsky's lovely melodies contrive to combine Wagner's chromaticism with the whole-tone flavour of Debussy and the pentatonic orientalism of Mahler's 'Lied'. Their harmonic atmosphere is closely related to that of Berg's early songs, of which the second Storm song was a belated echo. In its turn this song expresses the same kind of longing for a love-union in death that permeates the libretto of *Tristan* and the poems underlying Zemlinsky's symphony. The concealed vocality of Berg's *Lyric Suite* is seen in the exclusively vocal character of its avowed models of style (*Tristan*, Mahler's 'Lied' and Zemlinsky's symphony) and by the vocal character of its quotations. This is borne out by the second pivotal quotation in the *Lyric Suite*, the initial bars of Wagner's *Tristan* prelude, which occur in Movement IV, bars 26/27. F. Bouquet[1] has traced the quotation back to a segment of the viola passage:

[1]Cf. *Melos*, Aug.-Sept., 1948.

Example 127

which is nothing but a retrograde version of the Basic Shape of the *Lyric Suite* (cf. infra). However, the tone-poetical and philosophical connotations of that famous motive are closely related to the oriental poetry of Mahler's and Zemlinsky's compositions. This seems underlined by Wagner's own comment on the *Tristan* motive: 'However, Nirvana changes for me quickly into Tristan. You know the Buddhistic theory of genesis? A breath blurs the clarity of the heavens:

Example 128

It grows, condenses and solidifies, until finally the whole world confronts me again in all its impenetrable bulk.'[1] These words could stand as poetic motto of Berg's *Lyric Suite*. They paraphrase the ecstasy and despair of the last twenty bars (which follow directly after the quotation from *Tristan*, in the last movement) more convincingly than do the words from Stefan George's poem *Litanei*: 'Take love from me, but give me your happiness', set to music in the third movement of Schoenberg's String Quartet with soprano solo, Op. 10, which T. W. Adorno has applied also to Berg's *Lyric Suite*. Schoenberg's Quartet, with its programmatic undertones, may well have influenced Berg, subconsciously, in the designing of his Suite. But the music of Schoenberg's early work, with its strong emphasis on tonality and its final transfiguration in an Isolde-like hymn of ecstasy, is miles removed from Berg's inconsolable

[1] Letter of March 3, 1860, to Mathilde Wesendonk.

143

despair, so eloquently expressed in the viola's soliloquy, as
forlorn as the triplets of the harp in Mahler's *Lied von der Erde*:

Example 129

The close relationship between the second Storm song and
the *Lyric Suite* has been described in an earlier chapter. Both are
based on the same peculiar twelve-note series, the so-called 'All-
Intervallreihe'. The specific quality of its Basic Shape *A* (cf.
Example 116) is that its second half (notes 7-12) is identical with
a transposition of the retrograde motion of its first half (notes
1-6). This inherent tendency of the series to mirror-reflection
becomes evident in the notation suggested by Hanns Jelinek:

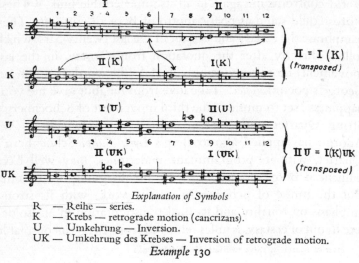

Explanation of Symbols

R — Reihe — series.
K — Krebs — retrograde motion (cancrizans).
U — Umkehrung — Inversion.
UK — Umkehrung des Krebses — Inversion of retrograde motion.

Example 130

144

The harmonic possibilities of this series suggest themselves at once, when the notes of the series are combined in chordal form:

R   (K)   U   (UK)

Example 131

Not all the movements of the *Lyric Suite* are rigorously dodecaphonic. Some of them are based on thematic reminiscences, or dependent on the common Basic Shape without adhering closely to strict dodecaphony. The following sections of the work are strictly twelve-tone music:

Movements I and VI (in their entirety);
Movement III (only the exposition and recapitulation);
Movement V (the 'tenebroso' middle section).

In a freer style are:

Movements II[1] and IV (throughout);
Movement III (the 'Trio estatico');
Movement V[1] (the 'presto delirando').

Series (*A*) (cf. Example 116), on which the dodecaphonic parts of the work are based, is subject to certain modifications, as previous analysts have pointed out. These variants of the Basic Shape are chiefly responsible for certain features of thematic variation.

Series (*A*) is a re-arrangement of the primordial series (*X*) which is the basis of the 'chaotic' bar 1 (cf. Example 124 a). (*X*), re-arranged as a scale, results in (*Y*), the perfect twelve-note row of the chromatic scale, which in turn represents the source from which all dodecaphonic 'matter' is drawn. It is also the thematic source, as it were, of bar 1. From that point of view

---

[1]However, these two movements are very closely related to the processes of twelve-tone technique, as will be shown later.

(*A*) appears as a special selective variant of (*Y*). It is turned into a manageable thematic subject for Movement I by octave-transposition of its notes 5, 7 and 12 (cf. Example 119, b). However, already in bars 7-8 Berg makes use of the possibilities of exchange, within the framework of the series, by allotting the function of 'alpha' to 'beta' (cf. Example 121). Bar 13 already uses a chordal organization of (*A*) and bars 18/19 utilize in the first violin part the inversion of (*A*) = *c* (Example 130, (*U*)). Although Movements II and III are less rigorously subjected to serial discipline, they too are fertilized by the intervallic determinants of (*A*). In fact, they are based on a variant of it (*A* 1), as may be seen from the following graph:

A1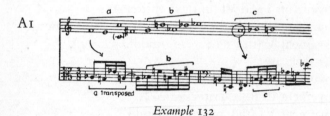

Example 132

The same applies to the insect-like thematic growth of the mysterious Movement III, whose ant-like microcosm rests thematically on the retrograde motion of (*A* 1), transposed down a semitone:

Example 133

(*A*) yields another variant in Movements V ('tenebroso' section) and VI. The strictly serial chords of the 'tenebroso' are derivatives of the following variant of (*A* 1):

146

Example 134

The chief subject of Movement VI ('Largo desolato'), given out by the cello in bars 1-2, is nothing but a transposition of the retrograde motion of the inversion of *A* (cf. Example 130).

Apart from these close serial relationships between the six movements of the *Lyric Suite*, a number of self-quotations and reminiscences should be mentioned, which act as a kind of psychological link between them. Perhaps the most striking of these are: (1) the (non-dodecaphonic) 'Trio estatico', which recurs again in Movement IV (bars 12-13); (2) the chief melody of the (non-dodecaphonic) 'Andante amoroso', which also reappears in Movement IV (bars 30-31); (3) the scale-like passage of chromatic chords of the sixth, moving either up or down, but always with a quasi-cadential function.

The inner cohesion of the work does not depend only on the fact that its thematic material is derived from a common dodecaphonic source. This pre-conceived and co-ordinated thematic material begets individual motives and thematic characters, which are called upon to function as actors in a play, entering the stage at a given cue, vanishing again out of sight, or submitting occasionally even to the minor roles of walkers-on. This concealed dramatic tendency of the motives affects also the construction of the Suite. If Movement I is preludial (it is a sonata movement without a development section), Movements II, III and V could be considered as Scherzos, with extended Trio-episodes. The 'Andante amoroso' (II) has been called a Rondo with two contrasting episodes (Tempos II and III), but this movement, with its *Ländler*-rhythm in episode I and the nightmarish *chiaroscuro* of its second episode, is strongly reminiscent of the Mahlerian scherzo-type referred to earlier. The psychological climax of the whole work is surely Movement IV ('Adagio appassionato'). It is loosely constructed, composed in a style free from the rigours of dodecaphony, is strongly reliant on the effect of thematic reminiscence, and culminates in the double quotation from Zemlinsky's *Lyric Symphony*. It ends (like its forerunner, the non-serial Movement II) on a suspension-chord with a distinct cadential flavour which might be classified as a dominant preparation for the tonic of F major. In Movement V, which also belongs temperamentally and thematically to the Mahlerian Scherzo-type, the Suite's hidden drama comes to its catastrophic crisis. A wistful epilogue is finally intoned by the rhapsodizing free strains of the concluding 'Largo desolato'.

In the preludial Movement I ('Allegretto gioviale'), the dodecaphonic aspect of which has already been discussed, a technical feature is found which becomes increasingly characteristic of Berg's later music: the splitting of the serial subject (*A*) into two or more independent motives:

Example 135

The same kind of split, resulting in a dialogue-like Alternativo

148

between two complementary parts, leads in Movement III to the genesis of a four-note motive which re-appears in Movement VI as a reminiscence of *Tristan*.

The last bar of Movement I contains, like its first bar, all the twelve notes of the chromatic scale. In contrast to their deliberately 'chaotic' presentation in the initial bar, they exude an almost cadential flavour in this last bar, an effect which is more enhanced than disturbed by the chromatic blur on the final chord of B major. For the A sharp of that chord can be understood as a kind of 'border-sound', comparable to the Neapolitan implications which blur the inherent diatonicism of the penultimate chord in D minor at the very end of the String Quartet, Op. 3:

Example 136

The Scherzo Rondo of Movement II ('Andante amoroso') changes the sanguine mood of Movement I to elegiac wistfulness, although it suffers two interruptions in the rustic *Ländler*-episode (Tempo II) and the threatening knocking (viola) of Tempo III. As has been mentioned, the melody of this non-dodecaphonic movement is really a proper twelve-note growth, based not on (A), but on its ancestral form (Y), i.e. the chromatic scale. Thereby it seems closely linked with the very close of

149

Movement I, which is really nothing but a different presentation of the serial properties of the chromatic scale. This movement also ends in a cadence aiming at an imaginary tonic (F major) which never materializes in actual sound.[1] Here is the final chord and its fictitious cadential interpretation:

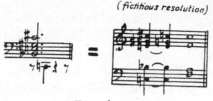

Example 137

The mysterious whisper of the artfully intertwined canonic imitations of Movement III ('Allegro misterioso') recalls the instrumental introduction to the vocal finale of Schoenberg's String Quartet, Op. 10. Berg's movement, too, seems to suggest 'air from another planet'.

The first part is repeated in exact retrograde motion from bar 93 on. Between exposition and its cancrizans recapitulation occurs the explosion of the 'Trio estatico', of which the ferocious intervallic leaps form a shattering contrast to the ghostly flanking sections.

Movement IV ('Adagio appassionato') is conspicuous for its passionate character and forms the climactic centre of the whole work. Serial technique is here replaced by strong reliance on canonic imitation (cf. bars 1-4) and by a subtle system of reminiscences and quotations. The 'Trio estatico' from Movement III interrupts the exposition already at bar 12, but its thematic incipit:

[1]Like the A minor tonic (by implication but not in actual sound) in the prelude to *Tristan.*

is identical with an integral link of the movement's chief thematic character:

Example 138

A quotation from the languorous chief melody of the 'Andante amoroso' (Movement II) at bar 30 is followed by the first quotation of Zemlinsky's cry of passionate desire, 'Du bist mein Eigen', at bar 32 ff. The Tristanesque parallel chords of the tritone (bar 36) prepare for the romantic nostalgia of the solo viola ('Molto tranquillo', bar 45), which in turn leads to the second quotation from Zemlinsky's Symphony (bars 46–50). This movement too ends its Coda (full of post-Wagnerian chords of the seventh and ninth) on a chromatically augmented chord of the dominant which seems to cry out for a resolution in the tonic of F major. The constant denial of this craving gives the music here a positively morbid tint:

Example 139

The spidery flexibility of Movement V ('Presto delirando')
is offset by the sphinx-like chordal symbols of its 'Tenebroso'
episodes. They recall in some ways the unearthly mood of the
'Allegro misterioso' of Movement III. The *flautando* harmonics
of these episodes, drawn like an inverted pedalpoint through
the obscurities of this amorphous musical landscape, are among
Berg's boldest experiments in rarified sonorities. Leibowitz has
rightly drawn attention to the metrical irregularity of the
movement's chief subject, of which the periodical structure in
3+4+5 beats is mainly responsible for the polyrhythmical variety
of the Coda (from bar 44 on). The chief thematic subject is
dodecaphonic and an obvious offspring of (*A*):

Example 140

This movement also includes reminiscences from previous
movements (cf. the return of the threatening knocking at bar
15, a reminiscence of the viola motive of Movement II, bar 56).
A truly extraordinary example of Berg's skilful integration of
tonal elements into his new dodecaphonic orbit is the Coda of
this movement which steers into the clear waters of a I-V-II
(IV)-V-I tonal cadence (cf. cello part from bar 446 on). The
Coda begins at bar 441 ('A tempo') in clear F minor, with a

return to the chief subject in the upper strings (cf. Example 140). The cello accompanies this canonically intertwined 'stretto' with the knocking motive (cf. Movement II):

Example 141

presenting it as a projection of all the notes of (*A*) and simultaneously as a tonal cadence in C major. The rhapsodic style and hopeless nostalgia of the 'Largo desolato' (Movement VI) recall in mood, if not in thematic subject-matter, the 'suicidal' 'Lento-Finale' of Bartok's second String Quartet, Op. 17, and also the tired 'dying out' of Mahler's late Adagios. The movement is dodecaphonic, but by no means exclusively so. Like Movement IV, to which it forms an epilogue, it relies chiefly on reminiscences and self-quotations. Shortly before the last convulsive climax starts, the initial bar of the prelude to *Tristan* appears, floating on the surface, as it were, of a tempestuous sea of conflicting motivic and dodecaphonic allusions (bars 26-28). The climax collapses on the romantic $\frac{6}{4}$ chord at bar 34, only to slide into the Coda, in which a round-dance of thematic ghosts gradually fades away into shadow. Nothing is more moving in this wistful retrospect than the final gesture of farewell, with the gradual sinking into silence of the four instruments. At last only the monotonous murmur of the viola's persistently reiterated 'D flat-F' remains, 'all passion spent'.

The *Lyric Suite* is, then, a work of farewell. A farewell to love, perhaps, and certainly a farewell to youth, whose sonorous symbols are called up here from Lethe, in dream-like incantation. The work says 'farewell' to Berg's early lyricism, for which, in the work of his remaining years, there will be little or no more room. The deep-seated affinity between the *Lyric Suite* and Mahler's last symphonies is nowhere more poignantly apparent than in its epilogue, the pages of which seem inscribed with the despairing words found on the manuscript of Mahler's unfinished tenth symphony: 'Farewell, my lyre. . . .'

CHAPTER VI

Der Wein: lyrical prologue to Lulu

THE composition of the Concert Aria with orchestra *Der Wein* was suggested by Frau Ružena Herlinger, a Viennese soprano well-known for her advanced views and musical sympathies. Berg accepted her commission in the spring of 1929, after he had decided to compose *Lulu* and while he was already working on its libretto. His correspondence with Schoenberg and Webern shows that the first sketches of *Der Wein* were set down at Trahütten in the latter part of May, 1929. The work was finished in full score by August 23—less than three months later. Evidently Frau Herlinger's suggestion was put forward at a favourable moment. Berg was still enveloped in the lyrical mood which had prompted the orchestral version of the *Seven Early Songs* (first performed in November 1928) and his interest in the special problems of the song with orchestra had been further stimulated by the problems presented by his future opera, involving a reorganization of the relations between voice and orchestra.

Der Wein is a setting of poems by Baudelaire, in the free German translation by Stefan George. It was first performed at Königsberg at the annual festival of the Allgemeine Deutsche Musikverein on June 4, 1930, under Hermann Scherchen and with Ružena Herlinger as soloist. The success of this first performance and its heartening effect on Berg are reflected in a

155

letter to the singer, reproduced in facsimile facing page 160. Two years later the work was given its first performance in Vienna at a symphony concert conducted by Webern, on June 21, 1932. This performance must have particularly pleased the composer, judging by his humorous marginal notes in a copy of the programme, reproduced in facsimile facing page 161. Frau Herlinger, who had handsomely paid for an option on the performance of *Der Wein* for the first two years of its existence, sang the work repeatedly under Scherchen's direction, and notably at the music festivals at Venice (1934) and Brussels (1936). The Nazis tried to prevent its inclusion in the Venice festival, their intrigues being brought to nothing at the last moment by the intervention of Casella and Malipiero.

Berg's modest remark, in his letter of appreciation to Frau Herlinger, that he had composed *Der Wein* with special regard to her vocal qualities, represents the truth, but not the whole truth. The work, conceived at the crucial moment of preparation for *Lulu*, was rather a preliminary experiment in the vocal style to be adopted in the opera, the heroine of which would be played by a coloratura soprano of Frau Herlinger's type. Thus *Der Wein* was the stylistic forerunner of *Lulu*, as, in a more modest way, the second Storm song had been the forerunner of the *Lyric Suite*. That this kinship with *Lulu* is more than a conjectural assumption *a posteriori* is shown by the choice of the text of the Aria, by its basic organization and by its colour and scoring.

The choice of Baudelaire's cycle of poems, *Le Vin*, was a logical step for a composer intent on submerging himself in the depths of Wedekind's satanic satire. These poems are an expression of social revolt, akin to Wedekind's. They are linked, too, by their dates of composition, with the smouldering 'Vormärz' period of Büchner's *Wozzeck*. For these five poems constituting

Le Vin, published in the *Fleurs du Mal* of 1857, only to be proscribed and suppressed immediately by the French public prosecutor, had actually been written far back in the early 1840's. Two of them, 'Le vin du assassin' and 'L'ame du vin', had already been published separately in French periodicals in 1848 and 1850. Moreover, a line of the latter poem had been used as a motto by Theodore de Banville in 1844, for his own poem 'Le chanson de vin' (*Les Stalactites*). Although 'Le vin du assassin' was specially attacked by the public prosecutor in 1857, neither it nor any of the other poems of the cycle were among those subsequently expunged from the edition of *Les Fleurs du Mal* of 1861.

Baudelaire, the Parnassian emerging from the orbit of Banville and Laprade, the enthusiast for Wagner's *Tannhäuser* Bacchanale, the 'frondeur' by habit and inclination, wrote these poems in a spirit of revolt, aimed at the complacent philistinism of his epoch, and anticipating Wedekind's later indictment of the bourgeoisie of the 'fin de siècle'. The dionysiac powers of the grape are reflected in the soul of the 'Disinherited', in the intoxication of the rag-and-bone man and the triumph of the common murderer, in the pleasures of the solitary and the ecstasies of young lovers. Berg omitted the poems about the rag-and-bone man and the murderer, choosing only to set 'L'ame du vin', 'Le vin du solitaire' and 'Le vin des amants', which gave him a tripartite musical structure.

It is a pity that Berg, whose knowledge of French seems to have been only elementary, became acquainted with Baudelaire's poems in Stefan George's translations, in which the poetical climate is radically changed. Baudelaire's elegant obscenities are often transposed to a lower key of severe solemnity, and some of the lines deliberately inaccurately rendered. By changing the original positions of Baudelaire's fourth and fifth poem, 'Le vin du solitaire' and 'Le vin des amants', Berg was able to make the former, with its allusion to the temptations of 'wine, women and dice', a logical and realistic reprise of the first poem 'L'ame du vin'. Between these two poems the lightweight doggerel of 'Le vin des amants' makes an admirable Scherzo. So great is the discrepancy between Baudelaire's original and George's translations that Berg's work is 'one big *Ossia*', to quote a caustic remark by T. W. Adorno.[1] The published vocal score is bilingual throughout and has two separate staves for the vocal part, adjusted to the scansion of the French original and the German translation. However, it is unquestionable that Berg received the decisive stimulus from George's free adaptation rather than from the original.[2]

Der Wein is strictly dodecaphonic, like two works that were to follow it, *Lulu* and the Violin Concerto. It shares with the Concerto a distinctive feature of its Basic Set, which admits also of a tonal interpretation. It shares, too, with the twelve-note series of the Concerto the scale-like rising tendency of its row:

Example 142

If note 7 is enharmonically changed to C sharp, section (*a*) represents the complete 'harmonic' scale of D minor, whereas section (*b*) becomes the G flat (= F sharp), scale if the positions of notes 6-12 are suitably rearranged:

<hr />

[1]Cf. W. Reich, Op. cit., p. 106.
[2]This becomes specially evident in bars 189 ff., where the entry of the solo violin was surely prompted by George's totally inaccurate verses, and unfortunately not by Baudelaire's original. Baudelaire nowhere refers to a violin, but speaks instead of 'Les sons d'une musique enervante et caline. . . .'

Example 143

The tonal implications in a chordal re-arrangement of the notes of this series are evident. Here, as in the Violin Concerto, Berg's tendency to integrate tonal elements into his dodecaphonic world leads to the construction of a tonally impregnated series.[1]

The mediant relationship D—F sharp, noticeable in Examples 142 and 143, acted as an even stronger catalytic agent for Berg's creative imagination than the fictitious F major tonality in the *Lyric Suite*. The chordal and melodic consequences of the intervallic arrangements of Examples 142 and 143 determine already the very first bar of the Aria. Berg makes this introductory bar the sum total of all the serial notes, in chordal and melodic simultaneity:

Example 144

The Basic Shape of the row appears already in the orchestral prelude (bars 8-10) and again in the initial bars of the voice part (bars 16 ff.). The structure of the Aria is strictly ternary (i.e. A-B-A1), in conformity with the poetic triptych of the text. Again, as in the *Chamber Concerto* and the *Lyric Suite*, the re-capitulation and its reminiscences and self-quotations, as well as the sectional repetition in retrograde motion, are integral

[1]Cf. J. Rufer (cf. Bibl.), p. 97 ff.

structural devices. Again, as in the *Lyric Suite*, it is the middle movement (section II) which is turned back, crab-fashion, thereby preparing for the inevitable return of section I.[1] Again, as in the Rondo of the *Chamber Concerto* and the 'Largo desolato' of the *Lyric Suite*, extensive passages of section I recur in the final section in literal quotation. Most important for the deeper understanding of the work is the main part of section I (bars 1-87), which has been called a complete Sonata-exposition, with an orchestral prelude based on a Basso Ostinato on the serial notes 1, 2, 3, 12 (bars 1-7).[2] The implications of the Basic Set are chiefly responsible for the often impressionistic hues of its harmonies.

A surprising novelty is the use of Jazz instruments and Jazz rhythms, for the first time in Berg's work. It is remarkable enough that Jazz elements could be integrated at all into Berg's mature idiom. According to Adorno,[3] Berg only became acquainted with Jazz in or about 1925 and took to it reluctantly. However, Berg's widow asserts that he delighted in listening to Jazz bands on his wireless set. The latter assertion is supported by the important part allotted to Jazz music in *Lulu* and by the use of the saxophone even in the Violin Concerto. Berg's penchant for Jazz is all the more remarkable in that neither Schoenberg nor Webern paid more than casual attention to it.[4] Jazz is used in *Der Wein*, as later on in *Lulu*, as a sound symbol of moral decay and depravity. It remains here and later a medium for the characterization of special social conditions. Berg, like Stravinsky in *The Soldier's Tale*, uses only the older, obsolescent types of Tango, Ragtime and English

[1]Section II consists of: Scherzo, bars 88-96; Trio, bars 97-122; Scherzo reprise, bars 123-141; retrograde motion, bars 142-172; Scherzo reprise, bars 140-112.
[2]Cf. R. Leibowitz (cf. Bibl.), pp. 161-62.
[3]Cf. W. Reich, op. cit., p. 102 ff.
[4]Apart from the contemporaneous use of jazz instruments in Schoenberg's *Von Heute auf Morgen* (1930) and in Webern's Quartet Op. 22 (1930).

Facsimile of a Letter by Alban Berg to Ružena Herlinger, the first
singer of 'Der Wein' (June 1930)
(By courtesy of Mrs Ruzena Herlinger)

10 Briefe ~~~

Dienstag, 21. Juni 1932, 19.30 Uhr
im Großen Musikvereins-Saal

ZU EHREN DES ZEHNTEN INTERNATIONALEN MUSIKFESTES

ORCHESTER-KONZERT

SCHÖNBERG . . . . . . a) Friede auf Erden (Gedicht von C. F. Meyer)
b) Begleitmusik zu einer Lichtspielszene

BERG . . . . Der Wein (Gedicht von Baudelaire) für Sopransolo
und großes Orchester (Erste Aufführung in Wien)

MAHLER . . . . Zweite Sinfonie

Ausführende:
Ružena Herlinger (Sopran)/Enid Szantho, Staatsoper Wien (Alt)/Freie Typographia/Der Singverein der Kunststelle/Das Wiener Sinfonieorchester

Dirigent: ANTON WEBERN

PREIS DIESES PROGRAMMES 40 GROSCHEN

Facsimile of a Concert Programme issued for a Concert in which
Anton Webern conducted the first performance in Vienna of
Berg's Concert Aria 'Der Wein' (1932)
The Programme contains words of praise in Berg's hand who
signs humoristically as 'The Butler'
(By courtesy of Mrs Ruzena Herlinger)

Waltz, ignoring the more modern Charleston and Blues, which had only recently inspired Ernst Krenek's Jazz opera *Johnny spielt auf* (1927). The thematic relationship of the Jazz enclaves in *Der Wein* with the Jazz music in *Lulu* is based as much on skilful use of cross bar rhythms as on the constitutional element of the interval of the fourth. The latter is here used (as earlier in *Wozzeck*) as a symbol of the musically primitive:

Example 145

Compare this with the following extract from the English Waltz from *Lulu*:

Example 146

Example 145 is confined to the piano which, together with alto saxophone, muted trumpet and banjo-like pizzicato strings, forms a kind of imaginary Jazz band, foreshadowing the very aura of sound emanating from the Jazz band employed in *Lulu* (Act 1). This Jazz music, which illustrates in section I 'le refrain des dimanches', returns in recapitulatory fashion in section III (transposed down a third) at the words 'Un baiser libertin de la maigre Adeline'.

In sharp contrast to the angular rhythms of the Jazz sections is the ecstatic scintillation of the Scherzo, with its unique combination of high-pitched sounds (high coloratura soprano, backed by flutter-tonguing flutes and high-pitched violins). It is especially this dream-like vision of the Scherzo (section II) which anticipates in an almost somnambulistic manner the future musical atmosphere of *Lulu* and its heroine's erotic fascination.

CHAPTER VII

LULU

The Opera of Social Protest and Compassion—II

I. THE LIBRETTO

BERG was a son of Darkest Austria, and his creative achievements have their roots in his basic opposition to the decaying empire in which his youth was spent. The subjects of his two great operas are centred in two symbolic figures, indicative of the sufferings of the socially down-trodden in his home-country. The enslavement and humiliation of poor Wozzeck, the inarticulate infantryman, are matched by the death-dance of social machinery in which Lulu, the prostitute, is slowly atomized.

Two theatrical performances provided the igniting spark that set Berg's imagination burning and led eventually to the creation of these operas. The performance of Wedekind's *Pandora's Box* at the Trianontheater on May 29, 1905, and the exhumation of Büchner's *Woyzeck* at the *Wiener Kammerspiele* in May 1914 were events on the fringe of Vienna's artistic life. They were intended to be protests against a fictitious social and artistic world, and against the fermenting erotic cynicism of its 'fin de siècle' literature.[1] The revolutionary social criticism implied in both plays profoundly affected Berg and his conception of the opera of social protest and compassion, which he

[1] *e.g.* Arthur Schnitzler's frivolous dramatic dialogues *Anatol* and *Reigen*.

163

was to create in the very hour of Imperial Austria's doom. Both operas are linked with the political catastrophe of Austria by virtue of a truly remarkable coincidence of dates. Berg decided to set Büchner's *Woyzeck* to music on the eve of the assassination of the Archduke Franz Ferdinand at Sarajevo. The opera was planned, written and published during the years of the first World War and its revolutionary aftermath, which led to the birth of 'little' Republican Austria. *Lulu* was conceived and composed in the twilight years of post-war Austria's independence. During the months of fratricidal struggle between Socialists and *Heimwehr*, culminating in the rising of February 1934, the last bars of the short score of *Lulu* were written. Berg died less than two years later, in a Vienna increasingly faithless to his ideals, leaving to posterity the unfinished full score of his opera. Meanwhile the political decomposition of Austria had progressed so rapidly that the two completed acts of *Lulu* could only be performed in free Switzerland (at Zurich, June 20, 1937). Nine months later, in Hitler's Austria of March 1938, the very name of Alban Berg was proscribed.

In the literary work of Frank Wedekind the struggle of the sexes is the dominating theme, as it is in the writings of August Strindberg, whose mixture of erotic satanism and pungent social satire seems reflected in the life story and creative bias of his younger German contemporary. Wedekind's favourite subject, the demoniacal *hubris* of the female element, inspiring but also destroying men, is most convincingly presented in two plays of which Lulu is the central character: *Earth Spirit* (1893) and *Pandora's Box* (1901). They had been preceded by *Frühlings Erwachen* (1891), a tragedy of premature sex-fulfilment among schoolchildren. This play, a dream-like succession of short scenes, admittedly modelled on Büchner's *Woyzeck*, was for fourteen years banished from the German stage, a fate that was to befall the two 'Lulu' plays as well. They were condemned in three courts of law as immoral and inartistic and copies were destroyed by order of the police.

The man who aroused this storm of protest and conflicting reactions in law, police and public was born in Hanover on July 24, 1864. His father, a doctor, had married in San Francisco, late in life, a German actress much younger than himself, while on a tour round the world. The family seems to have been notorious for eccentric behaviour and internal feuds. Some critics believe that their quarrels are reflected in Gerhart Hauptmann's early play *Das Friedensfest*. Wedekind was a tragic figure from the very outset of his career. One of his brothers committed suicide and he himself seems to have suffered from the malady of the Romantics and their spiritual heirs: a Faustian ambivalence. His life and work move, as it were, in an incessant spiral of antitheses. He was lame from birth, yet became a remarkable actor. Despite, or perhaps because of, this physical handicap, he was attracted by the circus and especially by men of athletic build. He tried his hand desultorily at various occupations: journalism, circus work in Switzerland, and work for the modern German realistic stage. With Bierbaum, Wolzogen and others he joined the first German literary cabaret, 'Die elf Scharfrichter', and on its miniature stage at Munich made his *début* as *chansonnier*, accompanying on the lute his cynical little ballads, set to melodies of his own. One of these *Lautenlieder* was afterwards employed by Berg in the third act of *Lulu*. As poet and cabaret-singer Wedekind became a hit and soon he also won his spurs as an actor in straight plays. In later years he acted chiefly in his own plays, opposite his gifted wife, Tilly Newes, an actress of great beauty and charm.[1]

---

[1]In later years Wedekind repeatedly acted in *Earth Spirit* and *Pandora's Box*, playing in turn the parts of Dr Schön, Jack, and the Lion-tamer who recites the 'prologue'.

In the majority of Wedekind's plays the characters are drawn from the bohemian world of the circus, the theatre and *demimonde* (*Der Kammersänger*, 1897; *Der Marquis von Keith*, 1901; *Hidalla*, 1904; *Musik*, 1906). However, the plays embodying the quintessence of his post-Nietzschian philosophy of human renewal through the purgatory of untrammelled sexuality, chiefly concentrate on the perverse aberrations of love, on prostitution, and on procurers and nymphomaniacs (*Totentanz*, 1906, *Franziska*, 1911). It is in *Totentanz* (a play that has more than just the title in common with Strindberg) that the heartless procurer Casti-Piani, Lulu's evil genius, returns to the stage and, in the end, commits suicide. Wedekind never surpassed the *succès de scandale* of *Earth Spirit* and its sequel, and died, prematurely aged and already eclipsed as a writer by the vanguard of German expressionism, in Munich on March 8, 1918.

Wedekind conceived the two parts of his 'Lulu' drama as a feminine parallel, as it were, to Goethe's *Faust*. Like Goethe's hero, Lulu runs through the whole gamut of passion. She climbs the social ladder, only to topple over from its dizzy heights into the abyss of prostitution, illness and crime. Her companion is the Countess Geschwitz who, with her sterile Lesbian infatuation with Lulu, represents something akin to Mephistopheles's principle of negation ('Der Geist, der stets verneint'). Wedekind underlined the parallel with Goethe's play by opening 'Pandora's Box' with a 'Prologue in the bookshop', closely modelled on Goethe's 'Prologue on the stage' down to the doggerel rhymes *à la* Hans Sachs. Some element of the poetic programme underlying the tremendous adventure of Goethe's *Faust* is embodied in the famous final lines of the 'Prologue on the stage':

Und wandelt mit bedächtiger Schnelle
Vom Himmel durch die Welt zur Hölle!

This is re-echoed in the impertinent stanzas of the little poem
'Earth Spirit', found among Wedekind's lyric poems but not
included in the 'Lulu' plays:

> Greife wacker nach der Sünde,
> Aus der Sünde wächst Genuss.
> Ach, du gleichest einem Kinde,
> Dem man alles zeigen muss.
>
> Meide nicht die ird'schen Schätze:
> Wo sie liegen, nimm sie mit.
> Hat die Welt doch nur Gesetze,
> Dass man sie mit Füssen tritt.
>
> Glücklich, wer geschickt und heiter
> Über frische Gräber hopst.
> Tanzend auf der Galgenleiter
> Hat sich keiner noch gemopst.

The parallel with Goethe's *Faust* culminates in the dramatic
function of the Countess Geschwitz who, telescoping, as it
were, the roles of the cheated Mephistopheles and *Una poeniten-
tium* (alias Gretchen), intercedes for the sinner Lulu in the face
of death. Wedekind himself encouraged an interpretation on
these lines by his own assessment of his chief characters[1]:

> Lulu . . . plays in all three acts a purely passive role; the Countess
> Geschwitz, however, offers proof in the first act of a superhuman
> degree of self-sacrifice. Nevertheless, the curse of perversity alone
> would not have induced me to treat this problem in dramatic
> form. I did so because I found that this fatal destiny had never yet
> been made the subject of a tragedy.

The refinement in the drawing of the Countess's character in
Berg's libretto is in line with Wedekind's own self-interpreta-
tion.

[1] In his preface to *Pandora's Box*, 1906.

Wedekind's 'Lulu' reaches its poetical apex in the ecstatic glorification of the 'Eternal Feminine' ('Das Ewig-Weibliche' of Goethe's final Chorus Mysticus), symbolized in the figure of the naïve she-demon, the incarnation of amorality and unlimited sensuality. It is this note of hedonism which distinguishes *Lulu* from the contemporary plays of the pessimistic anti-feminist Strindberg. The philosophical and, indeed, ethical ground-bass of Wedekind's 'Lulu' plays evidently passed unnoticed when the public prosecutor hurled his indictment against their author. A rehabilitation of Wedekind, as moralist, preacher and playwright, occurred only in 1905, when *Pandora's Box* received its first performance in Vienna, with Wedekind himself and his wife in the parts, respectively, of Jack the Ripper and Lulu. Karl Kraus gave an introductory lecture and appeared as the sinister negro chieftain Kungu Poti. As we know, the twenty-year-old Alban Berg attended this performance. He decided to set the two 'Lulu' plays to music only after prolonged hesitation, and after setting aside various other projects, including an operatic version of Hauptmann's *Und Pippa tanzt*. The following pages give, in tabulated form, the history of *Lulu* before and after the composer's death:

May 29, 1905	First performance of *Pandora's Box* in Vienna.
Spring 1928	Berg decides to set Wedekind's 'Lulu' plays to music.
Spring 1929	Completion of the libretto. Composition begun, but temporarily interrupted by work on *Der Wein*.
August 1929	Agreement with Wedekind's heirs signed.
June 4, 1930	First performance of *Der Wein*.

December 1933	'Das Lied der Lulu' (Act 2), dedicated to Webern on his fiftieth birthday.
April 1934	*Lulu* completed in short score.
Late April 1934	Dedicatory letter and passage in vocal score 'Eine Seele, die sich im Jenseits den Schlaf aus den Augen reibt. . . .' (*Lulu*, II/1, bars 317 ff.) sent to Karl Kraus on his sixtieth birthday. This same passage had played an important part in Kraus's introductory lecture to *Pandora's Box* in 1905.[1]
August 28, 1934	Autograph of the 'Prologue' to *Lulu* sent to Schoenberg, and the opera dedicated to him, for his sixtieth birthday on September 13.
Summer 1934	Compilation of the so-called 'Lulu-symphony' (published early in 1935).
November 30, 1934	First performance in Berlin of the 'Lulu-symphony' under Erich Kleiber.
Winter 1934-35	Work continued on the orchestration of *Lulu*.
Spring 1935	Orchestration of *Lulu* interrupted by the composition of the Violin Concerto (completed on or about August 11, 1935).
End of August 1935	Orchestration of *Lulu* resumed.
December 11, 1935	First performance of the 'Lulu-symphony' in Vienna, in the presence of the composer. Berg, mortally ill, hears for the first and last time fragments from his opera.

[1]Cf. Karl Kraus, *Literatur und Lüge* (Vienna, 1929).

169

December 24, 1935 Death of Berg in Vienna.
April 19, 1936 First performance of the Violin Con-
certo, in Barcelona.
June 2, 1937 Première of *Lulu* at the Stadttheater,
Zürich.

The Symphonic Fragments from *Lulu* ('Lulu-symphony')
were published in full score by Universal Edition, Vienna, in
1935. A vocal score of the first two acts of the opera, piano-
reduction by Erwin Stein, was published by Universal Edition
in 1936. The libretto of the first two acts was published in 1937.
The vocal score and the libretto include a brief synopsis of the
third act.

Before Wedekind's plays could be set to music, Berg had to
subject their texts to a literary and dramaturgical 'streamlining',
much more drastic than that to which *Wozzeck* had been subjected. He reduced the seven acts and two prologues of the two
semi-independent plays to three acts (seven scenes), and one
prologue. This process of concentration entailed the excision of
numerous scenes and several episodic characters. The scenes cut
include the Faustian 'Prologue in the bookshop' to *Pandora's
Box* and the expository scenes 1 and 2 of the first act of *Earth
Spirit*.[1] The characters omitted include the reporter, the maid
and Dr Hilti, the grotesque Swiss University lecturer, one of
Lulu's last customers. Other figures of special importance for the
demonstration of Lulu's social rise, *Medizinalrat* Dr Goll, her
first husband, and Prince Ecserny, the African explorer, were
turned into shadowy characters, losing much of their individuality, together with their surnames. Dramatic attention
was focussed on the painter, Dr Schön, Alwa and Schigolch,

[1]It is interesting to note that there exists an authorized edition of Wedekind's plays
condensed into one, under the title 'Lulu'.

among the male characters of the two plays. The structure of
Berg's libretto emphasizes the decisive phases of Lulu's develop-
ment much better than the caesuras of Wedekind's many acts.
The final curtain of Berg's Act I underlines Lulu's triumph over
Dr Schön. His Act 2 is played without change of scenery in
Dr Schön's house, and amalgamates Act 4 of 'Earth Spirit' with
Act I of *Pandora's Box*. By this fusion it abolishes the overlong
caesura between Wedekind's two plays. The two scenes of this
act are linked by means of a musical interlude which, synchronized with the track of a silent film, narrates Lulu's turbulent
adventures between the killing of Dr Schön and her escape
from prison. The main episodes of the film are: Lulu's arrest,
remand for trial, legal proceedings, ending in her being sen-
tenced to imprisonment; prison; escape, through the devotion
of the Countess Geschwitz, who smuggles Lulu into an isolation-hospital for cholera cases; illness (cholera); escape from the
hospital. These episodes represent in flash-like abbreviations the
gist of the ponderous dialogue of the first half of *Pandora's Box*,
Act I. They are accompanied by music, the retrograde motion
of which underlines Lulu's triumphant return to her former
haunts. Responsible for the deaths of three husbands, Lulu re-
appears, phoenix-like and as seductive as ever, before her next
victim, Alwa. Unchanged by trial, prison and cholera,[1] she has
now reached the apex of her victorious feminity. This is
exultantly expressed by her union with Alwa at the end of
Act 2. The big caesura between Acts 2 and 3 of Berg's libretto
indicates the end of an episode in Lulu's life more forcibly than
the less significant hiatus between Acts I and 2 of Wedekind's
Pandora. Between Berg's Acts I and 2 the marriage of Lulu and
Dr Schön takes place. Similarly, between Acts 2 and 3 Lulu's

---

[1]According to a remark by Rodrigo in *Pandora's Box*, Act I, p. 137, Lulu is still
only in her twentieth year.

love affair with his son Alwa is more or less legalized, resulting in their joint escape from Germany and their subsequent new life in a shady Parisian *demi-monde* environment. Lulu, from now on, is for ever excluded from bourgeois respectability. Berg's caesura between Acts 2 and 3 also underscores the ageing of Lulu, who reappears in the first scene of Act 3 as a woman of about thirty, having led the life of a Parisian 'Grande Cocotte' for about ten years. Lulu and Alwa's flight from the German police at the end of Act 2 and their escape from Paris at the end of the first scene of Act 3, when the blackmailer Casti-Piani threatens to expose them to the police, form a conclusive parallel. Finally, Berg's second scene of Act 3 presents Lulu ageing, sick and debauched, in her ultimate disguise as a London prostitute.

The structural economy of the libretto is matched by its verbal condensation, by which all the polemical longeurs of Wedekind, the sermonizing satanist, are shed.[1] However, the composer's encroachment on the poet's preserve does not end here. Berg also boldly transferred the action from the 'fin de siècle' atmosphere of the 1890's to the 1920's. This modernization of Wedekind can only be understood as an act of self-identification, deep down in Berg's subconscious, with the character Alwa. Dr Schön's gifted son, the poet of *Earth Spirit*, author of a play in which Lulu appears as a dancer, who intends, too, to write an interesting play on Lulu herself (*Earth Spirit*, III/2), is transformed in the libretto into a poet-composer of a 'gruesome opera' (*Lulu* II/2, p. 84). He is scornfully apostrophized as 'your composer' by Casti-Piani (*Lulu*, III/1, Chorale Variation No. 5). Berg finally unmasks his relation to Alwa completely in musical self-quotation, when the initial bar of

[1] A more detailed account of Berg's revision of Wedekind's dialogue is given in the German edition of this book.

Wozzeck accompanies Alwa's words: 'Über die liesse sich freilich eine interessante Oper schreiben':[1]

Example 147

As in the case of *Wozzeck*, Berg was here confronted time and again with sections of text difficult or impossible to set to music—a predicament familiar to all composers who, like Strauss and Puccini, have decided to turn straight plays into operas. In *Lulu* these residual dialogue sections are more frequent than in *Wozzeck*. In the later work they occasionally tend to bring the music to a complete standstill.[2] However, Berg was unendingly resourceful in turning casual phrases of Wedekind's dialogue into musicogenic material.[3] The number of different vocal devices used in *Lulu* is prodigious. A passage such as the following (III/1, cue 477), with its clear distinction of four vocal techniques: (*a*) speaking on pitch, (*b*) recitative, (*c*) parlando-singing, (*d*) bel canto:

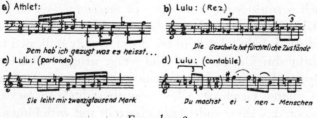

Example 148

recalls the multitude of recitative and arioso-types prevalent in

---

[1]'To be sure, she could become the subject of an interesting opera' (*Lulu*, 1/3, cue 1095).
[2]Cf. *Lulu*, I/2, cue 407, II/2, cue 1021 b, III/1, cue 55.
[3]Cf. the words to the vocal ensembles of III/1.

early opera. The sections in *Lulu* produced by '*Sprechstimme*' are indicated in the notation 𝄌 and take their cue from Schoenberg's early 'mélodrames'.[1] Berg's imagination was undoubtedly stimulated by the fact that he conceived the part of Lulu for a coloratura soprano. The effects demanded range from a whispered shriek to the passionate whistling sound of hysteria. This can best be studied in the scene of Lulu's clash with the Countess Geschwitz (III/1). Lulu's rage and frustration are reflected in the almost unproducible pitch of the following bars:

Weiss . Gott nein! Aber wenn du kommst so ge — he ich ____

Example 149

The numerous minor changes in Wedekind's plays include the less antisemitic presentation of the banker in III/1 and the less provocative 'male dress' of the Lesbian Countess. The rearrangement of the final scene of Lulu's assassination should be specially mentioned. While Berg is evidently intent on reproducing in III/2 the gruesome atmosphere of Grand-Guignol which permeates the final scene of *Pandora's Box*, he lets the actual murder take place *behind* the scenes, in contrast to Wedekind. Lulu's death, in the opera, is only indicated by her frightful shriek at cue 1268. The savage struggle with Jack the Ripper is here mercifully curtailed and attention focussed on the Countess Geschwitz who, mortally stabbed by Jack on his way out, dies alone under Lulu's portrait and with Lulu's name on her lips.

The opinion expressed above, that the libretto of *Lulu* represents an even greater literary achievement than the libretto of *Wozzeck*, is supported by a passage from a letter of Berg's to

[1] Cf. the chapter on *Wozzeck* in this book, p. 74 ff.

Schoenberg, dated August 7, 1930,[1] where he describes the difficulties of transforming Wedekind's text into the substance of an opera:

... Of my new opera I can only report that I am still in the first Act. Apart from the composition, the twelve-note style of which does not yet permit me to work quickly, it is the libretto that holds me up so much. Its formation progresses alongside the composition. As I have to cut out four-fifths of Wedekind's original, the selection of the remaining one-fifth is enough of a torture.[2] And what further torture when I try to adapt that selection to the larger and smaller musical structures and to avoid destroying Wedekind's idiomatic characteristics in the process! Hence I could only send you the 'text' of the parts already composed; however, I prefer to wait until the whole text is settled.

Despite this clinging to detail, the libretto as a whole has, of course, been quite clear to me for a long while. That applies to the musical proportions as well as to the dramatic structure. The scenario can be briefly presented thus:

The two plays	*The opera*
Act I: Studio of the painter, in which Dr Goll, Lulu's husband, dies of an apoplectic stroke.	
Earth Spirit — Act II: The flat of Lulu and her second husband, the painter, who commits suicide.	Act I 3 scenes
Act III: The dressing-room in a theatre, of Lulu, the dancer, to whom Dr Schön proposes marriage.	
Act IV: Schön's flat, where he is killed by Lulu. She is arrested by the police.	
	Act II Scene I
After 10 years in prison[3] Lulu is released by Alwa (Schön's son) and Geschwitz. She returns ...	separated from scene 2 by a long interlude.
... in Act I to Schön's flat (scene as before). She becomes Alwa's mistress.	
Pandora's Box — Act II: Gambling-den in Paris. Lulu has to flee.	Act III. 2 scenes.
Act III: In an attic in London.	

[1] First published by R. S. Hill (*Musical Quarterly*, Jan. 1953, p. 134 ff.).
[2] Compare this with Willi Reich's astonishing assertion (*Melos*, 1952, No. 12) that Berg set Wedekind's text 'without altering a word'.
[3] The 'ten years in prison' were altered to 'one year in prison' in the final form of the libretto.

The brackets (right and left) indicate how scenes are deliberately combined in my text which were separated in Wedekind's plays, which, after all, are *two* plays. The interlude which bridges the gap between the last act of 'Earth Spirit' and the first act of 'Pandora' is also the focal point of the whole tragedy. In it begins, after the ascent of the preceding acts or scenes, the descent of the following scenes, the inversion. (By the way: the four men who visit Lulu in her attic have to be represented in the opera by those singers who have represented the men who become Lulu's victims in the first half of the opera—in inverted order of appearance, to be sure . . .)[1]

2. THE MUSIC

Berg's two operas are set apart from almost all other contemporary works by their pitiless realism. The hero of *Wozzeck* and the heroine of *Lulu* are both murderers, in the common sense of the word. But in both operas the murderer is clearly presented as a victim of environment and social conditions.

The music in both works is subject to a rigid formal discipline, in strong contrast to the loose texture of post-Wagnerian opera in general. In Berg's works the music retains an independent life of its own. This is emphasized in the vocal scores of *Wozzeck* and *Lulu* by sub-titles which draw attention to the use of the forms of 'absolute' music, as often as not of an archaic nature: Passacaglia, Canon, Chorale-Variation, Sonata, etc. The episodic character and puppet-like atmosphere of *Wozzeck* made it difficult to establish a system of characteristic *leitmotive*. But in the case of *Lulu* the almost continuous presence of no less than seven chief characters seemed to call for a much more

[1] These dramatic correlations correspond in turn with musical reminiscences extending over III/2. See page 192ff.

systematic employment of these devices. To be sure, the characteristic motives of *Lulu* are very different from Wagnerian *leitmotive*. They frequently present themselves only in the form of a sonorous aura, indicative of a certain dramatic mood. Thus the banging of chord-clusters on the piano is associated with the athlete, the solo violin with Casti-Piani, the chamber orchestra with Schigolch, and pentatonic harmonic progressions with the Countess Geschwitz. Similarly, the atmosphere of the theatre (I/3) is indicated by the sound of Jazz music and that of the London slums by the strains of a barrel-organ grinding out the melody of Wedekind's *Lautenlied* (III/2). A 'leit-rhythm' (*sit venia verbo*) plays an integral role in *Lulu*, as in *Wozzeck*.[1]

The motives and sound combinations associated with certain characters in *Lulu* are more closely related than are the motives in Wagner's operas, where basic relationships are often established by the use of certain determinant keys. The motives in *Lulu* are all derived from a single twelve-note series, except for such extraneous matter as Wedekind's ballad tune in Act 3. Whereas *Wozzeck* achieved rigid formal control, in the sense of strict serial composition, only in isolated episodes (I/4: Passacaglia; III/1: Fugue), *Lulu* applies dodecaphonic technique consistently, if not exclusively. Berg employs here a mature technique which permits the establishment of a system of subtle thematic correspondences, such as had been increasingly characteristic of his music since the Chamber Concerto. But even more than in that work and its successors, the music of *Lulu* is constructed on the principle of symphonic recapitulations and correspondences, involving whole scenes in that process of repetition and self-quotation. In that sense Act 3 of *Lulu*

---

[1]Indicated by 'RH' ('Hauptrhythmus') in the score. Even the smallest rhythmic 'events'—for instance, Lulu's stamping her feet (I/1) or the knock on the door when the Negro, Kungu Poti, enters (III/2)—are subject to its organizing control.

can be understood as a symphonic recapitulation of Acts 1 and 2, with long sections of I/1 returning in III/2 in literal quotation. Berg's increasing inclination towards self-quotation and subtle allusion becomes more noticeable than ever before. These musical correspondences may refer to whole movements (the Canzonetta of I/1, which returns as the Arietta of II/2) or to musico-poetical purple patches (cf. Alwa's passage: 'A soul rubbing sleep from its eyes in Heaven', in II/1, bar 317 ff, which returns in literal quotation at Lulu's sentence: 'If only your great infant eyes did not exist', in II/2, bar 1000).

This complicated system of motivic allusion, of self-quotation and self-revelation by purely musical means is made possible by the fact that the entire thematic substance is derived from one basic serial row. The characteristics of the twelve-note row determine the choice of intervals, such as the fourth, fifth and ninth, used for the purpose of dramatic characterization. In particular, sequences of fourths, developed from certain permutations of the Basic Shape of the series, give the whole opera its hall-mark. They underlie the passionate episodes as much as the interludes of jaunty Jazz music. Sequences of chords of the seventh and ninth (almost in the luscious manner of Scriabin) express the magic of sensuality. Berg's predilection for formal correspondences is also responsible for the frequent use of retrograde inversions, as well suited to the accompaniment of the bizarre film as to the dialectical antinomies of the text (as in Lulu's song, II/1, where every line contains also its dialectical antithesis).

The possibilities of the technique used by Berg in the composition of his twelve-note opera had been explored and tested some years earlier by Schoenberg. His little opera *Von Heute auf Morgen*, on a text by Max Blonda, was composed in 1928/29 and first performed at Frankfurt-on-Main on February 1, 1930.

It was published early in 1930 in a facsimile reproduction of the autograph score, and there is no doubt that it influenced Berg very much.[1] Features of *Lulu* anticipated in Schoenberg's opera include the use of archaic forms, such as Canon, Duet, Quartet, Recitative and Arioso, the parodistic employment of Jazz instruments, especially the saxophone, and the systematic application of dodecaphonic technique. Schoenberg's music is controlled by the formal demands of each respective 'set piece' and by the imposed thematic derivation from the basic series. Every bar of this little domestic comedy[2] is determined by these fundamental principles of musical organization, which were taken over fully (if not perhaps wholly consciously) by Berg for use in *Lulu*. The structural pattern of *Lulu* having been expounded in great detail by earlier commentators,[3] the following explanation can do little more than epitomize their findings.

Here is the Basic Set *R*, which yields the musical symbols related to the opera's heroine:

Example 150

If the notes of *R* are re-organized vertically the result is a short chordal sequence:

[1] Cf. the little Canon composed by Berg on the occasion of the fiftieth anniversary of the Frankfurt Opera House, jointly commemorating the first performance of Schoenberg's opera there. It is based on the twelve-note series used by Schoenberg and alludes to the title of the opera in its text. It was published in the appendix to Willi Reich's book of 1937, p. 16. Berg sent the autograph of the Canon to Schoenberg, together with a letter in which he apologized for the incorrect use of the twelve-note series of Schoenberg's opera in his own opusculum.

[2] The insipidity of the libretto is probably responsible for the oblivion which has overtaken the opera.

[3] Cf. W. Reich, Op. cit., also *Musical Quarterly*, XXII/4, 1936 and Grove's Dictionary, Supplementary volume, 1940. Cf. also R. Leibowitz, Op. cit.

Example 151

These chords ('Bildharmonien') present the essence, as it were, of Lulu's character. They are associated with the painted portrait of her that plays a symbolical role in the opera, reminiscent of that of the portrait in Wilde's *Dorian Gray*. A scale motive is produced if the three 'voices' of the 'portrait harmonies' are strung out horizontally:

Example 152

In a rhythmic variant the above example is transformed into a dance-like motive, expressive of Lulu, the demoniac ballerina, pirouetting over social prejudices, death, love and hate with equal grace and fascination:

Example 153

If *R* is continuously repeated, with every seventh note singled out for a special accent, the graph of the sequence of accented notes yields a new theme:

Example 154

180

This derivative of *R* is eventually turned into the Alwa motive, with its characteristic feature, the interval of the minor third:

Andante

Example 155

If an accepted rhythmical series of five notes each is superimposed on *R* the result is:

Example 156

The principle of pentatonic organization used here (which had already been employed in Schoenberg's earliest serial composition, the piano pieces Op. 23) can be associated with the pentatonic system of Ancient Greece, and thus with Greek tendencies to homosexual love (Lesbos). Motives derived from Example 156, such as:

Example 157

become the musical symbol of the unnatural tendencies of the Lesbian Countess Geschwitz.

Another mode of permutation applied to *R* yields the series:

Example 158

181

out of which the energetic Sonata-theme of Dr Schön is developed:

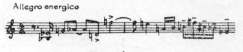

Example 159

Even the 'Leit-rhythm' (RH) can be understood as a variant of R. This RH (which as 'Monoritmica' plays a big part in the scene of the painter's death, I/2, and again in the final scene, III/2) may be reduced to the formula:[1]

This rhythmic scheme is distilled out of certain variants of the Basic Set, as is shown here:

Example 160

RH determines also, as rhythmical backbone, the structure of the fatalistic motive which recurs at all the turning-points of Lulu's erotic career:

Example 161

[1] The formula is closely related to the RH in *Wozzeck* (III/3), as also to the RH in the Chamber Concerto (last movement). Their common source is, of course, in the RH of Mahler's ninth symphony (first movement).

By a similar process of thematic 'atom-splitting' Berg obtains
the chromatic mosaic of motive-particles from which Schigolch's creeping figures are constructed:

Example 162

Certain characteristic intervals are derived from the Basic Set
and its variants. For instance, the intervals of the seventh and
ninth in the upper and lower parts of the portrait-harmonies
(Example 151), and the heaped-up intervals of the fourth which
result from the following process of permutation and elimination on the basis of R:

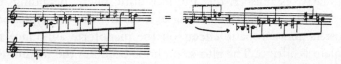

Example 163

These fourths are easily recognizable as the *Earth Spirit* fourths,
symbolizing the primordial urge of the Faustian Lulu in all her
guises.

   The peculiarities of the *Lulu* orchestra had been foreshadowed
in *Der Wein*. Berg's last opera shares with its immediate precursor, as with Schoenberg's *Von Heute auf Morgen*, the incorporation of Jazz instruments into the normal orchestra.[1] With
the exception of particularly vulgar types, such as Flexaton and
Swannee Whistle, all the favourite Jazz instruments of 1930 are
represented. They include: alto saxophone in E flat (an important melodic instrument in *Lulu*, linking oboes and clarinets),

   [1]Some of these instruments are meant to play only in the Jazz band, *behind* the
scenes (I/3). However, for smaller theatres they are cued into the respective parts of
the main orchestra.

183

tenor saxophone, Jazz trumpets and trombones (with mutes), sousaphone (alternating with tuba and bass-saxhorn), violins with 'Jazz funnels', double-basses treated percussively, banjo, pianoforte and a large percussion group, amalgamating the Jazz types with the more conventional instruments.

In rhythmic style and orchestration the Jazz episodes of *Lulu* correspond to the obsolescent types of 'Ragtime' and 'English Waltz'. By excluding any allusion to the more modern species of 'Blues', which had become universally popular by 1930, they seem deliberately to renounce cheap topicality of effect. Alto saxophone, percussively treated pianoforte and vibraphone (none of which are employed in *Wozzeck*) are given significant dramatic functions in this score. The vibraphone regularly establishes the musical atmosphere heralding the appearance of Lulu (Cf. Prologue, 1 bar before cue 15). Chordclusters and acrobatic effects on the pianoforte announce the athlete Rodrigo. The alto saxophone becomes the medium of voluptuous passion (II/2, Hymn, 2 bars before cue 110).

Another feature of the score is the deliberate overclouding of root triads, achieved through a kind of orchestral pedal-effect of blurring character and through subtle infiltration of 'foreign' notes into the orbit of clearly defined tonalities. This is seen in the penultimate bar of Act 1, where the tonic D flat is threatened in its harmonic existence by the intrusion of a D natural and the effect of the echo of the piano pedal, mixing with the tremolo of the vibraphone and a 'flautando' cantilena in clarinet and saxophone:

Example 164

The part of Lulu is written for a high coloratura soprano. It calls for extensive passages of bel canto singing, as do the parts of Dr Schön and Alwa, in strong contrast to the vocal style of *Wozzeck* in general. The sensual atmosphere of *Lulu* determined this radical change in the treatment of the voice.[1] On the other hand, the long stretches of bare dialogue tax the ability of the average opera-singer to assume the role of a straight actor. The ensembles in *Lulu* (Duet-canon, I/I Trio-canon, II/I, Choral ensemble, III/I) surpass similar passages in *Wozzeck* by their increased polyphonic subtlety.

* * *

The three scenes of the first act of Berg's opera correspond with the action of the first three acts of Wedekind's *Earth Spirit*. The composer's infallible feeling for dramatic effect is seen in this elimination of the opening scenes of the play and plunge into the demoniacal vortex of Lulu's erotic adventures. The painter (Schwarz) falls madly in love with Lulu while painting her portrait in fancy dress, as Pierrette. Lulu's husband, Dr Goll, gate-crashes into a turbulent love-scene. Rage and excitement bring about an apoplectic stroke and he dies on the spot, Lulu thus becoming a wealthy young widow who almost automatically marries the bewildered painter.[2] Schwarz proves unequal to his allotted role of accommodating husband. Once he has certain proof that Lulu has deceived him, and that she has been the mistress of her so-called 'Father' Schigolch, as well as of her fatherly protector Dr Schön, he cuts his throat (I/2), bequeathing his matrimonial burden to Dr Schön, the most forceful male character in the opera. Schön tries to rid himself of Lulu by becoming engaged to a respectable young lady. But

[1] Realistic effects in the style of *Wozzeck* are occasionally admitted. They re-appear in the scene where Dr Goll dies of an apoplectic stroke. They accompany also Schigolch's asthmatic panting and the athlete's noisy bravado.
[2] Cf. plate opposite page 192.

185

Lulu is intent on having her cake and eating it. She plans to become Schön's lawfully wedded wife herself. By simulating a fainting fit during a theatrical show at which she appears as a dancer, she lures Schön into her dressing room, where he finally becomes so compromised that he weakly submits to Lulu's demand that he should break off his engagement. At the end of the first act Schön, tricked into submission, writes a farewell letter to his *fiancée* under Lulu's dictation. He actually marries Lulu soon after the curtain falls.

This first act is preceded by a Prologue, spoken and sung in turn by the Lion-tamer. In it all the motives and characters of the play are introduced. This Prologue presents Wedekind's erotic philosophy in a nutshell. The part of the Lion-tamer is taken by the singer who is to appear later as Rodrigo, the athlete. Berg's music to this Prologue offers a fascinating cross-section of the music of the whole opera. The chief characters are described (and in Lulu's case visually presented) as exhibits in a menagerie. It is here that their 'animalistic' characteristics (Lulu the snake, Dr Schön the tiger, etc.) are made to correspond to certain intervals. The part of the Lion-tamer makes use of every device from straight speaking voice to shouting and bel canto singing. Nearly all the leading motives of the opera appear in the Prologue—incidentally, the last part of the score to be composed. The opera begins with the 'Earth Spirit' fourths in progressively rising pitch[1]:

Example 165

[1]Cf. page 183 where its association with the Basic Series R is explained.

186

The Lion-tamer is immediately identified by the sequence of chord clusters on the piano which are to accompany Rodrigo throughout the opera:

Example 166

The Prologue's allusion to the 'tiger's leap' is based on Dr Schön's motive, with its characteristic upward leap of a tenth:

Example 167

Finally the Lion-tamer asks for the Boa constrictor to be brought on the stage. Lulu is carried in by a stage-hand, in seductive tights, in fancy dress, as Pierrette, as she will appear subsequently in the first scene of the first act. She is cynically apostrophized by the Lion-tamer as 'sweet innocence' while the orchestra intones her hymn-like motive:

Example 168

187

The music of the first scene of the first act includes the 'mélodrame' of Dr Goll's death from apoplexy, which is mainly based on the Leit-rhythm RH.[1] Already in this preliminary scene of the opera sharply defined formal musical patterns are employed, such as 'Canon' and 'Canzonetta'. The scene is linked with the following one by an orchestral interlude (bar 257 ff.) in the manner of the development section of a symphonic movement. Its thematic relationship to the preceding scene is reminiscent of similar relationships between scene and interlude in *Wozzeck*.

The second scene, in the elegant flat of the painter, may be divided musically into three distinct sub-sections:

1. Duettino: Lulu and the painter;
2. Chamber music (a Nonet for woodwind): Lulu and Schigolch;
3. Sonata: Dr Schön's entry. In this is interpolated the so-called 'Monoritmica' section, connected with the painter's suicide.

The coda of the 'Sonata' is resumed at the fall of the curtain (*Grave*, bar 957) and continued in a symphonic interlude, of which the last bars, in turn, are invaded by the sound of the 'Ragtime' played by the Jazz band off-stage. The deliberately primitive musical character of the 'Ragtime' is based on the interval of the major fourth, and its chief motive is clearly a derivative from the 'jazzy' section of *Der Wein*:

Example 169

[1]Cf. page 161 and Example 160.

The third scene includes the 'English Waltz', played by the Jazz band, the recurrent 'portrait harmonies' and a set of highly original 'Chorale Variations' (CH), which accompany the dialogue between Prince Ecserny and Alwa. The climax of the music of this scene is reached during the great show-down between Dr Schön and Lulu, musically expressed in terms of a development section within Schön's 'Sonata'. When Schön signs his farewell letter (and with it his own death warrant) the music intones the sinister RH rhythm, floating indeterminately over the vague chord of the added sixth, ending the act, as it were, with a huge question mark.

The second act represents the peripeteia of Lulu's existence. She has become Schön's lawfully-wedded wife and has climbed to the top rung of the ladder of social success. But she is already in love with Schön's son Alwa and this new love-affair can only prosper after Schön's forcible removal. Scene 1 of Act 2 is identical with the last act of Wedekind's *Earth Spirit*. From now on Lulu's dizzy ascent changes to a catastrophic decline. The approaching crisis is heralded by the introduction of the play's tragic figure *par excellence*, the Countess Geschwitz, who entertains feelings of unnatural passion for Lulu. The hopelessness of her position links her with the triumvirate of Lulu's unsuccessful admirers, the athlete, the school-boy and the butler. Lulu, now at the very pinnacle of her success, flirts unashamedly with her admirers under Schön's very eyes. She also makes the preliminary moves of a future grand love-affair with Alwa. Schön who, torn by jealous despair, lies in ambush for Lulu's admirers and who, in the course of the act, discovers the Countess in her ridiculous hide-out behind the fire-screen, eventually draws a pistol. The pistol comes into Lulu's hands and she fires it five times at her husband. The dying Schön, with the clairvoyance of the moribund, whispers to his son:

'Don't let her make a get-away; you are her next victim . . .'
At the end of this first scene Lulu is arrested by the police, in
the presence of the outraged Alwa and despite the vociferous
protests of her four admirers. Lulu's arrest, apparently approved
by Alwa, seals her fate. Here begins the decline, and the slow
and subtle process of physical disintegration. The silent film,
leading to the second scene, presents the retrograde motion of
Lulu's life from her arrest onwards—imprisonment, isolation-
hospital, cholera—to her escape and return to Alwa's house, the
scene of her former triumphs and misdeeds. This film-strip is
accompanied by corresponding music in retrograde motion.[1]

Scene 2 of Act 2 corresponds to Act 1 of Wedekind's
Pandora's Box. The plot to contrive Lulu's escape is about to
succeed, chiefly owing to the self-sacrifice of the Countess
Geschwitz, who, risking cholera, changes places with Lulu in
the isolation-hospital. Rodrigo wants to marry Lulu, only to
renounce his claim when confronted with her after her release.
She bamboozles him into the belief that she has lost her good
looks by play-acting the ravaged cholera victim. As soon as she
has rid herself of him and the Countess, and faces Alwa alone,
she throws off the mask of sickness and radiates beauty, health
and youth again. In a passionate love-scene, culminating in
Alwa's hymn, Lulu becomes his mistress on the very settee on
which his father had breathed his last. This signifies the gruesome finale of Lulu's mock-respectability. Soon they are to flee
across the German frontier, with the police hot on their trail.

The music of the second act can be assessed as a big symphonic recapitulation of the music of the first act, with little new
thematic material. Only the newly-introduced figure of the Lesbian Countess claims a musical motive of her own, constructed
of parallel pentatonic fifths of a deliberately 'foreign' character:

[1]Cf. p. 171.

Example 170

The musical 'numbers' of this act underline its reprise-like character. Schön's 'Arioso' and Lulu's 'Ostinato' quote extensively from sections of I/1 and I/2. The climax of their second and final show-down is marked by 'Lulu's song'. It is the first 'set piece' in the opera to utilize the Basic Shape of the twelve-note series R, which is here transposed a tone higher, beginning thus with *c*:

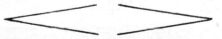

Example 171

The music to the silent film (orchestral interlude No. 3) is a large-scale ostinato movement, progressing dynamically on the lines of this figure:

Its serial technique of retrograde motion links it with the Adagio of the Chamber Concerto and with the ghostly third movement of the Lyric Suite, with the distinction, however, that the *cancrizans* motion is here clearly dictated by the 'flash-back' nature of the film-strip.

The music to the second scene emphasizes, even more than that to the first scene, the recapitulatory, reminiscent nature of this act. The whole scene hovers, as it were, uneasily in the 'no man's land' between unfulfilled past and indeterminate future. It lacks all sense of present time, and its ghostliness is wonder-fully expressed by the veiled character of the music. It chiefly alludes to the music of earlier scenes, quoting them sleepily in a kind of 'slow-motion' manner (Schigolch's entry, Largo, II/2, bar 788). Alwa's ecstatic hymn (bar 1097 ff.) concludes Act 2, ending with the same indeterminate chord of the added sixth and the same fatal knocking of RH as had been heard at the end of Act 1.

The thematic content and structure of Act 3 correspond to those of the two preceding acts in the way that the recapitula-tion of a classical symphony movement corresponds to the exposition. This becomes especially evident in the numerous reminiscences of, and thematic allusions to, Acts 1 and 2. The chief thematic addition in Act 3 is Wedekind's 'Lautenlied' No. 10, chosen by Berg to symbolize Lulu's decline. It crops up for the first time in Casti-Piani's 'Procurer's song' (III/1, cue 103, i.e. after Chorale Variation 3):

Solo Vln . (*throughout on G string*)

Example 172

Lulu and the Painter
Dr Goll Dies of a Stroke
(*Lulu*, Act I/1)

Next to it in importance is the theme of these Chorale Variations itself. This too appears in III/1 for the first time, as Chorale theme, but it derives from the Basic Set R, as can be shown:

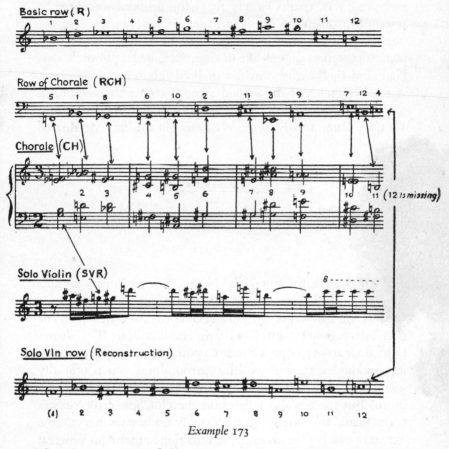

Example 173

The Circus music of the Lion-tamer's Prologue becomes the chief thematic source for the 'society' ensembles of III/1, revealing finally its full dramatic significance. Both the Circus music and the Lute song are subjected to variation and frightening distortion, in the 'Grand Guignol' musical atmosphere of this act. This atmosphere, totally different from that of the two preceding acts, results largely from the prominence given to certain instruments. Vibraphone and saxophone represent the 'society' stratum of the Parisian 'Demi-monde', violin and pianoforte reflect the eel-like flexibility of the loathsome Casti-Piani and the bulging muscles of Rodrigo. The barrel-organ at the beginning of the second scene becomes the symbol in sound of the poverty-stricken, whore-infested London slums. The Jazz drum, finally, sombrely beats out the 'fate' rhythm of RH:

Example 174

in the nightmarish scene of the Negro, Kungu Poti, who kills Alwa with the callous indifference of a drunk.

The two final stages of Lulu's decline are associated with the two international centres of Paris and London. III 1 shows Lulu, now an over-ripe 'Grande Cocotte' of about thirty, basking for the last time in wealthy surroundings. She is officially still living with Alwa, who by now has sunk to the level of a pimp. But she has also fallen into the clutches of the sinister Casti-Piani, the bogus Marquis who dominates her to the extent of making her his mistress, infecting her with his venereal disease and successfully tricking her out of the rest of her money and social standing. Three tortuously involved dialogue-episodes with Casti-Piani, Rodrigo and Schigolch reveal Lulu as

194

the hunted prey of her former lovers, who try in turn to black-mail her into parting with her last possessions. She loses the rest of her money as the result of a disastrous fall in the value of her shares in the 'Jungfrau railway'. Lulu's struggle with the black-mailing ghosts of her past is seen against a background of tur-bulent society-scenes, peopled with stock jobbers, tuft-hunting demi-mondaines, cocottes and pimps. At the end of the first scene Lulu is bankrupt and threatened with exposure and arrest at the instigation of the villainous Casti-Piani, who wants to sell her against her will to an Egyptian brothel. She flees for her life to London, repeating on a lower level the flight from Ger-many to Paris at the end of Act 2. She escapes in the clothes of her youthful groom, the last servant to fall in love with her. But she is unable to shake off all the spectres of her past: Alwa, Schigolch and, last but not least, the faithful Countess Gesch-witz follow her to London. The Countess had consented to become Rodrigo's mistress for a night, in order to distract temporarily his blackmailing attentions from the frantic Lulu.

The music of this scene III/1 shows extraordinary variety of form and structural resourcefulness. Its climax is undoubtedly the cycle of Chorale Variations accompanying the struggle be-tween Lulu and Casti-Piani. Deeply moving is the musical expression of Lulu's imminent fall into the abyss, achieved with the simple means of a chain of chords of the ninth, linked to one another by virtue of their function as dominants. These intimate passages are offset by the noise and bustle of two 12-part ensembles, reflecting the shallow excitement of the gambling tables and the stock exchange. The third ensemble, based on the words 'The whole world loses', signifies Lulu's impending doom. She escapes in male disguise on the fluttering wings of her descending scale-motive:

Example 175

The police are only able to arrest her groom, grinning sheepishly in Lulu's frock. It is her last victory over the 'pillars of society'. The big orchestral interlude which links III/1 and III/2 takes the form of a set of variations, based on the 'Lute song' (Example 172). The theme appears afresh in every variation, in a different key and given out by a different group of instruments. At the very end—i.e. when the curtain is about to rise on III/2—Example 172 is heard once more, this time in a realistic imitation of a wheezy barrel-organ (bar 715 ff.)[1] evoking the monotonous hopelessness of a rainy day in the London slums.

The filthy attic of a London street-walker supplies the sombre background for Lulu's end. Its shabbiness follows tellingly on the bogus elegance of the Parisian 'Salon' of the first scene. The bundles of shares and bank-notes, the gaudy jewellery, clattering gambling chips and sparkling champagne are replaced by a monotonous prospect of petrol lamp and brandy bottle, the professional tools of a débutante of vice. Lulu's first and last day as a London prostitute passes in the endless rotation of her clients. They appear and disappear in a kind of round, interrupted by the disillusioned gossip of Schigolch and Alwa —two stranded pimps, banking in vain on Lulu's faded charms.

The music is admirably contrived to illustrate this macabre scene. It takes the form of a kind of extended Rondo, in which

---

[1] The orchestration, for piccolo, flute, clarinet, bass-clarinet and double bassoon, clearly harks back to the barrel-organ device in Stravinsky's *Petrushka*.

Example 172 acts as the eternally recurring theme, interrupted by episodes bringing various thematic reminiscences from Acts 1 and 2. The psychological climax of the scene occurs with the surprising reappearance of the Countess Geschwitz, who brings her most cherished treasure, Lulu's famous portrait of I/1, into the dismal attic. Lulu finds the contrast between the picture and her own present condition unbearable. The whole scene was evidently planned as a vocal quartet, as the surviving short score shows. Lulu's three clients—the Professor, the negro and Jack the Ripper—form a macabre parallel to the three black-mailers of III/1. Lulu fails to obtain even financial satisfaction from them. Kungu Poti, the negro, smashes Alwa's skull when he attempts to interfere. An object lesson in 'Aristotelian irony' is the use of hauntingly beautiful reminiscences of the music which previously accompanied Lulu's love scenes with Alwa during the scenes between her and her murderer. He enters the stage at bar 1162, fulfilling Lulu's childhood dream that she would become the victim of a sexual maniac. The whole scene is dominated by the tango rhythm:

of the Cavatina of Act 2 (bar 61) and, with tragic mockery, Lulu's luscious suspension-chords now accompany hollow phrases of professional prostitution. The music of Lulu's death, culminating in her dreadful shriek (bar 1268), is identical with the 'Finale' of the *Lulu Symphony*, which Berg had completed in full score in 1934. The Countess Geschwitz, who dies by the hands of Jack the Ripper in a last attempt to save Lulu, epitomizes her love in a melodic phrase borrowed from Marie in *Wozzeck* and sung to the earlier opera's Leitmotive of compassion:

197

Ich bin dir nah

Example 176

The opera ends with the Countess's pentatonic fifths, with Example 176 in the horns and with Marie's tritone triplets on the harp. However, the fatal rhythm has the very last word and the opera ends with it and the indeterminate vagueness of an unresolved Tristanesque $\frac{5}{6}$ chord.

★   ★   ★

As in the case of *Wozzeck*, Berg decided to put together some symphonic extracts from his opera which could be performed in the concert-hall, and which might arouse interest in the whole work. These extracts were completed in the summer of 1934 and published early in 1935. The full score of this *Lulu Symphony* (a title not of Berg's choice, but accepted by him later on) was dedicated to Schoenberg, as well the opera as a whole. Willi Reich has praised the organic nature of this *Lulu Symphony*, which he likens to a late symphony by Mahler. He believes that the love of Lulu and Alwa is here elevated to a sphere of poetic isolation, in the way that the tragedy of Marie is presented in condensed form in the symphonic fragments from *Wozzeck*. However, the parallel does not quite tally with the facts. The *Wozzeck* fragments are, save for a few bars at the beginning and end of scenes, completely identical with the music of the opera. But the music of *Lulu* was thoroughly revised and modified for incorporation in the *Lulu Symphony*. Collation of the Rondo of the Symphony (Andante and Hymn), itself a compound of fragments of the music from

198

scenes 1 and 2 of the second act, with the corresponding sections of the opera, shows how much the music has been simplified and freed from the interruptions of dialogue and action. The music of the *Lulu Symphony* has a value of its own; it can be assessed as a separate creative achievement, but it is hardly comparable with the colossal canvas of a symphony by Mahler.

The symphony consists of five sections:

    1. RONDO (Andante and Hymn)
    2. OSTINATO (Allegro)
    3. LULU'S SONG
    4. VARIATIONS
    5. ADAGIO

The third and fifth sections include vocal parts.

Section 1 is a condensation of two scenes between Lulu and Alwa in Act 2, with an introduction of its own.
Section 2 is the interlude between II/1 and II/2, accompanying the film, unchanged.
Section 3 is Lulu's song (II/1, bar 491 ff.), unchanged except for the highly characteristic entry on the vibraphone, which re-appears in inversion as the conclusion of the song. It includes the harmonic inversion of the 'Earth Spirit' fourths:

(Vibraphone)   (Vibraphone)

Example 177

Section 4 is identical with the orchestral interlude between III/1 and III/2. It is introduced by the dodecaphonic Chorale tune of III/1 (cf. Example 173). The movement is rounded

199

off by a Coda of nine bars, with a re-statement of the CH series. Section 5 represents a symphonic telescoping of the last scene of the opera. Its conclusion, with the last words of the dying Countess actually sung, is completely identical with the actual end of the opera, as found in Berg's sketch in short score.

★ ★ ★

The Première of Lulu, after several postponements, took place on June 2, 1937, at the Stadttheater, Zürich, where Hindemith's Mathis der Maler, another opera proscribed in Germany, was to be heard a year later. The Swiss, despite their political independence, were subjected to a continuous blast of 'cultural' propaganda from the Reich. Their feelings were expressed by K. H. David, former editor of the Schweizerische Musikzeitung, who wrote: 'It is a sign of the times that this work could be brought to performance only in Zürich. Yet it is in no way politically dangerous; it is a purely artistically exceptional work, to be hailed or condemned as such.' Despite its great success at the first performance, reflected in the enthusiastic reports of connoisseurs like Ernest Krenek, Darius Milhaud and others, the opera's fate was sealed. It remained proscribed in Germany and Austria for the duration of Hitler's reign.

Unlike Busoni's Doktor Faust and Puccini's Turandot, which were completed by disciples and subsequently published in complete form, Lulu was made known as a 'Fragment'.[1] After the end of the second act, at the Zürich performance, the producer appeared on the stage and gave a synopsis of the third act. Only those parts of the Lulu Symphony related to this third act were played by the orchestra and the final murder

---

[1]The vocal score, published in 1937, promised in a prefatory note the publication of the opera in complete form at a later date.

scene was then sung and acted against a backdrop depicting Lulu's attic.

The revival of *Lulu* after the second world war had to wait until March 7, 1953, when a performance of great merit was given at Essen.[1] On that occasion an attempt was made to perform more of Wedekind's action of III/2, accompanied by those sections of the music which Berg had scored for use in the 'symphony'. H. H. Stuckenschmidt's critical report in *Die Neue Zeitung* for March 9, 1953, makes clear that this solution was found unsatisfactory and detrimental to Berg's artistic intentions. Many of Berg's admirers have never ceased to ask why the opera should be presented always as a fragment, when Willi Reich, Berg's first biographer, had written:[2] 'The opera is nearly complete in short score. The vocal parts are written out fully, except for an ensemble in Act 3.'

Is Act 3 performable? The question was raised and answered in the affirmative by Willi Reich himself, back in 1936. Yet although Schoenberg, Webern and Erwin Stein were approached in turn by Berg's widow, they could not make up their minds how to complete the score. In my own opinion (shared by a good many *cognoscenti*) the task of orchestrating the rest of Act 3 on the basis of the surviving sketch in short score is not beyond the capacity of a musician thoroughly familiar with Berg's style and methods of composition.

The musical sketches and fragments of Act 3 consist of:

(A) A complete draft in short score, in Berg's hand.

(B) The fragmentary full score, 43 pages, breaking off at bar 268 of scene 1.

(C) The complete libretto, in Berg's hand.

---

[1]Fragmentary performances and a complete radio performance (which was recorded) had already taken place in 1949 and earlier in 1953.
[2]*Melos*, December 1952.

(D) Those parts of the *Lulu Symphony* which incorporate parts of the music of Act 3 (i.e. sections 4 and 5 of the symphony).

Only (D) has been published, so far. Sixty pages of Erwin Stein's piano arrangement of (A) were engraved, but they have remained unpublished. Stein's arrangement includes Berg's own indications of his intended orchestration. It would be possible to score the later part of Act 3 (i.e. bars 1209-1300, down to the Adagio of the *Lulu Symphony*) because it includes a number of recapitulations and transpositions of episodes from I/2 and III/1, which could easily be used as stylistic and structural models.[1] A much more difficult task awaits the future editor in the vocal quartet beginning with the re-appearance of the Countess Geschwitz (III/2, after bar 861). But even in that section the continuity of the sketch in short score is unbroken. The passages for which no corresponding models are to be found in the music of the previous acts are in a minority compared with those which are clearly based on reminiscences. The completion of Act 3 is therefore a distinct possibility, a task which will have to be undertaken before Berg's finest and most mature work can become part of the international repertory of operatic masterpieces.

[1] The third ensemble of III/1, for instance, (bar 542 ff.), is a complete replica of the second ensemble, which exists in full score in the composer's hand (cf. (B).). Similarly, the sketch of Lulu's scenes with her three clients is for the most part based on literal quotations from the music of Acts 1 and 2.

CHAPTER VIII

The Violin Concerto: postludium in excelsis

BERG'S last work, the Violin Concerto, was commissioned by the American violinist Louis Krasner specially for himself. The suggestion may have elicited in the composer a sympathetic response because of the earlier stimulating experience of writing *concertante* music for the voice in *Der Wein*. The Concert Aria had passed beyond the limits of the original commission and become the prelude to Berg's last opera. Similarly the Violin Concerto went far beyond the original stipulations of the contracting parties. It became the composer's most poignant self-revelation in the face of impending death. It was the news of the death, from poliomyelitis, of Manon Gropius, the beautiful eighteen-year-old daughter of Alma Mahler, that provided, in April 1935, the igniting spark that set Berg's creative imagination aflame.[1] The Concerto, undertaken for Louis Krasner, became a 'Requiem for Manon', a moving dirge, inspired by 'the memory of an Angel'—hence the double dedication on the title-page of the full score.

Berg stopped work on the orchestration of the third act of *Lulu* when he started to compose the Concerto in April 1935 in the solitude of his 'Waldhaus'. The short score was all

[1] Manon had been struck down by the disease in the spring of 1934 while staying at Venice. Her fate hung in the balance for some time. Berg's letters to Webern reflect the measure of his affection for the girl and his concern for her mother.

203

but finished on July 12.[1] In a letter to Webern of August 7, Berg says: 'At present I am writing like a madman at my full score, in order to complete it by the middle of August'. According to Willi Reich,[2] who paid Berg a visit at that time, the full score was completed on August 11. A letter to Schoenberg of August 28[3] says: 'The Concerto was already completely finished a fortnight ago.' The same letter mentions the insect sting which caused the carbuncle on his back and goes on to say that the carbuncle had been tormenting him for the past fortnight. It is therefore possible to assume that the actual completion of the Concerto and the fatal sting all but coincided, between August 11 and 14. The Concerto was finished in record time and in a final and feverish marshalling of all his creative energies. The carbuncle and the ensuing blood-poisoning found Berg drained of strength and without recuperative powers.[4] His hope, expressed in a letter to Schoenberg, of completing the orchestration of *Lulu* in the following two or three months remained unfulfilled. When he returned to Vienna in the middle of November his condition was already grave. The last letter to Schoenberg, dated November 28,[5] was written in bed. Despite his ever increasing suffering he attended the first performance in Vienna of the *Lulu Symphony* on December 11 and even corrected the copy of Rita Kurzmann's piano arrangement of the Violin Concerto on December 14. Ten days later, on December 24, Berg passed away, without having heard a note of his last work, which was published and

[1] A letter to Webern of July 15 makes clear that the sketch was completed on the day on which Webern's transcription of Bach's 'Ricercare' from the *Musical Offering* was broadcast. That day was July 12. Incorrect dates, in connection with the history of the Concerto, are given by W. Reich.
[2] Op. cit. p. 17.
[3] Published in facsimile by J. Rufer in *Melos*, Feb. 1955.
[4] Berg had complained already in early June of being 'deadly tired, nervous and asthmatic'.
[5] Cf. previous footnote [3].

performed posthumously in the following year. The first performance, with Krasner as soloist, took place on April 19, 1936,
at the I.S.C.M. festival in Barcelona. Webern was to have conducted, but resigned during the rehearsals owing to increasingly strained relations between him and the orchestral players.
Almost literally at the last moment Hermann Scherchen took
over and, with his intimate knowledge of Berg's style, secured
for this *opus ultimum* the resounding success which has never
since deserted it.

The Violin Concerto—like the Chamber Concerto and the
Lyric Suite—grows out of the thematic cells of certain quotations from existing melodies, which thus become structural
determinants of the whole composition. As in the earlier works,
a system of subtle thematic associations and correspondences
enables the student to interpret the music's tone-poetical mean-
ing. The two extraneous melodic elements are a church chorale
and a traditional folktune, diametrically opposed to one
another. They appear separately, but in the end their apparent
incompatibilities are fused in the mystical *coincidentia opposi-
torum* of the Coda of the Concerto. In view of the inherent
dualism of Berg's work it is interesting to note that Bach's
church cantata O *Ewigkeit, du Donnerwort*, from which the
chorale is taken,[1] bears the sub-heading 'Dialogue between
Fear and Hope'. The struggle of conflicting emotions on the
very threshold of death finds resolution in the words of the
Holy Spirit: 'Blessed are those who die in the Lord'. It is this

[1] The chorale 'Es ist genug' is not by Bach, as repeatedly stated in writings about the
Violin Concerto, but by Johann Rudolph Ahle (1626-1673). The words are by Franz
Joseph Burmeister. Poem and tune date from 1662; Bach's Cantata, No. 60, dates
from 1732. Bach harmonized Ahle's lovely melody with the heart-searing poignancy
he had earlier given to another borrowed melody, transformed into the Passion chorale
'O Haupt voll Blut und Wunden'. Bach's earlier cantata, No. 20, 'O Ewigkeit . . .',
composed before 1727, does not make use of Ahle's melody at all. This explanation
seems necessary in view of the fact that references to Bach's Cantata create the misleading impression that only *one* cantata of this title exists.

blissful acceptance of the inevitable that is given expression in the final chorale: 'It is enough.' The Violin Concerto depends thematically and psychologically on this chorale, the funereal implications of which underline the Requiem-like character of Berg's last work.

The thematic elements of the Concerto are:

(A) The Basic Shape of its dodecaphonic series;

(B) The Carinthian folk-tune;

(C) The Bach-Ahle chorale melody.

They are presented below in tabulated form and thematic subjects derived from them are labelled accordingly A1, B1, C1, etc.

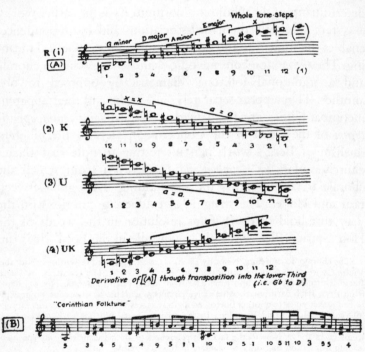

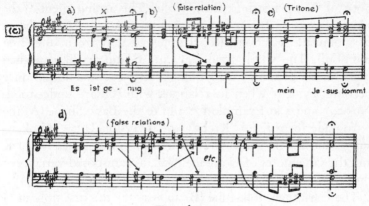

Example 178

The Basic Shape (A) belongs, like the series on which *Der Wein* is based, to those 'tonally coloured' sequences of notes which Schoenberg deliberately avoided, in the early days of his dodecaphonic period, because of their diatonic implications.[1]

(A) shares with the series of *Der Wein* a scale-like arrangement of rising notes. It is a sequence of rising thirds with an 'appendix' (*x*) of whole-tone steps. The chain of thirds implies chordal progressions of major and minor triads. Their harmonic possibilities (G-minor, D-major, A-minor, E-major), but also dissonant chordal combinations such as:

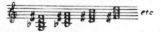

Example 179

can be easily extracted from (A) (cf. Example 178). The tonics of the four above-mentioned root-chords are identical with the

[1] He used them occasionally in his latest works (for instance, in the *Ode to Napoleon* Op. 41) and he had used them as far back as 1912 in his pre-dodecaphonic Op. 16, No. 1. There T. W. Adorno discovered the six-note row: which, if transposed to 'a', is identical with (A) (cf. Example 178).

notes of the open strings of the violin. This arrangement of the series permits the free use of the open strings and also the choice of violinistic 'positions' (serial notes 2, 4, 6 are in the 'first position'). The whole-tone segment 'x' appears like an alien body in its diatonic surroundings. Its structural importance becomes evident when its relations with (C) are understood. Nos 2, 3 and 4 in Example 178 add to the Basic Shape (A) the retrograde form K (= 'Krebs'), the inversion U (= 'Umkehrung') and the inversion of K. It transpires that notes 1–9 of K and the same notes of U are identical, as transposed variants of the series.[1]

The Carinthian folk-tune (B) appears for the first time in G flat major (bar 213), the first instance of the use of a key signature by Berg since the far-off days of his Op. 2. When transposed to D major it can easily be understood as a serial offspring of (A). This relationship is possibly quite fortuitous and probably as accidental as the amazing identity of the appendix 'x' with the incipit of the chorale (C)[a]. That the latter connection was in fact accidental is proved by Berg's letter, quoted earlier, of August 28, 1935. There he expressly called Schoenberg's attention to the 'quite accidental character' of this identity. The identity is again, as in the previous case of K and U, an identity of variants, brought about through transposition. Bach's version of Ahle's melody is in A major, while Berg's quotation of it is a semi-tone above (B flat).[2] Quite apart from the melody's affinity to Berg's series, Bach's harmonization of the chorale contains false relations, dissonances caused by the frequent use of the tritone, and gliding chromaticisms which are quite at home when transplanted into Berg's own musical landscape

---

[1](A) is frequently transposed to D, C sharp, etc., in the course of the work.

[2]Cf. part II, Adagio, bar 136, with the added traditional key-signatures, inserted in order to adjust the music better to the general tonal character, which oscillates chiefly between G minor and B flat major.

(Cf. Example 178 C). To the Chorale-incipit's identity with '*x*' (A) corresponds the identity of its tail-end '*x*' with the whole-tone appendix '*x*' in the serial variant (U) (cf. Example 178, figure 3).

The introduction of a chorale in Berg's Concerto was not itself surprising since, as has been shown, the chorale and chorale-variation play their part in Acts II and III of *Lulu*. Chorale-like themes were frequently used by Bruckner and Mahler at climaxes of their symphonies, and the psychological function of the chorale in Berg's Concerto seems also fore-shadowed by the role allotted to Klopstock's hymn 'Aufersteh'n' in the finale of Mahler's second symphony.

★ ★ ★

Berg described the structure of the Violin Concerto in the quoted letter of August 28, 1935, thus:

> It is in two parts: each part containing two movements:
> I (*a*) Andante (Preludium)
>   (*b*) Allegretto (Scherzo)
> II (*a*) Allegro (Cadenza)
>   (*b*) Adagio (Chorale variations).

One might bracket the two sub-divisions of I together, as being in the nature of a musical portrait of Manon Gropius. If that interpretation is accepted, then II represents the catastrophe of death and the transfiguration in heaven. As in *Wozzeck* and *Lulu*, a dotted *Leitrhythmus* RH symbolizes the catastrophic climax of the Concerto (II, cue 125):

Part I consists of a tripartite Andante, preceded by an introduction and followed by a Scherzo (Allegretto) with two Trios
and a reprise of Trio I—a scheme reminiscent of certain middle
movements by Mahler. The tender reverie of the introduction
shows Berg's skill in utilizing the characteristic intervals of his
series for specifically violinistic arpeggio-affects. The diatonic
intervals of (A) make possible a dodecaphonic exposition in
almost orthodox G-minor, cunningly based on a chordal
presentation of the series:

Example 180

Its melodic form follows with the entry of the solo violin at
bar 15. There the series is presented in the guise of a scale-like
ascending subject, whose curious skips over more than two
octaves at the very tail-end ('x') may be called a fingerprint of
the 'Second Viennese School'. It is juxtaposed to its ultimate
transformation at the end of the Concerto in the following
example:

Example 181

210

The Scherzo-Allegretto (I *b*) consists of three contrasting thematic *Ländler*-motives, labelled by the composer respectively
'scherzando', 'wienerisch' and 'rustico'. Their rhythms and
melodies prepare the way for the appearance of the folk-tune,
which breaks into the magic circle of dodecaphonically determined theme-combinations with the diatonic bluntness of its
G flat major tonality ('Come una pastorale', bar 213 ff). That
all three *Ländler*-motives are transposed derivations of (A) can
be easily seen from the following quotation and its serial
associations:

Example 182

The 'Viennese' motive:

Example 183

may derive from the mournful sigh of falling thirds in the first
movement of Mahler's ninth symphony, which was a life-long
favourite of Berg's.

Trios I and II are chiefly concerned with the same thematic material (acting like development sections in a sonata movement), until, during the recapitulation of Trio I (beginning at 'Quasi Tempo I', bar 173) the Carinthian folk-tune (B) (first noticeable in the horn at bar 213) joins in, restoring the original *Ländler*-character of the movement after the tempestuous aberrations of the Trio-sections. Part I ends on a *diminuendo* chord of velvety dissonance.[1]

Part II (*a*) is directed to be played 'with improvisatory freedom, like a cadenza'. Its explosive opening reminds one of the beginning of the 'Rondo ritmico' of the Chamber Concerto, but also of the stormy Finale of Mahler's first symphony. The Cadenza is divided into three parts. The first section is chiefly determined by RH (cf. page 209). The tripartite Solo Cadenza (section 2, beginning at bar 43) already intones in passing the Chorale-incipit *Es ist genug*. Sundry reminiscences from part I occur. The third section is shaped as a kind of recapitulation of the first section (Tempo I, bar 96), which, propelled by the inexorable RH, reaches its climax at bar 125. The catastrophic collapse of the music detaches the serial notes 11, 12, 10 from the rest, crystallizing them into an agonized call for help ('Zu Hilfe'), reiterated by the full orchestra with rapidly dwindling strength:

Example 184

[1] It is the first serial chord combination, as given in Example 179.

The transition from the Inferno of this 'Allegro' to the visionary final 'Chorale variations' is made with consummate mastery
by a gradual increase of melody-notes of the Chorale tune in
the solo violin, and a simultaneous dropping away of RH and
of the chordal combinations of (A).

The second section of II (Adagio) presents the unique case of
a set of Chorale variations, evidently inspired by certain organ
preludes by J. S. Bach, yet strictly subjected to dodecaphonic
discipline. The section can be divided into five sub-sections:

(1) Chorale (bar 134 ff., containing Ahle's melody with
    Bach's harmonies, given out by the woodwind in
    magical imitation of an organ stop)
(2) Variation I (bar 158 ff.)
(3) Variation II (bar 178 ff.)
(4) Reminiscences from Part I (Carinthian folk-tune at bar
    198)
(5) Coda (bar 214 ff.).

The numerous felicities of Berg's polyphony, especially dis-
played in canonic imitations in Variations I and II, could and
should be made the subject of detailed analysis, which, however, is outside the scope of this chapter. Mention must be made
of the dramatic highlight of the movement, heralded by the
return of the folk-tune, which grows out of the incipit of the
Chorale melody. The symbiosis of these apparently incom-
patible themes is the composer's final achievement:

Example 185

The Concerto dissolves in an aura of visionary transfiguration.
The violin gives out once more the chief serial melody (Cf.

213

Example 181 b), based on the conciliatory vagueness of the $\frac{5}{6}$ chord in B flat major, which has here an effect of touching inconclusiveness like that of its first cousin in the final bars of Mahler's *Lied von der Erde*. An atmosphere of unearthly serenity is created by the accompanying orchestra of this extraordinary work, which in its truly autumnal beauty rounds off, all too soon, Berg's creative career. A multitude of plans for the future[1] faded into limbo with his death.

[1]Mentioned by Willi Reich (*op. cit.*, p. 17 ff.) to whom Berg apparently spoke of these plans.

PART III: BIOGRAPHY

CHAPTER IX

The Life of Alban Berg

IT would be unrealistic to attempt an exhaustive biography of Alban Berg today, less than twenty years after his death. Before that can be done, several decades must pass. The future biographer will have to go far beyond the brief sketch contained in the following pages. He will have to trace the enigmatic undercurrents of Berg's life, and try to unravel the fascinating contradictions of the composer's personality, on the basis of the documentary evidence, unrestricted use of which will be open to him. His final task will be to solve certain psychological problems, the posing of which might be considered presumptuous today. Apparent enigmas will find their solution in Berg's correspondence—in his letters to Schoenberg and Webern, in those addressed to his *fiancé* and wife, and to intimate friends such as Hermann Watznauer, Joseph Polnauer, Erwin Stein, Alma Mahler-Werfel and others.[1] As long as these documents, and the replies they evoked, cannot be placed unreservedly at the disposal of

[1]Berg's letters to Schoenberg are today in the possession of the Music Division of the Library of Congress, Washington, in accordance with instructions in Schoenberg's will. The collection comprises 145 letters, 40 postcards, 4 telegrams, and a number of other autographed documents, covering a span of 23 years, 1912-1935. Some extracts from these letters are published in this book for the first time. I was able to study this correspondence through the kind assistance of Richard S. Hill, of the Music Division of the Library of Congress, who also generously placed at my disposal the results of his own Berg research. (cf. Richard S. Hill's article on Schoenberg, in the

scholars, any biography of Berg must necessarily be fragmentary and provisional.

With Raphael, Shelley, Chopin, and Oscar Wilde (whom he curiously resembled in the dionysiac femininity of his features), Alban Berg shares the secret of perpetual youth. A photograph of Berg at the age of fifty shows a face lined by physical suffering and spiritual upheavals, but revealing still, fundamentally unchanged, the features of the platonic ephebe of early portraits. This physical beauty, the aristocratic refinement of which was further emphasised by his tall, gaunt figure, was inherited from his father. Comparison of photographs of Konrad and Alban Berg in their 'teens reveals a degree of resemblance rarely found, even between father and son. The romantic good looks of Berg's Franconian father found a match in the Viennese charm of his mother, and their union resulted in Alban's 'late-coming' type, so characteristic of the culturally over-ripe, autumnal Austria of the late nineteenth century. In this Austria Alban Berg's whole existence was rooted. The hesitant bloom and youthful charm of this patrician artist suggest the silhouette of the poet Hofmannsthal, who to our retrospective glance appears as the quintessence of that entire epoch of Austrian culture. It was Berg's destiny, as it was Hofmannsthal's, to live in perpetual danger. The façade of his good looks and Austrian charm concealed a constitutional frailty which often proved unequal to the demands of the hour and the prevailing tension of its inhabiting spirit. Berg

'Quarterly Journal of Current Acquisitions, Library of Congress', for November 1952, p. 43 ff.). Berg's letters to Webern, covering the years 1910-1935, were saved from destruction in 1945 by Dr Werner Riemerschmid, of Mödling, near Vienna, one of Webern's personal friends. Dr Riemerschmid's typescript copy of these letters was discussed and quoted in extracts by Willi Reich in 1953, in the 'Schweizerische Musikzeitung'. Numerous additional passages from these letters are published here for the first time. It is still too early for the complete publication of Berg's correspondence with Schoenberg and Webern.

was a life-long invalid, forcing a recalcitrant body to supply him with enough stamina for artistic creation. This endless struggle with physical weakness gives the measure of the composer's achievement, of the man's fibre, and of the indomitable spirit's victory over the flesh.

Berg's precarious health partly explains the peculiarities of his artistic career; it affected his relations with his fellow men, and also determined the limitations of his creative work. Physical frailty was solely responsible for the restricted range of his musical activities./Berg never conducted an orchestra, he never appeared—as Schoenberg and Webern did—on a concert platform either as soloist or accompanist. Always he had to conserve his strength. This constant disability proved too much for him in the critical year of 1903, when he attempted to commit suicide after having failed his matriculation, and experienced at the same time the pangs of first love.

His debility became manifest in two forms; a tendency to develop abscesses, and an inclination to tidal waves of asthma. Both are described with uncanny self-observation in two letters to Webern, dating from the years 1911-1912. These letters establish a clinical picture of Berg, which reappears at regular intervals right up to the fatal autumn of 1935:

'. . . Apart from the fact that I am quite generally a bad traveller, I would run the risk of ruining the whole day following a night in which I had slept badly. At the same time, if I tried to stimulate myself artificially (a thing I could do very well with tea), I'd risk completely spoiling the next few days. I just have to take my rotten health always into account. I am, too, far from well at present. I am suffering from styes, *four* on one eyelid. The word "suffering" is no exaggeration, for this ridiculous and idiotic complaint causes a very painful inflammation of the eye and the whole left part of my face. . . .'

'I am very ill. It's not only the asthma, to which I have become almost accustomed. Now I've got jaundice again. At least I suppose so, as some of the symptoms fit into the picture. It is like a poisoning of the whole system. I have hardly the strength to lift my arm. I've got racking pains in my glands and muscles, and—worst of all—a constant splitting headache. I have tried to overcome this enigmatic illness by staying up, but high temperature and shivering have compelled me to remain in bed, whence I am writing to you now. . . .'

In the second quotation the sentence: 'It is like a poisoning of the whole system . . .' has an ominous ring. It sounds as if the twenty-seven-year-old Berg had a premonition of his end, which was to come about, catastrophically, through blood-poisoning.

Military service in the years 1915-18 proved detrimental to Berg's health, as is shown by letters from that period. His general condition deteriorated markedly in the oppressive atmosphere of the Austrian revolution and the aftermath of war. On June 19, 1919, he wrote to Webern:

. . . I'd like to get well again to the extent of regaining physical and spiritual efficiency. I have ruined my health so much since my call-up in 1915; that makes a total of four years, and demands a few months of recuperation. . . .

And in a letter to Webern, dated August 7, 1921, he bursts out with the desperate complaint: 'This never-to-be-quite-well-again is terribly depressing. . . .'

On the other hand, Berg tried again and again to master his illness by sheer will-power, especially under Schoenberg's virile influence. Characteristic in its realistic fortitude is a letter to Webern, dated August 9, 1913, re-echoing talks in which Schoenberg seems to have criticised Berg's attitude to his health:

. . . I am most curious to know what Schoenberg has written. I believe he thinks it not unlikely that in such illnesses the imagination, or, to put it better, auto-suggestion plays a large part. At least, he has always voiced that opinion when I have spoken of my asthma, which is certainly of a basically nervous nature. I would not, and could not, admit that, as this asthma has also appeared on occasions when I had *no premonition, no reason* to desire to be ill, at moments when I longed for nothing so much as to be well. . . .

At the time of the completion of *Wozzeck* Berg's asthma was made much worse by hay-fever and he was often compelled 'to sit the whole night on the edge of the bed, struggling for breath. . . .' In the middle 1920's a certain improvement took place; however in 1927, after the completion of the *Lyric Suite*, he was 'very ill, unable to work. . .'. The instability of his physical condition in the last years of his life is reflected in a passage from a letter written while he was working on the Violin Concerto, in which he says that he is '. . . feeling unwell all the time. . . . Asthmatic, with nervous heart trouble, and tired to death. . . .'

Very soon after occurred the fatal sting, which brought on the carbuncle which in turn precipitated the final blood-poisoning. This insect bite, reported in a letter dated August 27, 1935, had had sinister precursors in twenty or thirty stings, the result of an attack of a swarm of wasps, shortly before August 9, 1932. Who can say whether or not the condition of his blood attracted such a furious attack by these insects?

Berg's clinical history over twenty-five years of adult life reveals the silent heroism of his character. His fortitude in his perpetual struggle with ill-health shows one aspect of his nature, of which the other main attributes were enthusiasm, fanatical loyalty, fervent attachment to the chosen ideal and a child-like creative optimism. These found their fullest expression in his relationships to his teacher, Schoenberg, to his friend Webern, and to his wife. Berg's loving attachment to these three human beings determined his life and its simple contours. This trinity of creative love formed the main centre of gravity of his earthly *curriculum vitae*, to which the following pages are chiefly dedicated.

Berg's life may be divided into four sections of unequal length:

1. Childhood and adolescence in his parental home, 1885–1904.

2. Studies with Schoenberg, 1904–1910.

3. First independent compositions; marriage, military service; planning *Wozzeck*, 1911–1919.

4. Establishment in Vienna as a teacher of composition and Schoenberg's principal lieutenant; creative maturity, 1919–1935.

The first world war was a critical turning point for Berg, as it was for most of his generation. The grave political and social changes to which his native country was subjected from November 1918 onwards deeply affected his mode of life. They caused a short period of hectic re-adjustment, 1918–1920, but finally led to his establishing himself in Vienna as a composer, free and independent. The underlying rhythm of Berg's life seems to have been determined by the alternating attractions of town and country. He developed the typical city-dweller's longing for the cool purity of alpine heights, despite the fact that these heights were sometimes more harmful in their effect on his strained nerves and asthmatic condition than the much-maligned metropolis.

An undated letter to Webern, presumably written after 1920, indicates Berg's ideological antagonism to the idea of the modern state, and proves that he was at heart a political rebel, despite his bourgeois upbringing. The letter sets out a characteristic formula for the typical Viennese malaise of his generation.

. . . I therefore repeat: I am far from asserting that the institution of the State appears to me as something 'obsolete, traditional and absurd', and that I therefore have to reject it *a priori* as being 'unmodern'. My whole grudge is aimed at the *manner* in which the State (or whatever assumes that name) asserts itself *today*. Likewise you should not imagine that when I complain about Vienna it is because it's the fashion today to grouse about Vienna. When I thus complain . . . I am always aware of the fact that I'd be much unhappier in any other city and that I'd long for Vienna. Only at present the idea of the modern city is so repugnant to me that I'd rail at *any* metropolis, wherever I might happen to be. On the other hand, I'd expect of it the very last perfection! If a metropolis, then a real metropolis! If it is to be my bad luck to rely on other means of transport than my own legs (which I much prefer and with which I'd live quite contentedly if I could live in the country instead of the city) then these means of transport should be the best imaginable. If I am denied the good fortune of living in a little house built by myself and enjoying my own fireside, and if I am condemned to live in a flat, then this should be easily heated, whereas with the stove I have now I am unable to get my study warm. If there is to be comfort, then I should not have to feel it to be an inconvenience. After all, comfort has been achieved by the sweat of humanity's brow. The trouble is, however, that in Vienna only the upper classes enjoy the fruits of comfort. . . . I am nowhere happier than where comfort does not exist—in the country; but to live as a country-dweller in the city I find very difficult. . . .

Whenever Berg was in the country and was called away again for business reasons he became depressed. This tug-of-war between city and country caused the rhythmic oscillation of his life, between his flat in the Trauttmannsdorfgasse, Vienna, the family estate, 'Berghof', on the Ossiachersee in Carinthia (later replaced by 'Waldhaus', at Auen near Velden on the Wörthersee) and the estate of the Nahowski family, his wife's parents, at Trahütten, near Deutsch-Landsberg, in south-western Styria. This regular exchange of familiar scenery was increasingly interrupted in later years by professional journeys, in connection with performances of *Wozzeck*, or the attendance of music festivals. These journeys led him as far south as Venice, as far west as Cambridge, and even as far east as Leningrad. The more conventional tourist centres in Italy, Switzerland, the French Riviera, and Tyrol had no attractions for Berg. His predilection, all his life, was for the south-eastern fringe of the Alps, whose famous peak, the Koralpe, he climbed despite his asthmatic condition in the early 1930's. Even his beloved motor-car, acquired in August, 1930, was used first and foremost as a means to connect him with the districts of the Semmering, the Carinthian lakes, and the south-eastern corner of Styria. Berg's attachment to the Eastern Alps of his homeland, expressed repeatedly in his letters to Webern, who was his companion and guide on many mountaineering trips before 1914, is deeply characteristic; he was firmly rooted in Austrian soil. This attachment links Berg with Schubert, Brahms and Mahler, all of whom drew inspiration from the lakes and mountains of Styria and Carinthia.

Alban Berg was the offspring of a union in which Bavarian-Franconian and Austrian racial peculiarities combined in an attractive new blend. Konrad, his father, descendant of a family of Bavarian civil servants and soldiers of high rank, was born at Nuremberg on August 31, 1846. He emigrated to Austria as early as 1867, established himself in Vienna as an export merchant and bookseller, and married into the Viennese *haute bourgeoisie*. His wife Johanna, daughter of the Court jeweller Franz Xaver Melchior Braun, was born in Vienna on February

Villa Nahowski, Trahütten

Alban Berg and Helene Berg

Alban Berg's Father   Alban Berg's Mother

Alban Berg's Paternal Grandfather

28, 1851. Johanna shared her husband's artistic leanings, and was, in fact, a talented painter and musician. There were four children of this marriage: Charley, b. 1881, d. 1952, Hermann, b. 1882, d. 1921, Alban, born in Vienna on February 9, 1885, and Smaragda, b. 1886/d. 1954. The fact that Smaragda played the piano, and Charley sang well, probably explains the existence of numerous songs dating from the year 1900 or thereabouts. Memories of that chaotic gestation period, in which these earliest compositions were produced, long before Berg had decided to become a professional musician, are to be found in a letter to Webern dated July 18, 1914:

> ... What you say about the mine interests me enormously. Tell me more about it. Is it something big, where one can walk about in intertwining galleries under the earth for hours on end? I was once in the mine at Bleiburg; that impressed me so much that I wrote a whole play about it. As a youngster, of course, under the influence of Ibsen's plays! Nice, don't you think? Before I started to compose I wanted to become a poet. And I remember whole epics, inspired by the literature we studied at school. And, further back still, as a child I used to paint and draw, prompted by a certain manual skill which I mistook for talent. ...

'Before I started to compose I wanted to become a poet.' The faculty of poetic vision did not desert the maturing artist, as a passage such as this, in a letter to Webern, about the year 1911, clearly shows:

> ... my longing for an ideal aeroplane (the aeroplanes of today are mere toys and certainly far from a solution of the problem) so as to be able to fly, is, although surprising successes have been attained already, not a desire for mere *technical* achievement ... but a longing for the 'Above'. Only imagine: to be able to float above the highest mountain peak! Where no terrestrial sounds can reach one—not even cowbells—wonderful—wonderful!

P   225

From that early period of poetic aspirations Berg derived a sensitive feeling for literary values; in later life his favourite authors included Balzac, Strindberg, Dostoievsky, Karl Kraus and Peter Altenberg. His re-discovery of Georg Büchner's *Wozzeck*, and his creation of the *Lulu* libretto by conflation of two plays by Frank Wedekind, are literary achievements of a high order. His own original writings on music reveal a real mastery of German prose.

Berg grew up in a Roman Catholic household. His father, in his later years, owned a shop near St Stephen's Cathedral for the sale of saints' pictures and Catholic church furnishings. This business was carried on by his widow after Konrad's early death on March 20, 1900. It seems necessary to point out this Catholic component in Berg's spiritual heritage, especially in view of the fact that he has repeatedly been claimed for Protestantism by certain writers.[1]

His inclination to mysticism, which increased with advancing years, his predilection for Balzac's mystic novel *Seraphita*, for the works of Swedenborg, and the ceremonial of the Roman ritual, are explained by it, and the incorporation of a Lutheran chorale into the texture of his last composition is certainly no proof to the contrary.[2]

Berg's religious faith finds expression in a card to his *fiancée*, Helene Nahowski:

'Adieu, *A Dieu*, dear Helene. *He* will not abandon us, even if the "all too human" beings, the too little godlike-ones, may have done so.'

In his ability to make friends for life Berg resembled Schubert and Hugo Wolf. In early years his elder brother Charley and

---

[1] By Mosco Carner among others.
[2] It is worth mentioning in this connection that Max Reger, a Roman Catholic, was the most famous composer of Lutheran church music of his day.

his sister Smaragda were nearest to him. It was Charley who drew Alban's attention to a newspaper advertisement of Schoenberg as a teacher of composition. It was he who aroused Schoenberg's interest by secretly showing him some of Alban's early manuscripts. These so attracted Schoenberg that he invited Berg in the autumn of 1904 to become his private pupil (without payment until 1906) and attend his courses of composition. Other friends of Berg's early years were Hermann Watznauer (ten years older than Alban), and Paul Hohenberg, many of whose poems he set to music. Through Schoenberg he met Anton Webern, a fellow-pupil, only a little older than Berg himself, who soon became his most intimate and cherished friend. Throughout his life, Berg never felt a deeper regard for anybody. No other friend ever meant as much to him as the precociously mature, singularly reserved and severe Webern; he became Alban's model of a fanatical and uncompromising artist devoted to his exalted ideals. The influence of Webern on Berg, especially in the formative decade of 1910-1920, is of incalculable importance. Other events of these early years remain to be told. Berg's musical inclinations had first become noticeable about 1899, but the death of his father, in the following year, destroyed his hopes of successfully developing his talents in financial security. In the year of his father's death, 1900, the fifteen year old boy had his first attack of asthma. In the years 1901-1903, Berg's friendship with Watznauer deepened, and he wrote about seventy songs and duets. Ibsen was studied, and school work neglected, so it is not surprising that in the summer of 1903, Berg failed his matriculation examination.

As already mentioned, in the autumn of that year he attempted to commit suicide, having been frustrated in some youthful passion. However, in the summer of 1904, he passed his examination, and at the age of nineteen, he was still composing songs, and enthusing over Ibsen's plays and Mahler's symphonies. In the following October, he took an unpaid post as a probationer-accountant at the Lower Austrian *Statthalterei*, thereby shouldering a burden that many other poets and composers of the past have had to carry—the yoke of Civil Service in Imperial Austria. At the same time, he somehow managed to surmount this handicap, for a most important event took place; he began his studies in composition with Arnold Schoenberg in October, 1904.[1]

The years of study with Schoenberg laid the foundations for Berg's own creative activities. His compositions, at first largely determined in character and scope by his teacher's friendly advice, gradually became more ambitious and individual. New music which, during this period, made a deep impression on him, included Strauss's *Salome*, Mahler's second and sixth symphonies, and the cross-section of Schoenberg's work up to the *Kammersymphonie*, Op. 9, presented at the three famous Schoenberg concerts in 1907. Berg also attended the first performance of Wedekind's play, *Die Büch der Pandora* in 1905, and Mahler's farewell performance of *Fidelio* at the Vienna Opera House in October, 1907. He also made the acquaintance of Oscar Kokoschka and Peter Altenberg.

In 1906, Berg inherited enough money to enable him to leave the Civil Service and devote himself exclusively to music.

Berg's musical activities during these years of development were surprisingly varied; once at a private concert he appeared as his sister's accompanist, and he even joined Schoenberg's choral society. Besides 'school work', such as the double fugue

[1]Cf. Schoenberg's Commemorative article on Berg, first published in this book (Cf. page 280).

for string quartet and piano, six- and eight-part choruses and the variations for piano (published in the appendix to this volume), his first really original compositions, the *Seven Early Songs*, and the Piano Sonata, Op. 1, were written.

The first public performance of Berg's compositions took place at two pupils' concerts organized by Schoenberg, on November 7, 1907, and November 4, 1908. Works heard at these concerts included three of the *Seven Early Songs*, the double fugue, and the variations.

About this time, Berg met Helene Nahowski and fell in love with her immediately. During the years 1908-1910, his friendship with Webern developed and became very close. Webern's Passacaglia for orchestra, Op. 1, was first performed together with Berg's variations for piano at the concert of November 4, 1908. During Berg's final years of study, years that were transfigured and enhanced by his deepening love for Helene Nahowski, enduring impressions were made on him by the music of Paul Dukas, Alexander von Zemlinsky's comic opera, *Kleider machen Leute*, the early plays of Wedekind, the paintings of Kokoschka, and Schoenberg's String Quartet Op. 10 (which was received with 'cat-calls' at its first performance).

The songs on poems by Hebbel and Mombert, Op. 2, were composed in 1909, and it is significant that the last song of this group anticipates the mature style of Berg's String Quartet, Op. 3, written in 1910, when his studies with Schoenberg came to an end. About this time, he became formally engaged to Helene Nahowski.

On April 24, 1911, Berg's Piano Sonata, Op. 1, and String Quartet, Op. 3, were performed in public for the first time in Vienna. On May 3, 1911, Berg and Helene Nahowski were married. Two weeks later, on May 18, Mahler died in Vienna.

Although circumstances had not permitted any very close personal friendship with Mahler, and although it is doubtful whether the older composer ever heard any of Berg's music, at the same time Mahler remained an enduring influence and inspiration, and in 1910, Berg was able to study the full score of Mahler's still unpublished ninth symphony; in a letter Berg wrote to Helene, he gives a precise account of its style and psychological premises.[1]

Later on, Mahler's widow became a faithful and ever helpful friend of both Berg and his wife.

Earlier in this book, mention has been made of a certain degree of influence exercised by Schreker's interesting but artistically unequal first opera, *Der ferne Klang*, for which Berg prepared the vocal score for Universal Edition in 1911. Subsequent letters show that he did not always approve of Schreker's later development, though he retained sympathy for the man right up to his tragic end. Schoenberg himself admired *Der ferne Klang*, and it is not without significance that Schreker had employed a chamber orchestra in his ballet, 'The Birthday of the Infanta', at approximately the same time that Schoenberg composed his first *Kammersymphonie*, Op. 9. The realistic modern 'milieu' of Schreker's first opera, and its treatment in musical terms, make him a precursor of Berg in the history of the opera of social consciousness.

This is perhaps the most fitting place to discuss Berg's lifelong enthusiasm for Schoenberg and his music. This enthusiasm found practical expression in arrangements, analyses and critical essays, and was never more intense than in the years shortly before and after the first world war. Berg's association with Schoenberg as disciple and amanuensis found a kind of official

[1]Quoted extensively in the German edition of this book. Parts of this letter are published in my book, *Bruckner and Mahler*, London, 1955, on pp. 220/21.

recognition in his appointment as 'Vortragsmeister' of the Society for Private Performances, founded in Vienna by the older composer in November, 1918. This connection lasted for several years, on a salaried basis, and for Berg, as composer, this occupation with Schoenberg's orchestral scores developed into a 'master course' *post festum*. It gave him technical assurance and unrivalled insight into his master's ideas and the problems of their realization in performance.

During those years of loyal enthusiasm, when partisanship for Schoenberg was often rewarded by public ostracism, Berg fought tirelessly for his recognition and understanding. He was responsible for the vocal score of the *Gurrelieder*, and for an arrangement for voice and piano of the two vocal movements —'Litanei' and 'Entrückung'—of Schoenberg's second String Quartet, Op. 10; he wrote thematic analyses and guides to the *Gurrelieder*, *Pelleas und Melisande*, and the *Kammersymphonie*, Op. 9. He also contributed to the collective volume *Arnold Schoenberg*, published at Munich in 1912, and, as his correspondence with Webern proves, gave the initial impetus to the compilation of the special number of *Anbruch* for Schoenberg's fiftieth birthday and the *Festschrift* for his sixtieth birthday. In addition, he published numerous articles, polemical, enthusiastic and analytical by turns, and he delivered a cycle of lectures in Vienna in the winter of 1932-33 which were entirely devoted to Schoenberg's music.

Berg's letters reveal a worshipping adept's joy, uncertainty, despair and enthusiasm, but bear witness to his self-denying modesty, his self-effacing love for Schoenberg. As early as 1910, Berg had expressed his feelings for his master in a letter written to Webern:

> . . . How despondent you must be again, far away from all those divine experiences, having to forgo the walks with Schoenberg

ALBAN BERG

and miss the purport, gestures and cadences of his talk. . . . Twice
a week I wait for him at the Karlsplatz, before teaching at the
Conservatoire begins, and for the fifteen to thirty minutes walk in
the midst of the noise of the city, which is made inaudible by the
'roar' of his words. . . . Then twice a week outside the city in Ober
St Veit at his house, when to each lesson I bring the continuation
of the *Gurrelieder*, see his new paintings and look at songs by
Mahler. . . . But to tell you about all this is only to increase your
suffering and sense of privation. . . .

This letter refers to the preparation of the vocal score of the
Gurrelieder. A letter written to Schoenberg, dated July 5, 1912,[1]
shows Berg wrestling fiercely with the problems posed by the
transcription of the vocal movement of the String Quartet.
These problems were successfully overcome. But when he was
confronted with the necessity of inventing new closing-sections
and final *clausulae* for the separate publication of certain lyrical
'purple patches' of the *Gurrelieder*, Berg felt such a task to be
psychologically and technically impossible, at any rate for him.
A letter to Schoenberg dated December 3, 1913, reveals his
fundamental sincerity and courageous self-criticism, his inordin-
ate modesty and unbounded enthusiasm. Although the vocal
score as well as the thematic guide to the *Gurrelieder* had already
been published, he declared himself incapable of committing
the 'surgical' atrocities necessary to round off satisfactorily the
various 'song'-extracts considered suitable for separate publication.

The same letter refers to an arrangement of the *Kammersymphonie* Op. 9 for piano duet; this was not published, in fact it
was probably never completed.

How soul-stirring the first impact of Schoenberg's *Pierrot
Lunaire* and *George-Lieder*, Op. 15, was on Berg's impression-

[1] These letters to Schoenberg are quoted *in extenso* in the German edition of this
book.

232

able mind can be judged by the following letter, written on July 20, 1914:

> ... at long last a great joy has been allotted me; the George songs. It was—for me at least—high time they were published, for I have been longing for them for years, more than for anything. Now at last I can steep myself in their immeasurable splendour and the prospect of doing so beautifies my holidays. Perhaps in time I shall become riper for *Pierrot*. By 'riper' I mean that I feel now that I am very far from understanding the work as I'd like to, well knowing that when the moment comes for me to say: 'Now at last I fully understand it', I shall be utterly mistaken, for I shall realize a year later, when I again closely study the work (since the 'Führer'[1] I cannot abstain from analysis), that I hadn't understood it before at all. However, at present I haven't got that far: I only know that on the two occasions when I heard *Pierrot* I was conscious of the deepest impression *ever* made on me by a work of art, and that the enigmatic power of these pieces has left *indelible* traces on my mind. But when I look into the score the music still appears to me quite enigmatic and mysterious, and I cannot imagine that with my small technical ability (and my great shortcomings) I shall ever be able to approach this work of art, which seems to me like a miracle of nature. ... Here I miss, too, the help of a piano arrangement, which would enable me to present the music to myself connectedly. Such help has enabled me to become comparatively familiar with the 'Monodrama'.[2] That latter experience is among my most treasured memories: when I studied the piano arrangement slowly at home and then was permitted to play from it at each 'lesson', and you explained so much of it to me that in the end the thing came half to life at the piano. And so I live more in memories of the past than in the present, ... and more with you than with myself, and that helps me, perhaps, to endure in this horrible age. ...

This letter was written on the very eve of the first world war, which was to bring a long and painful interruption of Berg's

[1] Berg's guide to the *Gurrelieder*.
[2] *Erwartung*.

fervent propaganda on behalf of Schoenberg and his music. Meanwhile he had completed the Altenberg songs, Op. 4, the Clarinet pieces Op. 5, and the three Orchestral pieces, Op. 6. The first performance of some of the Altenberg songs in 1913 had led to scandalous scenes in the concert hall. In June of the same year Berg had gone to Berlin to see Schoenberg, and during this visit there had ensued a grave exchange of opinions between master and pupil, which led to a temporary spiritual crisis. This is echoed in a moving letter, dated June 14, 1913, written directly after his return from Berlin. The resulting tension overshadowed the first half of 1914, when Berg was working on the three orchestral pieces, which had pushed into the background earlier plans for a 'Seraphita' symphony (see p. 65). He intended to dedicate the orchestral pieces to his beloved teacher on the fortieth anniversary of his birthday (September 13, 1914), but was unable to complete them in time and work dragged on until the end of the year. A little earlier, after seeing several performances of Büchner's *Wozzeck* at the Wiener Kammerspiele, he had resolved to make it the subject of an opera.

Berg's war-fever flaring-up in a letter to Schoenberg, dated November 16, 1914, did not last very long: the same letter[1] also describes his work on the piano arrangement of the *Kammersymphonie*:

> ... I know only too well that today the study of maps is preferred to the study of musical scores, and that it costs enormous effort to occupy oneself with music (or with something at all unrelated to the war). ... Sometimes I find it downright wicked to think of anything else but war. If despite all this I was able to persuade myself first to complete my own score, which I sent you, and then to continue work on the *Kammersymphonie*-arrangement,

[1]The second part of this letter, about Berg's own Orchestral Pieces, Op. 6, has already been quoted in a previous chapter (see page 67).

with the firm intention not to desist until it is finished, that happened and continues to happen as a result of my concentrated will-power and decision (inspired by your admonishments of last spring) to tackle the job, once undertaken, *under all circumstances* and not to allow *anything at all* to deflect me from my purpose.

Something like war-weariness was revealed in a letter to Webern, dated May 19, 1915:

> . . . Let us hope that Italy does not enter the war, that Schoenberg will not be retained at tomorrow's medical examination . . . let us hope that it may at last start raining, so that the harvest may not turn out badly, but, more than all this, let us hope that at last, at long last, *peace* may come. . . .

A few months later, he was himself called-up. After having been trained for active service, he was declared unfit, and transferred to the War Ministry in Vienna. Just how much his health suffered under the impact of military service, how deeply he enjoyed his first leave—spent in the pastoral solitude of Trahütten, which he experienced as a kind of salvation—is expressed in a letter to Schoenberg, dated August 13, 1917. In this same letter, he makes his first reference to the composition of *Wozzeck*:

> . . . I've been here now for ten days. In the first week I was still suffering from the after-effects of years of slavery; attacks of asthma of such virulence that I believed, literally, that I could not last the night. But now things have much improved and there begins to stir in me the urge to work again, as in previous summer holidays. The musical setting, planned more than three years ago, of Büchner's play *Wozzeck* occupies me again. However, the coherent writing-down of a major section is beyond me; in another week my freedom is over and the slavery in Vienna recommences and may last for years. . . .

Willi Reich tells us that after the final collapse of Austria, on November 11, 1918, which abruptly terminated Berg's military service he was compelled, by inflation, to work for his living, which he did by running the family estate 'Berghof' on the Ossiachersee in Carinthia. However, he soon gave up uncongenial farm work in order to settle permanently in Vienna in the spring of 1919. Apart from giving lessons in composition, he was principally occupied with work in connection with Schoenberg's 'Society for Private Performances', his own Clarinet pieces, Op. 5, receiving their first performance at a meeting of this organization on October 17, 1919.

Berg's financial situation had reached a critical phase; that happened to many Austrians of his generation, who, having always had private means at their disposal, had never even thought about earning their own livelihood. 'Berghof' had to be sold in the spring of that year and Berg had nothing more to expect from his family in the way of financial support. 'I must concentrate more than ever on earning a living', is a recurrent phrase in his letters of this time. Economic considerations were mainly responsible for the gradual loosening of his connections with the Society for Private Performances, which involved him in exhausting work but could not guarantee him the living wage he needed more and more because of his indifferent health. Letters to Webern tell of his hopes and doubts about the prospect of becoming Editor of *Musikblätter des Anbruch*. He planned a propagandist explanatory pamphlet on Webern and his music, besides numerous articles for *Anbruch*. In 1920 there was published in this periodical one of his most dashing polemics, aimed at the ever-pugnacious Pfitzner, who had become embroiled in a perpetual feud with Busoni and Paul Bekker. Pfitzner had published the pamphlets, 'Die neue Aesthetik der musikalischen

Impotenz' and 'Futuristengefahr', and Berg replied with 'Die musikalische Impotenz der neuen Aesthetik Hans Pfitzners'.

The plan to become Editor of *Anbruch* came to nothing, and Berg never again attempted to find another such position. Office routine would have been quite alien to his temperament and dangerous to his health. The completion of the full score of *Wozzeck* and, later on, the preparation of the vocal score of the opera occupied all his time in the next few years, and as he became increasingly absorbed in the planning and composition of new works, teaching became more and more irksome. But despite his aversion to such mundane tasks, Berg as a teacher achieved magnificent results and worthily continued Schoenberg's educational tradition in forming a group of composers faithful to precepts of the second 'Viennese School'. The number of his pupils who gained distinction testify to his powers as a teacher, and many of these pupils are alive and still active; they include Joseph Rufer, author of a treatise on twelve-note composition; the composers H. E. Apostel and Hanns Jelinek; Joseph Polnauer; the conductors and musical educationists Hans Trauneck, J. Schmied, Fritz Mahler, S. Kassowitz, Bruno Seidlhofer and Otto Jokl; Willi Reich, who became Berg's first biographer; the theoreticians T. W. Adorno and F. H. Klein; Marko Rothmüller, the finest exponent of *Wozzeck*, Schoenberg's son-in-law Felix Greissle, and many others.

After the publication of *Wozzeck*, Berg's life, merged in his creative work, belongs to the main stream of post-war European cultural history. The last fifteen years represent the climax of his activity.

Biographical data concerning *Wozzeck*, *Lulu* and later instrumental works have been presented and discussed in earlier chapters. Some details of Berg's life still remain to be told. The vocal score of *Wozzeck* had originally been published by Berg, with the financial support of Mahler's widow, to whom the work was dedicated. In the spring of 1923, the opera was taken over by Universal Edition, Vienna, and from that time, relations with this publishing house were very cordial. In May 1927 a general agreement was signed, whereby the copyright in all his future compositions was assigned to Universal Edition, and Berg's financial position was thereby stabilized.

A few months before this great turning-point in Berg's life, his mother had died at the age of seventy-five; she had followed the changing fortunes of *Wozzeck* with the keenest interest, from its first performances during 1925 and 1926.

Among the few official honours accorded to Berg by his reluctant contemporaries, probably as a result of the ever increasing success of *Wozzeck* in Germany, was his nomination as a member of the Prussian Academy of Arts, on January 30, 1930—exactly three years before Hitler's appointment as Reichs-Chancellor automatically erased Berg's name and banished his works from the German musical world. In a letter to Webern, dated February 10, 1930, Berg humorously commented on his nomination, but not without an undertone of bitterness and an oblique glance towards the apathetic attitude of his Austrian homeland:

. . . Thanks for your congratulations to the 'Academician'. How it came about I don't myself know. I read it first in a newspaper, or rather, I heard about it from Paul Stefan, who had read it in a paper. No actual appointment is involved. But nevertheless it pleased me very much, especially on account of Vienna, i.e. of Austria, which, as is well known, has virtually overloaded us for years with honours and appointments. . . .

An invitation to become Professor of Composition at the

Berlin Conservatoire (at that time under the direction of Schreker) was declined in the spring of the same year.

In the summer of 1930, Berg passed his driving test and bought an English car, a Ford, the driving of which gave him the greatest enjoyment. As a member of the jury of the 'Allgemeine Deutsche Musikverein', and later, as representative of the Vienna section of the International Society for Contemporary Music, he was obliged to undertake numerous journeys during the remaining five years of his life. The actual causes of these journeys, jury-meetings and examinations of scores, for the most part filled him with disappointment and depression.

His purchase of a country house, 'Waldhaus', at Auen near Velden on the Wörthersee, was one of the last pleasures he was destined to enjoy. At 'Waldhaus', Berg composed *Lulu* and the Violin Concerto, despite increasing mental anguish caused by the growing terror of Hitlerism, and concern about his own and his wife's existence, threatened as this was at its foundations by the universal ban on his works throughout Germany since 1933. A curious twilight mood of happy domesticity, intertwined with a deep concern about the deteriorating political situation, is reflected in a letter Berg wrote to Webern, on June 29, 1933, of which a sentence may be quoted.

> . . . All this, and probably also my utter depression over *these* times, have for a long time now impaired my ability to work. Only now are things beginning to improve. For the rest, we are of the opinion that by the purchase of 'Waldhaus', we have done the right thing. . . .

Schoenberg's fate under the 'Third Reich' deeply moved Berg. On July 6, 1933, he wrote to Webern about it;

> . . . I enclose Schoenberg's letter, which I avidly devoured. Yes,

it is terrible, to be sure. What a fate! Now at the age of nearly sixty, expelled from the country where he could speak his mother tongue, homeless and uncertain *where*, and *on what*, to live, in a hotel room. . . .

In October, 1933, Schoenberg emigrated to the U.S.A.; he never saw either Berg or Webern again. This senseless separation, imposed by political terror, hurt Berg more deeply than anything else, especially as his own continued residence in an Austria increasingly infected with the Nazi virus was not easily understandable to the homeless emigrant. Few of the enforced refugees of 1933 could appreciate that there also existed a kind of 'mental emigration' for those who chose to remain behind; such a withdrawal was the pre-ordained fate of a man like Berg. A passage from a letter he wrote to Webern on January 28, 1934, reveals something of Berg's mental struggle in connection with his relationship to Schoenberg, and his intense suffering over Germany's disastrous political course;

> . . . I was tremendously moved by your news of Schoenberg's long and detailed letter. . . . Meanwhile I had written to him very fully, and I hope I was able to dispel his doubts. He wrote to me on September 21, from Boston: 'You have owed me an answer for so long that I began to fear . . . no, seriously I've never feared it . . . but in jest I may perhaps say it.' I understood this mysterious sentence quite *correctly*, then (*you* confirm this now to me), and so it was, I believe, right of me to reply jokingly that I am not, in fact, 'composing variations on the theme of the Horst Wessel song'.

Profound sadness permeates the next letter, written on February 15, in which he thanks Webern for a copy of the German version of Esther Meynell's *Little Chronicle of Anna Magdalena Bach*, adding a few sentences of such wistful beauty as are given only to those who have been 'expelled from the

Garden of Eden': a letter dated May 8, 1934, continues the melancholy story;

> ... Add to all this financial worries, and the necessity of reaching before long a decisive turning-point. This is of course closely linked with the problem of the first performance of 'Lulu'. In the second half of May I shall have replies to my letters to Furt-wängler and Tietjen. They will in any case have to show their colours. This silent exclusion of all our music from German con-cert programmes will either have to be rescinded or they will have to prove to me that our music is 'un-German'.

At that time, he still half-believed in the possibility of the performance of *Lulu* at a German opera house. But only a few weeks later he clearly understood that his music had no pros-pects whatever in Hitler's Germany: 'A performance cannot be thought of for the time being.' A ray of hope was kindled by Erich Kleiber's courageous first performance of the *Lulu-Symphonie* in Berlin on November 30.

On February 9, 1935, Berg celebrated his fiftieth birthday, and this last year of his life was devoted to hectic work, on the Violin Concerto and on the orchestration of the third act of *Lulu*—exertions which clearly depleted his waning physical strength at an alarming rate.

The last illness developing from an insect sting which brought on a carbuncle, had already begun by the end of August.

In spite of a temporary improvement, Berg felt unable to attend the Prague Festival of the International Society for Contemporary Music in September. On November 12, he returned to Vienna from 'Waldhaus', exhausted and ailing, and took part in the preparation for the first performance in Vienna of the *Lulu Symphony*, which he eventually attended, although gravely ill.

Berg's last days and hours have been movingly described by

Willi Reich, who was then much in his company. After a blood transfusion, the donor being a simple young Viennese, Berg jestingly expressed the fear that he would in consequence be turned into a composer of light-hearted Viennese operettas.

But the transfusion only delayed his end, and on September 24, just after one o'clock in the morning, Berg died in the arms of his wife, from the effects of pernicious blood-poisoning.

The circumstances of his death strangely resemble those of the death of Mahler, who had also died from blood-poisoning, and at precisely the same age, the lives of both composers being cut short exactly seven weeks before their respective fifty-first birthdays.

PART IV: APPENDICES

ARNOLD SCHOENBERG ON ALBAN BERG

(1949)

This article is here published for the first time, by kind permission of Mrs Gertrud Schoenberg. It was written in 1949, two years before Schoenberg's death, and it was mentioned in the Schoenberg-Bibliography of Josef Rufer's book 'Die Komposition mit zwölf Tönen', Berlin, 1952, Engl. version, London, 1955. The article was originally written in Schoenberg's peculiar English which is here faithfully reproduced.

H.F.R.

WHEN Alban Berg came to me in 1904, he was a very tall youngster and extremely timid. But when I saw the compositions he showed me—songs in a style between Hugo Wolf and Brahms—I recognized at once that he had real talent. Consequently I accepted him as pupil, though at this time he was unable to pay my fee. Later his mother inherited a great fortune and told Alban, as they have now money, he could enter the conservatory. I was told that Alban was so upset by this assumption that he started weeping and could not stop weeping before his mother had allowed him to continue with me.

He was always faithful to me and has remained so during all of his short life. Why did I tell this story? Because I was greatly surprised when this soft-hearted, timid young man had the courage to engage in a venture which seemed to invite misfortune: to compose *Wozzeck*, a drama of such extraordinary tragic (sic), that seemed forbidding to music. And even more: it contained scenes of every-day life which were contrary to the concept of the opera which still lived on stylized costumes

245

and conventionalized characters. He succeeded. *Wozzeck* was one of the greatest successes of opera.

And why? Because Berg, this timid man, was a strong character who was faithful to his ideas, just as he was faithful to me when he was almost forced to discontinue studying with me.

He succeeded with the opera as he succeeded in his insistence to study with me.

Making the belief in ideas one's own destiny is the quality which makes the great man.

ARNOLD SCHOENBERG

Facsimile of Berg's

Variations for Piano

on a theme of his own

(1908)

258

259

BERG'S LECTURE ON 'WOZZECK' (1929)

This lecture is published here for the first time in its entirety. It has been translated by the writer of this book, whose intention was to keep as close as possible to Berg's text. The lecture was originally intended to precede a performance in Oldenburg (March 1929). Later on, however, it was used by Berg in connection with other performances of his opera in Germany. A copy of the lecture was utilized by W. Reich (Cf. op. cit., p. 64, Note 1). The present complete publication of the Lecture is based on a revised copy of the typescript. This contains numerous corrections and insertions from Berg's own hand which sometimes amount to a complete change of opinion. In fact, this revised copy may be said to represent an improved version of the whole lecture. Notable among these changes is Berg's emphatic aloofness from the doctrines of French musical Impressionism.

WHEN I decided some fifteen years ago to compose 'Wozzeck' a peculiar situation in music existed. We of the Vienna school (under its leader Arnold Schoenberg) had just outgrown the infancy of that movement which was—quite erroneously—classified as the movement of Atonality. Composition in that style was primarily confined to the creation of musical miniatures —such as songs, pieces for the piano and for orchestra— or (in the case of more extensively planned works like Schoenberg's 'Pierrot' mélodrames or his two one-act operas) concentrating on a formal species which received its shape exclusively from its text and dramatic action. Until then works of bold dimensions—such as four-movement symphonies, oratorios and large-scale operas—were missing in the sphere of atonal composition. The reason for this deficiency? That style renounced Tonality and thereby gave up one of the most effective means of building either small or large musical structures.

On deciding at that juncture to compose a full-length opera I was confronted by a new problem, at least from the angle of harmony: How to achieve the same degree of cohesion and of structural unification without the use of the hitherto accepted medium of Tonality and of its creative potentialities?— cohesion, moreover, not only in the smaller forms of dramatic sections (of which more anon) but also the more difficult unification in the bigger formal units of a whole act and in the structure of the whole opera.

Libretto and dramatisation alone could not guarantee that unifying principle; least of all in the case of a work like Büchner's 'Woyzeck', consisting of many (twenty-three) loosely connected fragmentary scenes.[1]

Even a structural plan in three acts in which exposition, climax and catastrophe were clearly separated in three sections of 5 scenes each—achieving, as it were, structural unity and dramatic cohesion by force—did not necessarily guarantee musical unity and cohesion as well. In the course of my investigation we will notice the means used to achieve the latter. First of all I'd like to draw your attention to a phenomenon of Harmony, that is to say, to the closing harmonies of each Act.

The point where in a tonally conceived composition the return and confirmation of the main key becomes distinctly evident even for the layman, should also be the place where in an atonal work the circle of harmony comes to a full close. Such a confirmation has been achieved primarily through the fact that every Act of my opera closes into the same quasi-cadential chord, only to rest on it as on a Tonic. This is the

[1] Actually Büchner's fragment consists of twenty-seven scenes. (H.F.R.)

final chord at the close of Act I: (Vocal score, p. 81, bar 715 until the close of the Act.)

This is the chord at the close of Act II: v. sc. p. 180, bar 809 until end.

And this is the chord at the end of Act III: v. sc. p. 231, bar 389 until end.

You will have noticed (and you will notice it even more clearly when you hear it in the orchestra) that these final chords appear each time in a different shape although each time built up from the same notes. These changes in their sonority derive not only from the changed dramatic situation, but from something else as well. For the urge for musical unification and musical integration—as Schoenberg calls it—is equalled by the urge for musical diversion and variety of shape.

While Act I and II end with the simultaneity of these chords —I repeat: Act I: v. sc. p. 81, last bar; Act II: v. sc. p. 312, last bar—at the end of Act II this chord disintegrates more and more, v. sc. p. 180, bar 809 until end, leaving as its final residue the low 'B' behind.

By way of anticipation I'd like to add here that the 'B' in the bass (which accompanies the prophetic last words of Act II 'He is bleeding . . . One after the other . . .') becomes decisively important not only dramatically but also structurally for one of the most important among the later scenes of the opera.

To demonstrate more clearly how this musical integration as well as this musical variety becomes evident, I will now ask the orchestra to play the last scene of each act. I will then be able to add a word about the structurally important harmonies of the introductory bars of the acts, following these harmonies.

The action of the last scene of Act I is concerned with

Marie's seduction by the Drum-Major. The music to this scene is a rondo-like Andante affettuoso: v. sc. Act I, p. 73, from bar 656 to the end.

The very short orchestral introduction to the following Act II takes this final chord as its point of departure, playing it while the curtain is down: v. sc. Act II, p. 82, bars 1-6 (without the last quaver). Then the curtain rises for Act II.

The final scene of Act II presents the clash between the jealous Wozzeck and the Drum-Major, ending in the former's defeat. By the way: The struggle between the two men in this scene is musically identical with the struggle between Marie and the Drum-Major at the end of Act I, which ends in her seduction. Again a device to establish musical cohesion!

These (as well as other) parallels between the two closing scenes result—even if quite unconsciously—in a piece of musical parallelism. However, whereas in the former passionate Andante only a suggestion of the Rondo form could be detected, the latter scene presents a strictly organized Rondo, shaped by the experiences of military routine, a veritable 'Rondo marziale': v. sc. Act II, p. 173, bar 761 until end.

Finally, the last scene of Act III and of the whole opera is a perpetuum mobile-like movement in running quaver-triplets, reflecting the play of poor children, with the wholly unsuspecting child of Marie and Wozzeck among them—a child that has just become a poor orphan: v. sc. Act III, p. 229, bar 273, including the preceding upbeat, to the end.

With it the opera comes to an end. However, although the music steers again into the cadential haven of the final chord, it almost looks as if it was to go on. And it really does go on! As a matter of fact, the initial bars of the opera could easily link up with these final bars and thereby close the circle: v. sc. Act III, p. 231, last bar, and Act I, p. 9, bars 1-3.

264

That happened quite unintentionally. Much of what I tell you here has only now, after ten and more years, become clear to me in its relation to musical theory. For instance, regarding these two initial bars: they contain—before the drama begins to unfold—two short introductory string-chords. In order to underline the crescendo leading from the first to the second chord, a soft, but gradually increasing, roll on the side-drum bridges the two bars. This was a purely instrumental affair of musical sonorities. When I heard it for the first time, I noticed to my great surprise, that the general military atmosphere of the opera could hardly have been hinted at more poignantly and succinctly than by means of that little drum-roll.

Reverting once again to the tendency of my opera to be both integrated and diversified: you will have observed, when listening to the different beginnings and endings of the three Acts, that they differ considerably from one another, quite apart from the chordal variant mentioned above.

The curtain in Scene 1 is raised immediately after the first bar of the orchestra; it is lowered simultaneously with the closing bars at the end of Act I.

The curtain at the opening of Act II is only raised after the short orchestral prelude has finished which was played during this lecture a short while ago. When the music of Act II has finished, the scene remains open for a moment; only then the final curtain falls. Correspondingly (and with the intention of establishing dramatic cohesion), the curtain at the opening of Act III is raised in silence. The music only begins after a brief pause. The final curtain however is lowered before the music has finished; but its fall does not coincide with the diminishing final chord—as in Act I. Here it precedes the chord, which enters pianissimo and trails off.

Finally a word may be added about the general structure of

the opera and about my intention of achieving close formal integration. The manner in which I built up each single act could be understood as resulting from the venerable tripartite formal pattern a-b-a. This is proved by the fact that Act I and III show certain parallels (even if the latter act does not contain musical recapitulations of the first). Both flanking acts embrace, as it were, the much larger and weightier middle act symmetrically, by virtue of their shorter duration. While Act II (as we shall see) presents from the first to the last bar a musically coherent form, the structure of the two flanking acts is much more loose. It consists of five loosely linked music sections which correspond with the loosely connected scenes of the libretto. One could call the five scenes of Act I 'five musical character pieces', each characterizing—in accordance with the action—one chief character of the play in his relations with the hero of the opera, i.e.: the Captain, his superior officer; his friend and comrade Andres; his mistress Marie, the Doctor and the Drum-Major.

The five scenes of Act III correspond with five musical forms the cohesion of which is achieved through some or other unifying principle: be it the unifying function of a musical theme, subjected to variational treatment; be it a 'note', a 'chord', a 'rhythm' or an 'equalized motion' of notes.

The two flanking acts whose sequence of scenes is determined by a unifying idea (i.e. the five character-pieces of Act I, the five unifying principles of Act III) furnish the framework for the middle Act, like the element 'a' in the scheme of the tripartite 'Lied-form'. This Act II is musically much more closely integrated, its five scenes being inseparably linked like the movements of a symphony. They present a vivacious first Sonata-movement, followed by a Fantasia and Fugue based on three subjects: a slow movement (Largo), a Scherzo;

and finally the—already mentioned—'Rondo Marziale con Introduzione'. In this way the middle act could be likened to element 'b' in the tripartite form-scheme, differing from the two flanking acts (with their general parallelism of structure) by virtue of the fact that it represents emphatically the character of a middle section.

My discussion of the aspects of Harmony and Form in this opera will have informed you sufficiently about the formal cohesion of its music in general—a cohesion which, as has been stated earlier, had to be achieved without the medium of Tonality and without the latter's structural possibilities.

That structural cohesion was likewise necessary in the detail of the opera's musical fabric. In that connection the following simple trend of reasoning may have led to the frequently discussed employment of certain 'old forms' which has done more to disseminate widespread knowledge of this opera than its performances up to date. As I tried to achieve variety of musical means by avoiding the Wagnerian recipe of 'through-composing' each scene in similar manner, nothing else was left to me than to give a different shape to each of the opera's fifteen scenes. On the other hand, the formal integration of these scenes demanded an equal cohesion of their music. This again brought the necessity to secure for its varied shapes formal links, i.e. to find independent musical patterns for them.

The application of these patterns to the dramatic canvas emerged as naturally from this as the selection of special patterns for the purposes of dramatic characterization.

No antiquarian leanings prompted me therefore when I employed in this opera Variations, or even Passacaglias and Fugues. Even less correct would it be to connect this employment of old forms with the atavistic movement 'Back to . . .', which incidentally started much later. Indeed, I have not confined

267

myself to these more or less archaic form-types but I had to resort also to new forms, based on novel principles (as pointed out before), for instance, to principles based on a fundamental 'tone', rhythm or chord. Another circumstance, conducive to variety and multiplicity of shapes, was the comparatively high number of orchestral interludes, accompanying a change of scene, resulting from the threefold change of scene within each of the three acts. To compose for that purpose throughout symphonic transitions or Interludes (as I saw it done later on in the case of another contemporary opera involving frequent changes of scenery) would have run counter to my idea of musical drama and its legitimate claims, which I had retained as a composer for the theatre despite my admiration for absolute music. Also in this case I felt constrained to achieve variety of contrasts by composing these musical accompaniments to a change of scene, sometimes as transitions, sometimes as Coda of the preceding music or as introduction to the following scene, or finally by combining both functions. I achieved this aim in the end also by establishing inconspicuous links between the discrepant sections of the particular musical form or by favouring an often quite abrupt juxtaposition of contrasting elements. (We will later on listen to several musical examples, elucidating these points.)

I will now discuss each scene, not so much with the intention of enumerating all their musical forms (a task discharged for quite a time now by all daily papers and by those musical periodicals which have taken note of this opera), but in order to explain occasionally some feature which is less obvious than its conceptual shape.

The reason for the music of scene 1 being based on the form of a Suite may be found in the fact that the dialogue of this scene (in which nothing really happens) consists likewise only of loosely connected topics of discussion. It was a near guess to find for each topic a small formal type and to combine several of these types into a Suite. That this process resulted in a Suite of more or less stylized archaic dance-forms (such as Prelude, Pavane, Cadenza, Gigue, Gavotte with double-refrain) was no mere chance, although it happened quite unconsciously. Scene 1 receives through this Suite—albeit unintentionally—its proper and, as it were, historic colour, a consideration which weighed but little with me in other parts of this timeless dramatic subject. Listen, for instance, to the Gigue and to the cadenza-like Double Bassoon Solo, connecting it with the following Gavotte: v. sc. Act I, p. 15-19, bars 65-120 (first beat).

The formal end of the Suite is achieved—among other things by the fact that the introductory Prelude returns refrain-like at the tail-end of the Scene, however this time in retrograde motion. This means that it presents the notes literally from back to front and with that it reflects musically the dramatic peculiarity of the scene, the dialogue of which also returns in the end to its original starting-point. The following postlude is only a development-section, utilizing the chief thematic ideas of each section of the Suite.

If Scene 1 is based on an admittedly ancient form-type, Scene 2 is based on something totally different. The unifying principle of that scene is of an harmonic nature: these chords represent the harmonic vertebra of the scene: v. sc. Act I, p. 30, bars 203-204.

That a principle of that nature may become a form-generating element will be easily appreciated if Tonality itself is understood as a form-begetting device and if, in consequence thereof, these three chords are likened to the functions of Tonic, Dominant and Subdominant respectively. Of course, the manner in which these chords or harmonic sequences are presented is throughout variational and multiple. For instance: v. sc. Act I, p. 30, bars 201-207, or Act I, p. 32, bars 225 (or 227)-234.

Of course I did not miss any opportunity to write singable and song-like music, as suggested by the more operatic caesurae of a play. In fact, there are two songs to be found in this and the following scene. The first one, used as an interpolation within the more rhapsodic organization of the three-chord-section is Andres' Coloratura-song with its three stanzas; and the second in the next scene is the military march and Marie's Lullaby.

In this connection I should like to disclose the results of two observations.

The first concerning the treatment of the singing voice in this opera. It has frequently been pointed out that it is not a Bel Canto opera. However, there is no reason why much of what is purely vocally conceived should not be expressed by means of 'Bel cantare'. I have never renounced the possibilities of coloratura singing. To be sure, in my opera hardly any Recitative can be found. I believe to have compensated fully for this deficiency by having abundantly utilized for the first time in an opera Schoenberg's so-called 'rhythmic declamation', introduced by him nearly twenty years ago in the declamatory choruses of *Die Glückliche Hand* and in the mélodrames of his *Pierrot Lunaire*.

These made evident that this 'melodramatic' treatment[1] of the voice, while acknowledging all formal potentialities of absolute music which play no part in Recitative, with its fixation of melody, rhythm and dynamics within the framework of scanned declamation, represents one of the

[1] Not used here in the customary sense of the English term 'melodrama'. (H.F.R.)

most effective means of communication—a function occasionally allotted to speech even in opera. More: by embracing the whole gamut of expression from the off-pitch whisper to the veritable 'bel parlare' of its widely arched *Sprechmelodien*, it has undoubtedly enriched operatic music with an expressive device of high value and pure musical ancestry which forms a welcome and attractive sonorous contrast to straight bel canto singing.

The other result of my investigation refers to the manner in which I have coped with the necessity of including music of a 'folky' and singable character, i.e. with the necessity to establish an appreciable relationship between art-music and folk-music in this opera—a matter of course in a tonally conceived work. It was by no means easy to express their differentiation of levels in so-called atonal harmony. I believe I have succeeded by composing all sections requiring the atmosphere of *Volkstümlichkeit* in a primitive manner which applies equally to the style of Atonality. That particular manner favours a symmetrical arrangement of periods and sections, it utilizes harmonies in thirds and especially in fourths and a type of melody in which whole-tone scale and perfect fourths play an integral part, in contrast with the diminished and augmented intervals which usually dominate the atonal music of the 'Vienna School'.[1] Also the so-called polytonality may be counted among the devices of a more primitive brand of harmony. We find a popular element in them in the Military March (with its intentionally 'wrong basses') and in Marie's Lullaby (with its harmonies in fourths)—pieces which the orchestra will now play. During the performance I beg you to take note of the link between the two scenes to which I referred earlier.

I demonstrated to you the structural principle of the three

[1] Second Vienna School. (H.F.R.)

chords in scene 2: v. sc. Act I, p. 38, bar 286 (left hand more marked). The three thirds on which these chords are based are: v. sc. Act I, p. 38, bar 286 (the first two beats).

From these a more motive-like growth emerges in the description of the eerie sunset: v. sc. Act I, p. 38, bars 286-293 (first beat).

At another point the three chords become the basic harmony of a melody of wide span: v. sc. Act I, p. 39, bars 303-310 (or 312), which in turn, leading to the close of the second, rhapsodically constructed scene, becomes transformed into music accompanying the change of scene, into which the march of the approaching band infiltrates—the latter interrupted by Marie's song which follows now: v. sc. Act I, p. 38-48, bars 286-426.

I have let you hear the music up to this point only. I am interrupting it now in order to mention another device of dramatic composition the purpose of which is none other than to guarantee musical unity of design. These fifths: v. sc. Act I, p. 48, bars 425-426—together with other recurrent motives and musical patterns—belong to the figure of Marie (one could say, this particular quietus of Harmony expresses her aimless and indefinable attitude of waiting, an attitude that finds its final solution only in death). This musical idea is used several times, as it were, in the manner of a Leitmotif. Repetitions of this sort occur also in the case of other motifs, attached to different persons or to different situations. Thereby I only want to point out the fact that I have availed myself of this opportunity to establish cohesion and formal correspondences (and thereby to achieve again unity of design) by utilizing these Leitmotifs, or better, these musical reminiscences.

Such is the case, for instance, in the frequently mentioned chordal sequence of Scene 2: inanimate nature horrifying

Wozzeck; then, in the final scene of Act II: the realistic sound of snoring, coming from the soldiers sleeping in their barracks —here in the orchestra, there in the manner of a choral enunciation with closed lips intermingling with Wozzeck's groaning in his sleep: v. sc. Act II, p. 169, bars 737-743.

The Passacaglia, or Chaconne, of scene 4 (Act I) is based on a dodecaphonic subject: v. sc. Act I, p. 55, bars 486-487.

It is really superfluous to mention that the variational treatment of this subject does not follow mechanical, or even absolute, musical concepts. Rather is it intimately connected with the action of the opera. Already the presentation of the twelve-note series (see above) is transmuted into musical drama in that it accompanies the first words of the scene. In its first appearance it is nearly absorbed by the words of the Doctor and nearly totally concealed by the excited Rubato of a Cello-Recitative. v. sc. Act I, p. 55-56, bars 488-495.

This is followed by 21 variation-forms: v. sc. Act I, p. 57-72, bars 496-642.

The use of the expression 'Variation' is quite legitimate: for the one and only subject on which these sections are based represents the Doctor's obsessional 'idée fixe'. It is also re-echoed in the words of Wozzeck, the tortured victim of the Doctor's obsession. Cf. v. sc. Act I, p. 61 (with upbeat), bars 525-531 (first half).

When finally—in the last variation—the Doctor vociferously pleads for immortality (the most sublime of his many obsessions) the variational theme in the bass (which had been partially concealed throughout the development of the Passacaglia) now returns with emphasized distinctness in chorale-like harmonies. It winds up the whole section in the manner of a Stretto: v. sc. Act I, p. 72, bars 638-656.

It is closely followed by the 'Andante affettuoso'—already

273

played earlier during this lecture (v. sc. p. 73 ff.). Its initial bars open up the final scene of Act I.

Act II, beginning with the little introduction (which has also been played a short while ago—cf. v. sc. Act II, p. 82) contains a Sonata-movement as the first of its musical forms. It is perhaps more than mere chance that the three characters of this scene— Marie, her child and Wozzeck—correspond with the three thematic groups of an orthodox sonata-exposition. This circumstance permits on principle the subsequent use of strict Sonata-form. The whole dramatic deployment of this trinket scene, the twofold recurrence of certain situations, and finally, the head-on clash of the principal characters, are responsible for the continuing strict musical structure, which consists of a first recapitulation after the exposition, of a development section and finally of a second recapitulation. The following table will make this clear:

The principal subject...... v. sc. Act II, p. 83, bar 7 (with upbeat)-14;
The bridge-passage........ v. sc. Act II, p. 84, bars 29-36;
The cantabile-group...... v. sc. Act II, p. 85, bars 43-46;
The conclusion-group..... v. sc. Act II, p. 86, bars 55-59.
And with it the whole exposition (Cf. v. sc. Act II, p. 83/84, bar 7 with upbeat-59, except for the last beat).

Then follows the first recapitulation, repeating the exposition distinctly, even if in a variational and telescoped manner (Cf. v. sc. Act II, p. 87, bars 60 with upbeat-96, first beat).

The development section, i.e. the particular part of the scene in which the characters and their musical equivalents come to a head-on collision, leads up to the climax of the Sonata, i.e. to the musical reminiscence 'Wir arme Leut',[1] quoted earlier

[1] Cf. Music example No. 62. (H.F.R.)

in this Lecture, a motif which permeates the entire opera (Cf. v. sc. Act I, p. 22, bar 135).

The remaining music of this scene, as of the following change of scene (which belongs to the preceding scene on musical grounds and functions as its Coda), demonstrates how the last reprise of the Sonata can be reached and the Sonata concluded by way of the sustained chord of C-major which you have just heard. (How could the objectivity of money be more relevantly expressed than by this chord!)[1]

That this music of scenic transformation can boast of an independent musical life and therefore be classified as a small musical unit while simultaneously trying to coalesce with its succeeding section, may be the result of the following device: when the transition-music begins, a Glissando on the harp indicates its commencement; the same effect returns when the transition is ended, only the first time in a descending ff, the second time as an ascending pp. Please watch this, when the orchestra plays now the Sonata-recapitulation which grows out of that C-major chord: v. sc. Act II, p. 93-96, bars 122-170.

The following scene also depends on three dramatic characters which—to be sure—are less intimately inter-connected than the three figures of the preceding scene, linked together by ties of blood-relationship. While the former scene therefore engenders a musical form in which the limbs were linked together like members of a family, that is to say, Sonata-form, the latter scene demands a more artificial pattern consisting of more disparate elements, namely, an Invention and a Fugue with three subjects. The motival limitation of

[1] The bracketed sentence contains an important correction by Berg, pencilled into his typescript. The sentence, now referring to the 'Sachlichkeit' (objectivity) of money, ran originally thus: '. . . How could the "Nüchternheit" (prosiness) of money be more relevantly expressed . . .' etc. (H.R.F.).

these three subjects, in contradistinction to the tendency for a more melodic transition in the preceding Sonata-movement, calls for this strictly fugal form. Its severity, to be sure, is eased by the fact that the motifs are already well known. They are: the motif of the Captain, dominating already the very beginning of the first scene of the opera: v. sc. Act II, p. 97, bars 171–172 (right hand); then the motif of the Doctor, from Act I, scene 3: v. sc. Act II, p. 97, bars 171–174; and, finally, one of Wozzeck's motifs; the one which had been foreshadowed—without literal quotation—in the preceding Sonata-movement: v. sc. Act II, p. 108, bars 273–274.

The slow movement of this symphony-like Act II is a 'Largo'. Apart from the obvious thematic connections of its sectional and independent structure it contains one other peculiar feature: it is scored for a 'chamber orchestra' which is modelled on the Chamber Symphony No. 1 of Arnold Schoenberg. Incidentally, I intended thereby to pay homage to my teacher and master at this pivotal point of the opera.

On this occasion I'd like to mention that it has been my endeavour, here as in other sections of the opera, to satisfy my desire for unity and integration, as well as for variety and multiplicity of form, by utilizing the possibilities of orchestration and of instrumental combination. You will find not infrequently in this opera sections or even whole scenes (like this one) to which a specific sonorous body remains attached. In this way a small instrumental group—in the manner of an 'obbligato'—is attached to the little Suite-movement of scene 1, Act I, for instance: five woodwinds and three kettledrums and harp, or three flutes, or four brass instruments only, or the quartet of strings. One self-contained section of scene 2, Act I, is entirely concerned with the sonority of muted brass and strings playing col legno; a fugal episode of scene 1, Act III is limited to the sound of five solo strings only. Finally the orchestration of the very last scene of the opera might be mentioned, the scene of the playing children, from which oboes, bassoons, trombones and doublebasses are totally excluded.

To return once more to that 'Largo': the manner of its introduction and of its trailing-off could be called an example of the way to achieve a kind of musical cohesion by other means that the usual one of a return to the Tonic. The clarinet figurations which seem to emerge from the fugal subject-matter of the preceding scene—only to fade off—establish a link with this 'Largo' at the point where the figuration seems to congeal: chord: v. sc. Act II, p. 124, bar 367; representing the first harmony-basis of the Largo theme: v. sc. Act II, p. 124, bar 364-368.

The end of that 'Largo' closes into the same harmony which —transmuted again into movement—crystallizes retrogressively into the same clarinet-figuration from which that chord had emerged previously: v. sc. Act II, p.134, bars 406 (with upbeat)-411.

These figures of the clarinets form also a bridge to the succeeding music of transition: v. sc. Act II, p. 135-136.

I intend now to exemplify the symmetrical structure of this musical frame for a musico-dramatic scene from the angle of orchestral sonorities. I will do so by letting the orchestra first play the Introduction with the first Largo-idea and by adding afterwards its musical mirror-reflection with which this scene fades out, only to merge imperceptibly into the transition-music which in turn introduces the next scene with a slow Ländler-movement.

In this 'Ländler' and in the rest of the dance-music you may find sections which will strike you as being dissonant in a different way than that of strictly atonal music: dissonant, in the sense of the simultaneous sound of several pieces in different keys, as you may be used to hearing them at a fun-fair. This obvious dissonance which emerges from primitive polytonality is of course deliberate, but used not without judicious selection: for it not only derives from the dramatic situation, but is also the result of musical logistics.

An example: the antecedent of a Ländler in G minor— according to the rules of formal construction—either leads to the Dominant (D major) or back to the Tonic. The fact that both things happen simultaneously (who could blame the blind-fold rhapsodizings of an alcoholic band of beer fiddlers?) leads to musical chaos: cf. v. sc. Act II, p. 136, bars 424-425.

This chaos is prolonged when the section of the beer fiddlers which had reached the Dominant returns to the Tonic of G minor according to rule, whereas another section—with equal justification by the laws of modulation—turns into the mediant of E flat major: cf. v. sc. Act II, p. 126, bar 429.

It is a miracle that they manage to come together at the end of the Ländler! Listen to that now, please. The orchestra—as pointed out before—will play first the introduction to the Largo: Cf. v. sc. Act II, p. 123, bar 360 (with upbeat) until bar 372, and then the retrograde Coda with the succeeding Ländler: v. sc. Act II, p. 134, bar 403 (with long upbeat) until bar 442 (excluding the country-inn-music; cf. also p. 137, until bar 447 incl.).

I've already mentioned that the following scene represents the Scherzo within the framework of that dramatic symphony with which this Act II may be compared. The Ländler which you have just now heard is the first subject of this Scherzo. A song by the first of the two tramps would correspond with a 'first Trio', a Waltz played by the village-inn-band with a second Scherzo, the hunting chorus of the village lads would —as being the central portion of that whole section—represent a 'second Trio' in that connection. Now follows—in agreement with the strict construction of such Scherzo movements (think of those in Schumann's symphonies)—the repeat of the first tripartite Scherzo-group. To be sure, the repeat of the three little sections (Ländler, Lied, Waltz) is not a literal one, but as much as possible variational, in accordance with the progress of the play. Thus the Ländler is placed into quite new musical surroundings although its repeat is literal. Thus the 'first Trio' represented by the tramp's song is repeated in so outspoken a variation that its basic harmonies are unfolded, resulting in a Chorale-melody in sustained notes which—in its presentation by the Bombardon—forms the basis for a 'mélodrame'. This mélodrame, the harmless parody of a religious sermon, is therefore on the one hand the repeat of the 'first Trio', on the other hand a Chorale-Variation (albeit of a parodistical bent) and in five parts.

Finally, the repeat of the Waltz, played by the village band, reappears still in the form of a waltz; however, as it also functions as transition-music to the following scene its presentation conforms to the augmented form of a symphonic development-section played by the entire orchestra.

When that music breaks off suddenly, the snoring-chorus of the sleeping soldiers in the barracks is heard through the lowered curtain. With that section the Rondo Marziale (mentioned before) is introduced, which in turn concludes this Act with that very scene laid in the soldiers' barracks.

I have already discussed the different patterns of Act III and their form-generating principles. The principle of scene 1 is a theme, subjected to variational treatment. The strictness of architecture (I use this term deliberately) is responsible for the fact that this dual theme, with its antecedent and consequent, consists of seven bars, that it returns in sevenfold variation, and that the double fugue, consisting of two subjects in accordance with the dualism inherent in the original theme, is based on a theme consisting of seven notes. The mathematical character of this form might easily be scoffed at. That is what actually happened at the occasion of the first concert performance of this piece. It occurred in a review of a performance of this so called Bible-scene which never took place. Although not a single note of the music of that particular scene had actually been performed, the hyper-sensitive music critic was able to notice and duly to report to his readers the utter inefficiency of such an absurdly mathematical structure: Cf. v. sc. Act III, pp. 181-189, bars 1-12.

The low 'B' in the doublebasses which is here added to the final chord of this Fugue (we have become acquainted with it as being the last note of the significant concluding cadence of Act II), now becomes a unifying element and, indeed, the cohesive principle of the following scene of murder. It appears, of course, here also in manifold guises; as a pedal point, as sustained middle or treble part, doubled in one or more octaves, in short, in all possible positions and sonorous combinations. When finally the murder of Marie is committed to the sound of the *ff* drum beats on 'B', all motives connected with her are sounded precipitately, as may well happen in the very moment of death. They pass through her consciousness with lightning speed and in a macabre grimace, like the real characters which had permeated her life: The Lullaby from scene 1 (cf. v. sc. Act III, p. 296, bar 104); suggestions of the trinket-scene of Act II (v. sc. Act III, p. 196, bar 104); the drum major himself (see the same bar); the motif

280

of Marie bemoaning her wretched life (bar 105) which finally fades away in the moment of her last breath with the motif of the dreamy fifths (previously discussed), the motive of waiting in vain. . . . Cf. v. sc. Act III, p. 197, bars 106-107.

The short music of transition enunciates that 'B' once more and this time unisono in the higher octave, as the only note of the entire scale which belongs to *all* instruments of the orchestra (cf. v. sc. Act III, p. 197, bars 117-121). Now it starts in the softest pianissimo possible in the muted horn and increases its sonority through gradually louder orchestral entries (without percussion) up to the most powerful outburst. Regarding these entries it may be observed that they do not occur at regular intervals but assert themselves according to a peculiar law of rhythm. Entries of the winds as well as of the strings combined result in a kind of basic rhythmic pattern. Thereby both groups of these rhythmically ordered entries follow each other—canonically, as it were—in the time-span of a mere crotchet beat. This process produces the impression as if the resulting ostensible irregularity (which reaches the level of consciousness in the listener as little as does the logical order of the entries) imparted to that crescendo note on 'B' a special breath of life. It is a fact that this crescendo produces an even greater dynamic effect and intensity than does the repetition of that crescendo on 'B' on different levels of the scale, supported by the entire percussion-group.

The rhythm just mentioned, is, of course, not a matter of mere chance, but of thematic importance, like the chord arrived at by way of the crescendo-climax. This is the rhythmic pattern on which the following scene is based (v. sc. Act III, p. 198, b. 122-129), and which establishes cohesion and unity, as will become evident from every single bar. To be sure, that rhythm has not been superimposed on this scene, but is used in a manner permitting the highest degree of rhythmical and even metrical variability within the limits of this rhythmical monotony. This is achieved by using melodies entirely based on this rhythm, for instance the quick Polka of the carousing young men and women with which these scene begins (cf. v. sc. Act III, p. 198, bars 122-129), or by underpinning the accompaniment by this very rhythm (cf. v. sc. Act III, p. 199, bars 145-152), or, by augmenting or diminishing this rhythm or by shifting its accent, for instance: v. sc. Act III, p. 210, bars 152-159, or, finally, by superimposing another metre on this rhythm, by subdividing it into triplets or by presenting it in two or more dovetailed canonic entries.

A similar example of such utilization of musical substance which had proved its worth earlier in the case of a single note, a similar example of that form of objectivity (*Sachlichkeit*) (which is older than its modern connotations) can be found in the following scene, based on only one chord, or better, on a group of six simultaneous notes only (v. sc. Act III, p. 210, bar 220). Also this six-note chord has been announced (as has been mentioned before) in that earlier short transition-music with its great climax on 'B'. That chord, however, completes also harmonically the Coda of the preceding scene, resp. the change of scene (v. sc. Act III, p. 210, bars 219-220). Despite the fact that this scene is closely tied to this six-note group, it achieves variety and formal multiplicity through the fact that this six-note chord is subjected to all imaginable variations, i.e. divisions, inversions, regroupings and changes of position with regard to all its notes, exactly as the single note or rhythm earlier on had been subjected to it: v. sc. Act II, i p. 213, bar 247, or p. 217, bar 27. Even melodic divisions, i.e. re-interpretations of its notes into new melodies occur: v. sc. Act III, p. 217, bars 278-283. On the other hand, the formal structure in this piece is achieved by the old symmetrical three part-division of ancient merit. Thus this six-note chord appears in the flanking parts of each scene based only on one specific degree of the scale (but of course in all its variants), while in the middle section seeking also basic support from all other degrees of the chromatic scale. When this chord finally returns to its original position and, as it were, to its tonal centre, it functions simultaneously as a harmonic bridge to the following episode, the D minor tonality of which signifies almost the dissolution of that six-note chord: v. sc. Act II, pp. 223-4, with upbeat to D minor.

More of this anon. Here only a more general remark. It is obvious that music such as the foregoing, entirely based on harmony and on the simultaneity of chords, must needs reveal a strong impressionistic influence, despite all melodic variants. This is, of course, the natural result in the case of a dramatic action which comes so near to the elemental happenings of nature itself. For instance, the waves of the pond submerging the drowning Wozzeck, the croaking of toads: v. sc. Act III, p. 222, bars 297-305; the rising moon: v. sc. Act III, p. 222, bars 306-308, etc. Despite all this, no attempt has been made anywhere in this opera to establish a musical style which some listeners might be inclined to trace back to the French, perhaps to Debussy. For that ostensible Impressionism (using here again a famous artistic term of recent decades) which is allegedly to be detected here and there in my opera, can be found already in the works of the Classics and the Romantics of music, quite apart from Wagner's imperishable musical reflections of Nature. In fact, all that could here be called 'impressionistic' in the sense of the aforesaid term is miles removed from the vague and bottomless sonorities of that particular style. On the contrary:

all is here based on a strict musical principle, as I have explained earlier in this lecture. Here it is based on a thematic six-note group and in Act I, scene 2—discussed earlier—on an Ostinato of a progression of three chords. Also the final scene of this Act III (the scene of the playing children which you have just heard) with its continuous quaver-movement (I was able and, I believe, justified in calling it a 'perpetuum mobile' in accordance with the old traditions of form) thus obeys one of these laws of form which I had to promulgate myself first of all, in order to submit to it later on.

The final Scene (which we have heard already) is preceded by a somewhat longer orchestral piece. This should be understood from the dramatist's point of view as the Epilogue which follows Wozzeck's suicide; it should also be appreciated as the composer's confession, breaking through the framework of the dramatic plot and, likewise, even as an appeal to the audience, which is here meant to represent Humanity itself. From the musician's point of view this last orchestral interlude represents a thematic development-section, utilizing all the important musical characters related to Wozzeck. Its shape is tripartite and its unifying principle is—an exception to the rule of this opera—Tonality. This D minor key, the harmonically disintegrating function of which I have already previously mentioned, is, to be sure, extended to so vast an extent that it has become possible to reach the ultimate consequences of its augmented compass. This was achieved in the middle section of the piece, at its very climax, i.e. at the point where its developmental entries tighten up to a veritable 'Stretto'. This resulted in a sound-combination which—although it contained all the twelve notes of the chromatic scale—created in that particular context only the effect of a Dominant, leading naturally and inevitably back to the D minor of the recapitulation (v. sc. Act III, p. 228, bars 364-365).

Extending my heartfelt thanks to the orchestra, its conductor and the supporting singers of the Opera House in . . . for their collaboration, I beg the former now kindly to play this Epilogue as a conclusion to my lecture (v. sc. Act III, pp. 224-228, exclusive of the last beat). But before that I would like to express a request, addressed to the audience itself. Ladies and gentlemen—I beg you to forget all theory and musical aesthetics which have served my explanation, before you attend the Tuesday performance—or a later one—of the opera 'Wozzeck', staged at this opera house!

CATALOGUE OF WORKS

ORIGINAL COMPOSITIONS

I   *'Schliesse mir die Augen beide'*, 1 (Voice and Piano) 1900 (Storm). Published: Berlin, 1930, 'Die Musik',XXII/5. 1955 Universal Edition. Vienna (ed. Redlich). Autograph: lost. Note: dedicated to Emil Hertzka together with XV.

II   *Early Songs* (Voice and Piano). 1, 'Heilige Himmel', op. 1, (F. Evers); 2, 'Herbstgefühl' (Siegfried Fleischer); 3, 'Unter der Linden' (Walther v.d. Vogelweide); 4, 'Spielleute' (Ibsen); 5, 'Wo der Goldregen steht' (Lorenz); 6, 'Lied des Schiffermädels' (O. J. Bierbaum); 7, 'Abschied' (Monsterberg); 8, 'Liebeslied' (Dolorosa); 9, 'Über meinen Nächten' (Dolorosa); 10, 'Sehnsucht', I (Hohenberg); 11, 'Sternenfall' (Wilhelm); 12, 'Er klagt, dass der Frühling so kortz blüht' (Arno Holz); 13, 'Ich und du' (Busse); 14, 'Über Nacht' (Rognetti); 15, 'Verlassen' (Bohemian folksong); 16, 'Traurigkeit' (Peter Altenberg); 17, 'Hoffnung' (Peter Altenberg); 18, 'Flötenspielerin' (Peter Altenberg); 19, 'Spaziergang' (Mombert); 20, 'Soldatenbraut' (Mörike); 21, 'So regnet es sich langsam ein' (Caesar Flaischlen); 22, 'Grenzen der Menschheit' (Goethe); 23, 'Ballade des äusseren Lebens' (Hofmannsthal); 24, 'Im Walde' (Björnson); 25, 'Viel Träume' (Amerling); 26, 'Tiefe Sehnsucht'

287

(Liliencron); 27, 'Über den Berg' (Busse); 28, 'Am Strande' (G. Scherer); 29, 'Reiselied' (Hofmannsthal); 30, 'Spuk' (Hebbel); 31, 'Aus Pfingsten' (Evers); 32, 'Winter' (J. Schlaf); 33, 'O wär' mein Lieb ein Röslein rot' (Burns); 34, 'Sehnsucht', II (Hohenberg); 35, 'Ich liebe dich' (Grabbe); 36, 'Ferne Lieder' (Rückert); 37, 'Ich will die Fluren meiden' (Rückert); 38, 'Geliebte Schöne' (Heine); 39, 'Schattenleben' (Graf); 40, 'Am Abend' (Geibel); 41, 'Wenn Gespenster auferstehn' (Felix Dörmann); 42, 'Vom Ende' (Marie Madeleine); 43, 'Vorüber' (Wiesbacher); 44, 'Scheidelied' (Baumbach); 45, 'Eure Weisheit' (Fischer); 46, 'Schlummerlose Nacht' (Greif); 47, 'Nachtgesang' (O. J. Bierbaum); 48, 'Es wandelt, was wir schauen' (Eichendorff); 49, 'Liebe' (Rilke); 50, 'Wandert, ihr Wolken' (Avenarius); 51, 'Im Morgengrauen' (Stieler); 52, 'Grabschrift' (Jakobowski); 53, 'Traum' (Semmler); 54, 'Furcht' (Palma); 55, 'Augenblicke' (Hamerling); 56, 'Trinklied' (Rückl); 57, 'Fromm' (Gustav Falke); 58, 'Leben' (Evers); 59, 'Näherin' (Rilke); 60, 'Erster Verlust' (Goethe); 61, 'Süss sind mir die Schollen des Tales' (Knodt); 62, 'Der milde Herbst anno 45' (Max Mell); 63, 'Menschenherz' (delle Grazie); 64, 'Holophan' (Wallpach); 65, 'Mignon' (Goethe); 66, 'Läuterung' (Hohenberg); 67, 'Die Sorglichen' (Falke); 68, 'Das stille Königreich' (Busse); 69, 'Trinklied' (Henckell); 70, 'An Leukon' (Gleim). Dates of composition: Nos. 1 and 3: 1900. Nos. 2–25, and 27–34: *circa* 1902. No. 26: 1904 or 1905. Nos. 35–69: Summer 1904/5. No. 70: 1908. Autographs: in Helene Berg's possession. Published: No. 70 (c.f. W. Reich, op. cit., 1937,

Appendix p. 14). Note: No. 8 probably two songs; Nos. 23, 25 and 26 are duets. Autograph: Helene Berg.

III   *Seven Early Songs* (Voice and Piano). 1, 'Im Zimmer' (Johannes Schlaf); 2, 'Die Nachtigall' (Th. Storm); 3, 'Liebesode' (O. E. Hartleben); 4, 'Traumgekrönt' (R. M. Rilke); 5, 'Sommertage' (P. Hohenberg); 6, 'Nacht' (Karl Hauptmann); 7, 'Schilflied' (Lenau). Dates of composition: No. 1: Summer 1905; No. 2: Winter 1905/06; No. 3: Summer 1906; No. 4: Summer 1907; Nos. 5-7: Spring 1908. Autographs: Helene Berg (except No. 7, which is at the Gesellschaft der Musikfreunde, Wien). Publications: The revised Piano version was published 1928 by Universal Edition, Vienna. The version for orchestra was acquired by the same firm, but has remained unpublished so far. First performances: Nos. 2, 3 and 4 were first performed in Vienna on November 7, 1907, in a Concert by Schoenberg's pupils. The first performance of the orchestral version took place in Vienna on November 6, 1928. *Note:* The songs are dedicated to Helene Berg.

IV   *Fugue* (with three subjects) for String Quintet and Piano. Composed: Summer 1907. Autograph: lost. First performance: Vienna, November 7, 1907.

V   *Compositions for 6-8 part Chorus.* Composed: Summer 1907. Autograph: lost.

VI   *Twelve Variations for the Piano* on an original theme. Date of composition: presumably begun in 1907, completed 1908. Autograph: Helene Berg. Publication: Cf. Appendix 1. First performance: November 8, 1908, Vienna, in a Concert by Schoenberg's pupils.

VII   *Sonata for Pianoforte*, op. 1. Date of composition: Summer 1907 to Summer 1908. Autograph: lost. Published: 1910, Berlin, Robert Lienau; 1920, Vienna, C. Haslinger in a revised edition; 1927, Vienna, Universal Edition. First performance: April 24, 1911, Vienna.

VIII   *Four Songs for Voice and Piano*, op. 2, on poems by Hebbel and Mombert. No. 1: 'Schlafen, schlafen' (from Hebbel's poem 'Dem Schmerz sein Recht'). No. 2: Schlafend trägt man mich. . . . No. 3: Nun ich der Riesen Stärksten. . . . No. 4: Warm die Lüfte. . . . *Note:* Nos. 2, 3 and 4 are taken from Mombert's cycle of poems 'Der Glühende'. Date of composition: Begun early in 1909, completed spring 1910. Autograph: lost. Publications: 1910, Berlin, Robert Lienau; 1920, Vienna, C. Haslinger in a revised edition; 1927, Vienna, Universal Edition. *Note:* Orchestral version by R. Leibowitz (only available on L.P. record, cf. Appendix 5).

IX   *String Quartet*, op. 3. Composed: Spring to early Summer 1910. Autograph: lost. Publications: 1920, Vienna, C. Haslinger; 1924, Vienna, Universal Edition, in a second revised edition. First performance: April 24, 1911, Vienna. *Note:* Dedicated to Helene Berg.

X   *Five songs* on picture-postcard texts by Peter Altenberg, for voice and orchestra, op. 4. No. 1: Seele wie bist du schöner. . . . No. 2: Sahst du nach dem Gewitterregen. . . . No. 3: Über die Grenzen des All. . . . No. 4: Nichts ist gekommen. . . . No. 5: Hier ist Friede. Composed: Full score completed in the autumn of 1912. Autograph: Helene Berg and

Bodleian Library, Oxford (original drafts of Nos. 4 and 5). Publications: 1953, Vienna, Universal Edition (edition for voice and Pianoforte, ed. H. E. Apostel). No. 5 first published in the magazine 'Menschen', No. 5, 1921, Dresden. It was reprinted in 'Musical Quarterly', October issue, 1948, New York, G. Schirmer, ed. R. Leibowitz. The full score has remained unpublished so far. First performance: March 31, 1913, Vienna. It was prematurely broken off. First complete performances, conducted by Jasha Horenstein, in Rome and Paris, during the winter 1952/53.

XI   *Four pieces for Clarinet and Piano*, op. 5. Composed: Summer 1913. Autograph: Gottfried Kassowitz, Vienna. Publications: 1920, Vienna; C. Haslinger, 1924, Vienna, Universal Edition. First Performance: October 17, 1919, Vienna in Schoenberg's 'Verein für musikalische Privataufführungen'. *Note:* Dedicated to Arnold Schoenberg.

XII   *Three pieces for big orchestra*, op. 6. Praeludium, Reigen, Marsch. Composed: 1914. Full score of 'Praeludium' and 'Marsch' completed on September 8, 1914; full score of 'Reigen' completed in August 1915. Autograph: Universal Edition, Vienna (of the revision 1929/30). Publications: 1923, Vienna, Universal Edition, facsimile-reproduction of the autograph; 1930, revision undertaken which was published in 1954, Vienna, Universal Edition. Performances: First performance of 'Praeludium' and 'Reigen' on June 5, 1923, Berlin, conducted by Webern; first performance of all three pieces in Oldenburg, 1930, conducted by Johannes Schüler. *Note:* Dedicated

to Arnold Schoenberg, on the occasion of his 40th
birthday (September 14, 1914).

XIII   *WOZZECK*, op. 7. Opera in three acts, based on the
dramatic fragment by Georg Büchner. Dates of
composition: decision to set Büchner's fragment: May 1914; libretto completed: Summer 1917;
composition started: late Summer 1917; short score
completed: end of 1920; orchestration completed:
April 1921. Autograph: Library of Congress, Washington, D.C., U.S. (full score), Alma Mahler-
Werfel (U.S.A.) (short score). Publications: 1922,
vocal score (arr. F. H. Klein), by the composer himself; 1923, taken over by Universal Edition, Vienna.
1926, reprint of vocal score and publication of full
score, Universal Edition, Vienna. 1923, libretto published (Universal Edition). 1924, the 'Three fragments
for voice and orchestra' published, Universal Edition,
Vienna (full score and vocal score). 1956 publication
of pocket score, Universal Edition, Vienna-Zurich-
London. First performance: December 14, 1925,
Berlin; conductor: Erich Kleiber. First performances
of the 'Three fragments', June 1924, Frankfurt/Main,
conductor: Hermann Scherchen. *Note:* Dedicated to
Alma Maria Mahler.

XIV   *Chamber Concerto* for Piano, Violin and thirteen wind
players. Dates of composition: Sketch: Summer 1923
to February 9, 1925; orchestration completed: July
23, 1925. The second Movement 'Adagio' was
arranged as Trio for Violin, Clarinet and Piano in
1935 by the composer. Autograph: Full score:
Helene Berg; Trio—arr.: Universal Edition. Publications: 1925, Vienna, Universal Edition, facsimile of

the autograph; 1955, Vienna, Universal Edition, Trio—arr. 1956: pocket score (reprint), Universal Edition, Vienna. First performance: March 27, 1927, Berlin, conductor; Scherchen. First performance of the Trio—arr. of mov. 2, Vienna, 1936. *Note:* Dedicated to Arnold Schoenberg, on the occasion of his 50th birthday (September 14, 1924).

XV   *Schliesse mir die Augen beide* (Storm) II (cf. No. I). Composed: late Summer 1925. Autograph: Emil Hertzka's heirs. Publications: together with I,Berlin, 1930, Die Musik, XXII, February issue, 1930; Vienna, 1955, Universal Edition (ed. Redlich). *Note:* Cf. Note to No. I.

XVI   *Lyric Suite* for String Quartet. Dates of composition: October 1925 to October 1926; arrangement of the three middle movements 2, 3 and 4 for String Orchestra in 1928. Autographs: Full score: heirs of Alexander v. Zemlinsky; Arr. for str. orch.: Universal Edition, Vienna. Publications: Pocket score; 1927, Vienna, Universal Edition arr. for str. orch.: 1928, Vienna, Universal Edition. First performances: January 8, 1927, Vienna (Kolisch-Quartet). Arr. for str. orch.: January 31, 1929, Berlin (conductor: Horenstein). *Note:* Dedicated to Alexander v. Zemlinsky.

XVII   *Le Vin/Der Wein.* Concert Aria with orchestra, a setting of Baudelaire's poem, in the German translation by Stefan George. Composed: May to July 23, 1929; full score completed: August 23, 1929. Autograph: Ružena Herlinger. Publications: 1930, Vienna, Universal Edition (vocal score, arr. by E. Stein). Full score unpublished so far. First performances: June 4, 1930, Königsberg (Prussia), conductor: Scherchen, singer: Herlinger.

XVIII *Four-part Canon* 'Alban Berg an das Frankfurter Opernhaus' (words by the composer). Composed: Summer 1930. Autograph: Library of Congress, U.S. publication: 1937, cf. W. Reich, op. cit. Appendix, p. 16. First performance: February 1, 1930, Frankfurt/Main. *Note:* Composed for the celebration of the 50th anniversary of the opera house in Frankfurt/Main. It contains in text and music allusions to Schoenberg's Opera 'Von Heute auf Morgen', first performed in Frankfurt/Main in February 1930.

XIX *LULU.* Opera in 3 acts, based on Frank Wedekind's plays 'Earth Spirit' and 'Pandora's Box'. Dates of composition: Decision taken: Spring 1928; libretto complete: Spring 1929; agreement with Wedekind's heirs: August 1929; composition begun: Spring 1929; short score completed: April 1934; 'Lulu-Symphony' arranged: Summer 1934; orchestration of opera begun: Autumn 1934; interrupted until late August 1935, then resumed and carried on until the composer's death (December 24, 1935). The orchestration of Act III remains incomplete. Autograph: Helene Berg. Publications: 1936, Vienna, Universal Edition, vocal score (arr. E. Stein) of Acts I and II only. Act III unpublished. Full score also unpublished. Lulu-Symphony (containing Rondo, Ostinato, Lied der Lulu, Variations, Adagio), Vienna, 1935, Universal Edition (full score). Libretto published: 1937, Vienna, Universal Edition (Acts I and II only). First performance of Lulu-Symphony: November 30, 1934, conductor:

Kleiber. First performance of the opera-fragmen (Acts I and II and end of Act II only): June 2, 1937, Stadtheater Zürich (conductor: Denzler). *Note:* 'Das Lied der Lulu' is dedicated to Anton Webern, on the occasion of his 50th birthday (December 3, 1933); the the whole opera is dedicated to Arnold Schoenberg, on the occasion of his 60th birthday (September 14, 1934).

XX   *The Violin Concerto.* 'To the Memory of an Angel.' Composed: Short score: April to July 12, 1935: orchestration completed: August 11, 1935. Autograph: Louis Krasner, U.S.A. Publications: 1936, Vienna, Universal Edition (full score); 1938, Vienna, Universal Edition, piano arr. (R. Kurzmann), revised by Berg shortly before his death. First performance: April 19, 1936, Barcelona, conductor: Scherchen, soloist: Louis Krasner. *Note:* Dedicated to Louis Krasner.

ARRANGEMENTS OF COMPOSITIONS BY OTHERS

FRANZ SCHREKER: Der ferne Klang, vocal score with text 1911, Vienna, Universal Edition.

ARNOLD SCHOENBERG: Gurrelieder, vocal score with text, 1912, Vienna, Universal Edition.

'Litanei' and 'Entrückung' (middle movements of the String Quartet, op. 10), arr. for voice and Piano (completed in 1912, published in 1921), Vienna, Universal Edition.

Chamber Symphony op. 9, arr. for Piano Duet 1913/15, lost.

LONGER ARTICLES AND LECTURES

ARNOLD SCHOENBERG: 'Gurrelieder'. Thematic analysis and Guide, by Alban Berg. Published: Vienna, 1913, Universal Edition, No. 3695, also in a shortened edition, U. E. No. 52, 577.

Chamber Symphony, op. 9. Thematic analysis by Alban Berg. Published: 1913, Universal Edition, No. 6140.

Pelleas und Melisande, op. 5. Short thematic analysis by Alban Berg. Published: Universal Edition, No. 6268. A more detailed analysis was planned and perhaps sketched in 1920 and later. It is lost.

Lecture on WOZZECK. First given in 1929 in numerous German cities. First complete publication: Cf. Appendix 2.

'Was ist atonal?': Radio-Dialogue, spoken in the RAVAG, Vienna, on April 23, 1930. First published in the magazine '23', Vienna (ed. W. Reich), Nos. 26/27, June 1936.*).

Cycle of Lectures on Schoenberg's Music, delivered in Vienna in the winter 1932/33. Manuscript lost.

SHORTER ARTICLES (as far as published)

N.B.: R = Reprint by W. Reich, op. cit. 1937.
RO = Reprint in ital. transl. L. Rognoni, op. cit., 1954.

Dem Lehrer. Symposium 'Arnold Schoenberg', Munich, Piper & Co., 1912. (R)

---

* English transl. publ. in N. Slonimsky's 'Music since 1900', 3rd ed., 1949 and in 'Music Today', ed. R. H. Myers, London, 1949. Italian transl. publ. in L. Rognoni's 'Espressionismo e dodecafonia', Einaudi editori, Saggi 173, 1954. Condensed résumé publ. under the same title in H. Scherchen's 'Musica Viva', Brussels, 1936, II.

Der Verein für musikalische Privataufführungen in Wien. From the Society's leaflet, Feb. 1919. (R)

Erziehung des Zeitungslesers tut not. Fragment of an unpublished article written in Summer 1920, publ. W. Reich, 'Melos', July/August issue 1953, p. 219.

Warum ist Schoenbergs Musik so schwer verständlich? Special issue of the 'Anbruch' at the occasion of Schoenberg's 50th birthday, VI/August-Sept. issue, 1924. (R), Engl. edition under: 'Why is Schoenberg's Music so hard to understand?', transl. by Anton Swarowsky and Joseph H. Lederer, publ. in 'The Music Review', Cambridge, XIII/3, August 1952.

Verbindliche Antwort auf eine unverbindliche Rundfrage. From '25 Jahre Neue Musik', Jahrbuch 1926 der UE, Wien. (R)

A Word About 'Wozzeck'. Modern Music, U.S.A., V/1, Nov. 1927.

Credo. 'Die Musik', XXIV/5, January 1930. (R)

Vgl. *Wozzeck—Bemerkungen von Alban Berg* (1930), UE, Wien. Except for a new introduction paragraph, identical with the 'Pro Domo' section of 'Das Opernproblem', 1928.

Zum 60. Geburtstag. 'Festschrift für Arnold Schoenberg', UE, Wien, 1934. (R)

Die Stimme in der Oper. 'Gesang', Jahrbuch 1929 der UE, Wien. (R), (RO)

Praktische Anweisungen zur Einstudierung des 'Wozzeck' (1930). First publ. by W. Reich, op. cit. 1937, p. 166 ff.

Operntheater. Anbruch, Wien, X/8, October 1928. (R) (RO)

Das 'Opernproblem'. 'Neue Musik-Zeitung', Stuttgart, 1928. (R)

Die musikalischen Formen in meiner Oper 'Wozzeck'. 'Die Musik', Berlin, XVI/5, Feb. 1924. (R)

Open Letter to Arnold Schoenberg. (Thematic analysis of Berg's Chamber Concerto, by the composer). Vienna 1925, Uni-

versal Edition. ('Pult und Taktstock'), February issue, 1925. (R)
Die Musikalische Impotenz der 'neuen Ästhetik' Hans Pfitzners.
Anbruch, Wien, II/No. 11-12, June 1920. (R)
Händel und Bach. '23', No. 20-21, March 1935. (R)
Zu Franz Schuberts 100 Todestag. 'Unterhaltungsblatt' der Vossischen Zeitung, Berlin, 18 Nov. 1928. (R)
Vorstellung Ernst Kreneks. Ansprache, 3 January 1928. First publ. by W. Reich, op. cit. 1937.
Gedenkrede auf Emil Hertzka. Ansprache, 20 June, 1932. First publ. by W. Reich, op. cit., 1937.
An Adolf Loos. 'Festschrift zum 60. Geburtstag von Adolf Loos am 10 December 1930', Wien, Verlag der Buchhandlung Richard Lanyi, Wien. (R)
An Karl Kraus. 'Stimmen über Karl Kraus', zum 60. Geburtstag, 28 April, 1934, Verlag der Buchhandlung Richard Lanyi, Wien. (R)

DISCOGRAPHY

The following list is intended to be exhaustive. Inclusion of a catalogue number is no indication of present availability for which manufacturer's up-to-date catalogues should be consulted. Under each composition are listed the various recorded performances with the countries of issue, manufacturer and catalogue numbers.

*All records are 33⅓ r.p.m. microgroove except those marked * which are 78 r.p.m. coarse groove.*

This Discography, compiled by W. N. Aspinall, is based, by permission, on the 'World's Encyclopaedia of Recorded Music' by F. F. Clough and J. G. Cuming (Sidgwick and Jackson, London, 1952), the first and second supplements thereto, and unpublished material for the forthcoming third supplement supplied by the Authors.

The works are in chronological order of composition

THEODOR STORM–SONG	America, Dial, Dial 15
(1900 Version)	France, Classic, C6174
B. Beardslee (Sop.)	
J. L. Monod (Piano)	
SEVEN EARLY SONGS (1907)	America, Lyrichord, LL13
C. Rowe (Sop.)	
B. Tupas (Piano)	France, Eurochord, LPG628
B. Beardsley (Sop.)	America, Dial, Dial 15
J. L. Monod (Piano)	France Classic, C6174
SEVEN EARLY SONGS (Orchestrated)	America Concert Hall G12
K. Harvey (Sop.) Zurich Radio Orchestra W. Goehr.	
'AN LEUKON'—SONG (1908)	America, Dial, Dial 15
B. Beardslee (Sop.)	France, Classic, C6174
J. L. Monod (Piano)	

299

PIANO SONATA OP. 1 (1908)   America, Lyrichord LL13
   B. Tupas (Piano)   France, Eurochord LPG. 628
   T. Ury (Piano)   Great Britain, Argo ATM1006
       (Existence doubtful)

   A. Schier-Tiessen (Piano)   France, Polydor, 5032.*
       Germany, Deutsche Grammophon Gesellschaft, 72140.*

   Z. Skolowsky (Piano)   America, Columbia ML 4871
       Great Britain, Phillips NBL 5025
       International, Phillips NO2131L

   G. Gould (Piano)   Canada, Hallmark, RS3
   J. Manchon-Thies (Piano)   France, Ducretet-Thomson, LAP 1059
       Great Britain, Ducretet-Thomson, MEL 94008
       Germany, Telefunken TW30031

FOUR SONGS OP. 2 (1908/9)   America, Lyrichord, LL13
   C. Rowe (Sop.)   France, Eurochord, LPG 628
   B. Tupas (Piano)

FOUR SONGS OP. 2 (Orchestrated—René Leibowitz)
   I. Joachim (Sop.) Chamber   America, Dial, Dial 15 (L.P.)
   Orchestra—R. Leibowitz   France, Classic C2084*
       France, Classic C6174
       Great Britain, Esquire TW4-001*

STRING QUARTET OP. 3 (1910)
New Music Quartet

America, Bartók Recording
Soc., BRS906
(old no. BRS006)

Juilliard Quartet

America, Columbia, ML4737
(in set SL 188)
International, Phillips
AO1178L

FOUR PIECES FOR CLARINET AND
PIANO OP. 5 (1913)
S. Forrest (Clarinet)
B. Tupas (Piano)
E. Thomas (Clarinet)
J. L. Monod (Piano)
H. Tichmann (Clarinet)
R. Budnevich (Piano)

America, Lyrichord LL.13
France, Eurochord LPG628

America, Dial, Dial 15
France, Classic C6174
America, Concert Hall G.12

THEODOR STORM—SONG (1925
Version)
B. Beardslee (Sop.)
J. L. Monod (Piano)

America, Dial, Dial 15.
France, Classic, C.7164

'WOZZECK' (1925)
E. Farrell (Marie)
M. Harell (Wozzeck)
F. Jagel (Tambour-major)
R. Herbert (Doctor)
Chorus of the Schola Can-
torum, Philharmonic Sym-
phony Orchestra of New
York conducted by D. Mit-
ropoulos

America, Columbia, SL118(2)
France, Columbia, FCX157/8

THREE EXCERPTS FROM
  'WOZZECK'
  G. Ribla (Sop.)
  Philadelphia Orchestra—
  E. Ormandy

America, Columbia,
  Set MX347*
America, Columbia, ML2140
Great Britain, Columbia,
  LX1158/9*

C. Börner (Sop.) Jansen
Sym. Orch. of Los Angeles
—W. Jansen

America, Artist 1301/2*
  (Set J.S.12)*
America, Artist 500

Unknown soloist and
orchestra conducted by
Berendt

America, Allegro-Elite 3144

CHAMBER CONCERTO (1925)
  R. Charmy (Violin),
  J. L. Monod (Piano)
  Paris Chamber Orchestra
  —R. Leibowitz

America, Dial, Dial 9
France, Classic, C2107/12*
France, Classic, C609/8
Great Britain, Esquire,
  TW4-004/9*
Great Britain, Felsted, L89004

I. Gitlis (Violin)
G. Zelka (Piano)
Pro Musica Wind Inst.
Group—Byrns

America, Vox PL8660
Great Britain, Vox PL 8660

LYRIC SUITE FOR STRING
  QUARTET (1927)
  The (New) Pro-Arte
  Quartet

America, Dial, Dial 5
Sweden, Metronome,
  CL5003/5* (Set CL3)*
Sweden, Metronome
  CLP5003

Galimir Quartet	America, Vox, Set 181*
	France, Polydor, 595133/38*
	(Old Nos. 516659/62)*
	Great Britain, Decca, CA
	8244/47*
Juiliard Quartet	America, Columbia, Set MM
	957*
	America, Columbia, ML2148

LYRIC SUITE—ORCHESTRATED
Recording exists—no details known.

'DER WEIN'—CONCERT ARIA
(1928)
R. Herlinger (Sop.)—orchestra conducted by H. Scherchen
Manufacturer and Catalogue Number unknown

C. Boerner (Sop.)—Janssen	America, Capitol L8150
Sym. Orch. of Los Angeles	Great Britain, Capitol
—W. Janssen	CCL7515

'LULU' (1928-34)
I. Steingruber (Lulu)	America, Columbia,
W. Kmentt (Artist)	Set SL121(3)
O. Wiener (Dr Schön)	
Vienna Symphony Orches-	
tra conducted—H. Häffner	

VIOLIN CONCERTO (1934)
L. Krasner (Violin)	America, Columbia
	11589/1D* (Set M465)*
Cleveland Orchestra—	America, Columbia ML 4857
A. Rodzinsky	Australia, Columbia LOX
	594/6*

A. Gertler (Violin)
Philharmonia Orchestra—
P. Kletzki

America, Angel 35091
France, Columbia FCX 297
Great Britain, Columbia
33C1030

I. Gitlis (Violin)
Pro Musica Symphony—
W. Strickland

America, Vox PL 8660
Great Britain, Vox PL 8660

S. Goldberg (Violin)
Pittsburgh Sym. Orch.—
W. Steinberg.

America, Pittsburgh Festival
CB181

BIBLIOGRAPHY*

Musikblätter des ANBRUCH: Alban Berg's 'Wozzeck' und die Musikkritik (Musik der Gegenwart, Eine Flugblätterfolge, No. 9, UE, 1925)*

Kurt Blaukopf: Autobiographische Elemente in Alban Berg's 'Wozzeck', Vienna, 1954, Österr. Musikzeitschrift (May issue)

Fritz Bouquet: Alban Berg's 'Lyrische Suite'. Eine Studie über Gestalt, Klang und Ausdruck. (Melos, August–Sept. 1948, Mainz)

Mosco Carner: Alban Berg; Violin Concerto (in Ralph Hill's 'The Concerto', London, 1952, pp. 362–379.)

Study of 20th Century Harmony, 2nd ed. London, 1944.

P. Collaer—J. Weterings: Une nouvelle oeuvre d'Alban Berg: Loulou. (Revue Musicale, Paris, 1935)

K. H. David: 'Lulu' von Alban Berg (Schwz. Musikztg. 77. Jg. No. 13, 1 July, 1937, p. 397 ff.)

also: Vorbericht (Schwz. Musikztg. 77. Jg. No. 12, p. 385).

M. Deutsch: Le Concerto de Chambre d'Alban Berg (Schwz. Musikztg. 1949, No. 9).

H. Eimert: Alban Berg (Blätter der Städt. Bühnen Essen, Spielzeit 1952/53, Heft 13).

Roberto Gerhard: Berg's 'Wozzeck' (Foyer, No. 2, Staples Press, London, 1951/52).

Felix Greissle: Die formalen Grundlagen des Bläserquintetts von Arnold Schoenberg (Anbruch, 1925/2).

*Pamphlets and booklets have one asterisk, books have two.

D. J. Grout: A short History of Opera 2 Bd., U.S.A., 1947, pp. 5323/5.**

R. S. Hill: Report on the Berg-Schoenberg Correspondence (Quarterly Journal of Current Acquisitions, Library of Congress, Washington D.C., November 1952).

A Note on Schoenberg's Tone-Rows and the tonal system of the future (Musical Quarterly, January, 1936).

Berg: Lulu (review of LP record Columbia SL-121). (Mus. Qu., January, 1953, pp. 134 ff.)

P. Hindemith: Unterweisung im Tonsatz (Mainz, 1937).**

Hans Hollaender: Alban Berg (Mus. Q. XXII/4, Oct. 1936.)

Herbert Hübner: Alban Berg (in 'Musik in Geschichte u. Gegenwart', ed. F. Blume, Kassel, 1947 ff., Sp. 1681 ff.).

Hanns Jelinek: Versuch über den Sinn der Verwendung von Zwölftonreihen (Melos, Sept. Heft 1951, Mainz).

Anleitung zur Zwölftonkomposition* (UE, Wien, 1952).

F. H. Klein: Über den 'Mutterakkord' (Die Musik, Berlin, January, 1925).

Variationen über ein 'Modell-Typ II', das aus 12 verschiedenen Tönen und zugleich aus 11 verschiedenen Intervallen besteht (mit Vorwort und Analyse) Linz, 1924.

Pierre Jean Jouve and *Michel Fano*: Wozzeck ou le nouvel opera. (Paris, 1953.)**

P. J. Jouve: Matiére musicale de Wozzeck (Preuves, No. special, May 1952, pp. 2 ff.).

'Wozzeck' d'Alban Berg (Acte III, Sc. 4), pp. 87-98 (offprint of a chapter from the publication of 1952). (La Revue Musicale, April 1952, No. 212.)

Hans Keller: The eclecticism of Wozzeck (Music Review, Cambridge, XII/4, XIII/2, 3); XIV/1, pp. 55-59.

Correspondence with H. F. Redlich on 'Alban Berg and the C major triad' XIII/4, p. 332.

'Lulu' (Holland Festival 1931, XIV/4, p. 302 ff.).

Ernst Krenek: 'Fünf Orchesterlieder nach Ansichtskartentexten von Peter Altenberg op. 4' (in W. Reich's 'Alban Berg', Wien, 1937), p. 43 ff.

Über neue Musik (Wein, 1937).*

Zwölfton-Kontrapunktstudien, Schott, Mainz, 1952.

'New developments of the Twelve-Tone Technique.' (The Music Review, IV/q., May, 1943).

René Leibowitz: Schoenberg et son ecole. (Paris, 1947), Ed. Janin.**

Innovation and Tradition in contemporary music III: Alban Berg: or the seduction to Truth (Horizon, London, Heft 8, 1947).

Alban Berg's five orchestra songs op. 4 (with reprint of op. 4/No. 5) (Mus. Qu., October, 1948).

Qu'est-ce que la Musique de douze sons? (Ed. Dynamo, Liége, 1948).*

Schoenberg and his school, U.S.A., 1949 (transl. Dika Newlin).**

Introduction a la Musique de douze sons (Paris, L'Arche, 1949).**

Gian Francesco Malipiero: L'Opera di Gian Francesco Malipiero, con una introduzione di G. M. Gatti, Edizione di Treviso, 1952. (It contains two letters by Berg to Malipiero, dated July 17 and September 19, 1934, in Ital. transl.)

Zofja Lissa: Geschichtliche Vorform der Zwölftontechnik (Acta Musicologica, Vol. VII, 1935).

D. Mitchell: The Emancipation of the Dissonance. A selected Bibliography of the writings of Composers, Theorists, and

Critics (The Music Book, Vol. VII of Hinrichsen's Year
Book, London, 1952, pp. 141 ff.)
Dika Newlin: Bruckner, Mahler, Schoenberg (New York,
1947).**
Desiré Pacque: L'Atonalité ou mode chromatique unique (La
Revue Musicale, Jg. 11, 1930, Paris).
Emil Petschnig: Atonales Opernschaffen ('Die Musik', Berlin,
XVI, Febr., 1924).
G. Perle: Evolution of the Tone Row: The Twelve-Tone
Modal System (The Music Review, II/4, Nov. 1941,
pp. 280 ff.).
Twelve-Tone Tonality (The Monthly Musical Record,
October, 1943).
Schoenberg's late style (The Music Review, XIII/4, Nov.
1952, pp. 274 ff.).
Hans Pfitzner: Die neue Ästhetik der musikalischen Impotenz.
Ein Verwesungssymptom? (München, 1920).
Futuristengefahr, München, 1917.
K. Rankl: Arnold Schoenberg (The Score, No. 6, May 1952,
pp. 40 ff.).
H. F. Redlich: Gustav Mahler—eine Erkenntnis (Nuremberg,
1919).*
Die Welt der V., VI und VII. Symphonie (Anbruch, II/7-8,
Sonderheft 'Gustav Mahler').
Schoenberg's Tonalität.
Zu Schoenberg's Instrumentierung zweier Bachscher Choral-
vorspiele ('Pult & Taktstock', IV/March-April 1927, Sonder-
heft, 'Schoenberg u. seine Orchesterwerke'.)
Schoenberg's 'Erwartung' in Wiesbaden (Anbruch, X/2
February 1928).
Schoenberg's neue Oper ('Von Heute auf Morgen'). (Blätter
der Frankfurter Oper, Heft 3/4 Febr. 1930.)

'Von Heute auf Morgen' (Hamburgischer Correspondent, 4 Febr. 1930).

Mahler's Wirkung in Zeit und Raum. (Anbruch, XII/3, April 1930).

Alban Berg und der Schoenberg-Kreis (Lecture at the Volkshochschule Mannheim, 23 May 1932).

Arnold Schoenberg. (The Music Review, XII/4, Nov. 1951).

Alban Berg and the C major Triad. (Correspondence, The Music Review, XIII/3, August 1952.)

'Der Symphoniker Alban Berg' (history of the genesis of op. 6), Vienna, 1954, Österr. Musikzeitschrift, May issue.

'Alle guten Dinge'. . . (with letters by Berg on the genesis of the Chamber Concerto), Mainz, 1955, Melos (Schott), Febr. issue, 1955.

'Bruckner and Mahler' (Master Musicians, London, 1955, Dent's).★★

Willi Reich: 'Wozzeck'—a guide to the words and music of the Opera by Alban Berg (Modern Music, No. 2 of a series of Monographs, U.S.A., 1931).★

Reprint (together with Berg's 'A word about Wozzeck'), Modern Music, V/1, Nov. 1927) in Mus. Q. XXXVIII/1, Jan. 1952.

Alban Berg (Die Musik, Berlin, XXII/5, Febr. 1930) together with the two Storm-Lieder 'Schliesse mir die Augen beide'.

'Lulu'—the text and music (Modern Music, U.S.A., XII/3, April 1935).

Alban Berg's 'Lulu' (Mus. Q. XII/4, Oct. 1936).

Alban Berg (mit Bergs eigenen Schriften und Beiträgen von Theodor Wiesengrund-Adorno und Ernst Krenek), Wien, 1937.★★

Article 'Alban Berg' in Grove's Dict. of Music and Musicians, Suppl. 1940, pp. 38 ff.

Article 'Twelve Note Music' (Grove's Dict. Suppl. 1940, pp. 635 ff.).

Alban Berg's 'Lulu' (Zur Zürcher Uraufführung der Oper (Schweiz. Musikztg. 77. Jg. No. 11, June 1, 1937), Programme Stadttheater Zürich, June 1937.

Alban Berg's 'Lulu-Symphonie' (Neue Zürcher Zeitung, March 1936).

Alban Berg's Opera 'Lulu' (Melos, Heft 12, Dec. 1952).

Zur deutschen Erstaufführung von Alban Berg's 'Lulu' (Blätter der Essener Städt. Bühnen, Spielzeit 1952/53, Heft 13).

Versuch einer Geschichte der Zwölftonmusik (In 'Alte und neue Musik', Das Basler Kammerorchester, Atlantis Verlag, Zürich, 1952, p. 106 ff.).

Aus unbekannten Briefen von Alban Berg an Anton Webern (Schweiz. Musikztg. 93, Jg. No. 2, February 1953).

Alban Berg—Number of '23', eine Wiener Musikzeitschrift (ed. W. Reich), Nos. 24/25, February 1936.

'Aus Alban Berg's Jugendzeit', Mainz, 1955. 'Melos', Febr. issue, 1955.

Luigi Rognoni: Expressionismo e dodecaphonia (Giulio Einaudi, 1954), especially Chapters V and VI.

H. Rottweiler: Zur Lulu-Symphonie—Erinnerungen an den Lebenden ('23', Berg-Number, Nos. 24-26, 1936).

Josef Rufer: Die Komposition mit zwölf Tönen (Berlin, 1952).** (Engl. edition, London, 1955, Rockliff).

Dokumente einer Freundschaft (Berg's letters to Schoenberg, written in 1935), Mainz, 1955, 'Melos'.

R. Schaefke: Alban Berg's Opera 'Wozzeck' ('Melos', 1926).

Arnold Schoenberg: Harmonielehre, Vienna, 1911.

Brief an N. Slonimsky (in Slonimsky, 'Music since 1900'
New York, 1937).
Style and Idea (New York, 1950).
Alban Berg (Programmbuch der Düsseldorfer Oper, 1930,
reprint in W. Reich op. cit., p. 204, 1937).
Alban Berg (1949) (Cf. Appendix III).
Zu meinem 50. Geburtstag (Anbruch, Sonderheft 'Arnold
Schoenberg', VI, Aug.-Sept. 1924).
Walter Schrenk: Manfred Gurlitt's 'Wozzeck' (Anbruch, VIII/5,
1926).
Humphrey Searle: Alban Berg's Early Works (The Listener,
London).
Schoenberg and the Future (The Music Book, Hinrichsen,
Yearbook VII, 1952, pp. 134 ff.).
20th Century Counterpoint, London, 1955, Rockliff.
Matyas Seiber: Composing with Twelve Notes (Music Survey
IV/3, June 1952).
G. Sharp: 'Wozzeck' (The Music Review, XIII/1, p. 52),
Erwin Stein: Neue Formprinzipien (Anbruch, Sonderheft
'Arnold Schoenberg', VI, Aug.-Sept. Heft, 1924). (Re-
printed frequently.)
Einige Bemerkungen zu Schoenbergs Zwölftonreihen
(Anbruch, June-July issue, 1926).
Analyse der 'Lyrischen Suite' (Philharmonia score, No. 173,
UE, Wien, 1927).
Alban Berg u. Anton Webern (Chesterian, No. 10, 1922).
'Orpheus in New Guises', London 1953, Rockliff.★★
'Stimmen': Sonderheft, zum 75. Geburtstag Arnold Schoen-
berg's, Berlin, 1954, Stimmen, No. 16.
H. H. Stuckenschmidt: Neue Musik (Berlin, 1951).★★
Arnold Schoenberg (Zürich, 1951).★
O. Thompson: Obituary (Musical America, Jan. 10, 1936).

Ernst Viebig: Berg's 'Wozzeck' (Die Musik, Berlin, XV/7, April 1923).

Egon Wellesz: Arnold Schoenberg (Vienna-Leipzig, 1921).*
Die neue Instrumentation (2 vols.) Berlin, 1928/29.
An Alban Berg MS. at Oxford (Tempo, No. 6, London, 1946).

K. Westphal: A. Schoenberg's Weg zur Zwölftonmusik (Die Musik, Berlin, XXI/7, 1929, p. 491).

Th. Wiesengrund-Adorno[1]: Alban Berg: zur Uraufführung des Wozzeck (Anbruch, VII/12, 1925).
Zur Zwölftontechnik (Anbruch XI/7-8, 1929).
8 Analyses in W. Reich's 'A.B.', 1937 (Cf. infra).
Philosophie der neuen Musik (Tübingen, 1949).**
Versuch über Wagner (Berlin, 1952).**
Orchesterstücke op. 16 (Pult & Taktstock Sonderheft 'Schoenberg', March-April 1927).

K. H. Wörner: Article 'Expressionismus' (Musik in Gesch. & Gegenwart, 1947 ff.)
Musik der Gegenwart (Mainz, 1949.)**
'Neue Musik in der Entscheidung', Mainz, 1954.**

---

[1] Since 1945 he publishes under the name T. W. Adorno. This is the spelling adopted in this book.

INDEX

NOTE: Numbers refer to pages; numbers in parentheses, printed next to a page number, refer to footnotes on that page.

313

INDEX

Berg, Konrad (father), 218, 224ff, 226
Berg, Johanna (mother), 218, 224ff
Berg, Helene (wife), 229ff
Bouquet, Fritz, 142ff
Brahms, Johannes, 13(1), 14, 35ff, 45ff, 113, 113(1)
    Piano Quartet in A major, op. 20, 27
    Symphony IV, op. 98, 121
Bruckner, Anton, 13(1), 14, 66(1), 209
Büchner, Georg, 75ff, 78ff, 156, 163ff, 226
Burmeister, Franz Joachim, 205(1)
Busoni, Ferruccio, 55ff, 200, 236

Carner, Mosco, 226(1)
Carroll Lewis, 113
Casella Alfredo, 156
Chopin, Frédéric, 218

David, Karl Heinrich, 200
Debussy, Claude, 38
    Pelléas et Mélisande, 74ff, 91
Dostoievsky, Fedor, 226
Dukas, Paul, 229

Eisler, Hanns, 13(1)
Eliot, T. S., 113(2)

Franzos, Emil, 77ff, 79(1)

George, Stefan, 41, 143, 155ff
Gluck, Christoph Willibald, 96
Goethe, J. W. von, 166ff
Greissle, Felix, 114(1), 237
Gropius, Manon, 203ff, 203(1), 209
Gurlitt, Manfred, 107(1)

Hauptmann, Gerhart, 165ff, 168ff
Haydn, Joseph, 19
Hebbel, Friedrich, 79
Herlinger, Ružena, 155ff
Hill, R. S. 217(1)
Hindemith, Paul, 200
Hofmannsthal, Hugo von, 75ff, 218
Hohenberg, Paul, 227
Horenstein, Jasha, 60, 138
Horwitz, Karl, 66

Janaček, Leoš, 76(2), 87(1)
Jelinek, Hanns 13(1), 132, 144, 237
Jockl, Otto, 237

Kassowitz, Gottfried, 237
Kleiber, Erich, 110ff, 138, 169, 241
Klein, F. H., 130ff, 237
Kokoschka, Oskar, 228, 229
Kolisch Quartet, 138
Krasner, Louis, 203ff
Kraus, Karl, 168ff, 226
Krenek, Ernest, 161, 200
Kurzmann, Rita, 204ff

Leibowitz, René, 13ff, 41ff, 44(1), 60(1), 123(1), 126, 152, 179(3)
Lissa, Zofja, 25(1)
Liszt, Franz,
    Mephisto Waltz, 26
    Faust-symphony, 29, 38

Maeterlinck, Maurice, 75ff
Mahler-Werfel, Alma, 109ff, 203ff, 217, 229, 238
Mahler, Fritz, 237
Mahler, Gustav, 13(1), 55ff, 60, 65ff, 66(1), 69, 86ff, 138ff, 153, 198ff, 209 210, 228, 229ff, 242
    Symphony I, 212
        II, 209, 226
        III, 71
        V, 50
        VI, 70ff, 226
        VII, 25(1), 71
        VIII, 50ff
        IX, 57, 70ff, 182(1), 211
        X, 154
    Lied von der Erde, 140ff, 214
    Wunderhorn-songs, 87
Malipiero, Gian Francesco, 156
Méhul, Etienne Nicolas, 96
Milhaud, Darius, 71, 200
Monteverdi, Claudio, 96
Mombert, Alfred, 37, 40ff
Mozart, Wolfgang Amadeus, 19ff
    String Quartet in B flat major, KV, 589, 19ff
    Don Giovanni, 92ff

Pfitzner, Hans, 236ff
Polnauer, Josef, 217, 237
Pound, Ezra, 113(2)
Puccini, Giacomo, 200

Raphael, Sanzio, 218
Rankl, Karl, 77
Reger, Max, 226(2)

314

INDEX

315

ERRATA

[in the music examples]